The Selected Writings of Mordecai Noah

Mordecai M. Noah. Painting by John Wesley Jarvis. Used with permission of the Congregation Shearith Israel.

The Selected Writings of Mordecai Noah

Edited by
Michael Schuldiner
and Daniel J. Kleinfeld

Contributions in American Studies, Number 107

GREENWOOD PRESS
Westport, Connecticut • London

Library of Congress Cataloging-in-Publication Data

Noah, M. M. (Mordecai Manuel), 1785–1851.
[Selections. 1999]
The selected writings of Mordecai Noah / edited by Michael Schuldiner and Daniel J. Kleinfeld.
p. cm.—(Contributions in American studies, ISSN 0084–9227 ; no. 107)
Includes bibliographical references and index.
ISBN 0–313–31044–0 (alk. paper)
1. Noah, M. M. (Mordecai Manuel), 1785–1851. 2. Jews—New York (State)—New York—Biography. 3. Jewish authors—New York (State)—New York—Biography. 4. Jews—Restoration. 5. Grand Island (N.Y. : Island) 6. New York (N.Y.)—Biography. I. Schuldiner, Michael Joseph. II. Kleinfeld, Daniel J., 1974– . III. Title.
IV. Series.
F128.9.J5N632 1999
974.7'004924'0092—dc21
[B] 98–46813

British Library Cataloguing in Publication Data is available.

Library of Congress Catalog Card Number: 98–46813
ISBN: 0–313–31044–0
ISSN: 0084–9227

First published in 1999

Greenwood Press, 88 Post Road West, Westport, CT 06881
An imprint of Greenwood Publishing Group, Inc.
www.greenwood.com

Printed in the United States of America

The paper used in this book complies with the Permanent Paper Standard issued by the National Information Standards Organization (Z39.48–1984).

10 9 8 7 6 5 4 3 2 1

For our parents,

Andrew and Judith Kleinfeld

Max and Toby Schuldiner

Contents

Acknowledgments

A number of people have been especially helpful in the preparation of this text, and if it were possible we would thank all of them. As it is, space permits mention of only some of those individuals who come foremost to mind.

In the category of special assistance are Mr. Daniel M. Krauskopf, the late executive secretary of the United States–Israel Foundation, who provided the 1986 Fulbright award to Israel where the earliest formulations for a sampler of Noah's writings took place. Among those who offered their encouragement and resources was Jacob Rader Marcus, to whom we are indebted. In the category of individuals who provided their time to help in the collection of materials for us was Martha Oberle of American University who managed to get a photocopy of the Ararat address. It is thanks to her and to Karen Renninger, assistant chief of the Serial and Government Publications Division of the Library of Congress, that the Ararat address is produced here in its entirety for the first time since it appeared in the *Buffalo Patriot* on September 20, 1825. Jonathan Sarna of Brandeis University is also to be thanked on several counts. It was Sarna who first discovered Noah's important work, *Address Delivered at the Hebrew Synagogue in Crosby-Street, New-York, on Thanksgiving Day to Aid in the Erection of the Temple at Jerusalem* (1849), included in this sampler. Also, he graciously agreed to look over our work before going to press, and it is no doubt appreciably better for his critical attention. The editors of course take full responsibility for any shortcomings.

Among the individuals who contributed in very substantial ways were two students from the University of Alaska Fairbanks. The first is the late Dorothy Kelly who first pointed out to us that the figure of Christine in Noah's *She Would Be a Soldier* resembled Deborah Sampson Gannett. The second student to be thanked is Rebecca Wilson who has written a very fine and as yet unpublished essay on the fictive representations of Deborah Sampson Gannett in American literature. The parallels drawn here between Deborah Sampson Gannett and Noah's Christine were first identified in Wilson's paper.

Also, we are indebted to Ruth Schuldiner who helped proofread.

Lastly, we both owe a special and loving debt to those individuals identified in the dedication.

Introduction

Michael Schuldiner

Why read the writings of Mordecai Noah? Noah is hardly known today; and when he's spoken of at all, it is usually with reference to his abortive plan of 1824 to build a homeland for world Jewry on Grand Island in upstate New York. However, Noah was more shrewd, as well as more talented and complex an individual, than the portrait that commonly emerges from his "Ararat" venture might suggest.

First of all, Noah was an acknowledged leader among the literary men of his day. Playwright and essayist, as well as journalist, Noah was short-listed by his contemporaries as one of only a small number of American writers destined to share in the making of American literary history. When the *New York Mirror* ventured to identify in 1836 the American writers of the time whose works were of enduring value, among the writers included—along with James Fenimore Cooper and Washington Irving—was Mordecai Noah. Moreover, Arthur Hobson Quinn—one of the first modern American literary historians to share the enthusiasm of the early nineteenth century for creation of a national literary and cultural identity—identified Noah in 1945 as one of the two most important dramatists of American nationality to emerge in the early American period.

But Noah's activities were not confined to the written word. Noah had enormous energy. He was also a politician and a statesman: an influential member of Tamany Hall, sheriff for the county of New York, spokesman for a variety of religious and civic organizations, and U.S. consul to Tunis under President Madison. Moreover, Noah regarded himself as a spokesman for American Jewry, conducting correspondence with Presidents John Quincy Adams, Thomas Jefferson, as well as James Madison, and advocating for the rights of the Jewish citizenry of America. Like his liberal co-religionists in Europe, Noah was concerned with the question of how Judaism and Christianity could cohabit together, and how loyalties and allegiances were to be shared. These issues resolved themselves for Noah in the creation of a Jewish homeland that would be part of the United States. A number of American states had originally developed along religious lines. Massachusetts had been Puritan, Pennsylvania had been Quaker, Baltimore had been Roman Catholic, and Utah, of course, would later develop as a Mormon state. Why not a Jewish state in America? Later, as his visions of a Jewish haven in America waned, Noah turned his efforts toward advocating for a Jewish homeland in the Middle East.

Why read the writings of Noah? From a literary-historical standpoint, the period of monolithic constructions of American literary history has passed, and with it, the biases against female, non-Caucasian, non-British, as well as specifically non-Protestant writers. We now understand that American literature, especially early American literature, is the richer for the diversity of voices found within it. Emory Elliott's ground-breaking *Columbia Literary History of the United States* marked the beginning of a new era in literary historiography, and it is Elliott's work which inspires this and numerous other efforts currently being exerted to bring to contemporary audiences the noteworthy writings of early ethnic authors. In the next few years, it is likely that the first modern editions will appear of the writings of such authors as the very fine early Irish-American writer James McHenry and the earlier and very important German-American, Johann Conrad Beissel.

But the chief reason for reading Noah's writings is that they entertain, as well as provide instructive perspective on the character and manners of America in the early nineteenth century. Among the plays that Noah's Republican audiences found most entertaining, for example, was Noah's *She Would Be a Soldier* with its depiction of period types: the Federalist farmer-soldier who claimed Constitutional privilege to hide his cowardice during the War of 1812, or the foppish British captain searching the roadside inns of upstate New York for an anchovy and toast to satisfy his palette, and the frontier woman who reads French and handles a gun with equal skill and dexterity. So too Noah's journalistic pieces, collected in the *Essays of Howard,* offer amusing and, for the period, instructive social criticism, as in the Hogarthian tableau of New York City's well-to-do bloating themselves at fashionable midnight dinner-parties. But even when Noah is not being comical or satiric, his writings pique our interest. His speeches presenting his plans for the foundation of "Ararat," Noah's American arbor for the Jews of Europe; and his later proto-Zionist writings such as *Discourse on the Restoration of the Jews* and *Address . . . to Aid in the Erection of the Temple at Jerusalem* advocating that preliminary steps be taken toward the establishment of a Jewish homeland in the Middle East—these are rare curiosities today, interesting for what they tell us about the needs and aspirations of those first generations after the creation of the American republic.

The selections of Noah's work presented here are samples of his drama, and his social commentary and advocacy essays. Before proceeding to the selections, however, a brief biography, "Mordecai Manuel Noah," is provided by Daniel J. Kleinfeld. The section on "Noah's Drama" is introduced by Michael Schuldiner's essay, "The Historical Drama of Mordecai Manuel Noah," which contextualizes and explains the historical allusions in Noah's play *She Would Be a Soldier.* The selections consist of the text of Noah's *She Would Be a Soldier* and Noah's description of his theatrical career in "A Memoir of the Theatre." Daniel J. Kleinfeld's essay, "Noah on Behalf of Jew and Gentile" then follows, providing a discussion of the relationship between Noah's social criticism and advocacy for a Jewish homeland. The essay introduces the second and section of selections: "Noah's Social Commentary and Jewish Advocacy." Noah's social commentary is represented here by a number of journalistic pieces, ranging widely from a discussion of a need for more women's academies and the advantages that immigrant populations bring to America, to criticism of expensive fads that were popular in Noah's day. These pieces were collected in a volume titled the *Essays of Howard*, and it is from that volume that the selections are reprinted. Noah's advocacy on behalf of world Jewry is represented here in three pieces. *The Ararat Proclamation and Speech* is the entirety of Noah's remarks presented at the foundation ceremonies of what was to be the new Jewish colony in America. The address details Noah's plans for the government and financial basis of Ararat. The concluding selections present Noah's later efforts on behalf of a Jewish homeland in the Middle East. *Discourse on the Restoration of the Jews* identifies the historical and biblical bases for Noah's contention that a Jewish homeland is needed and viable, and the *Address Delivered at the Hebrew Synagogue in Crosby Street, New York . . . to Aid in the Erection of the Temple at Jerusalem* focuses specifically on the significance of the building of a temple in Jerusalem to the dawning of the Messianic age that seems to be at hand.

The intention in this selection of Noah's work, comprising only a small fraction of the total corpus, is to make available at least some of the writings of Noah to a substantially larger audience than his writings have hitherto been accessible to, with the hope that this audience will find his writings rewarding and efforts will begin toward publication of a complete edition of writings of the first important Jewish-American writer.

Mordecai Manuel Noah

Daniel J. Kleinfeld

Throughout his childhood, Mordecai Noah was acutely aware of his Jewishness. Orphaned at an early age, Noah spent much of his childhood in the care of his grandparents, who sent him for some time to the only Jewish school in New York, and who would regale him with tales of his family history. Grandfather Jonas Phillips, a successful Philadelphia merchant, had petitioned the Constitutional Convention to make sure that in the new United States, "all religious societies are on an equal footing" (Sarna 2). Phillips' strong belief in the need for religious freedom and his awareness of his own Jewish identity had a profound impact on Noah, shaping many of Noah's later ideas regarding the place of a Jew in America, and his notion of America itself.

Among the key influences on Americans in general and Noah in particular during this period was the theater. From his earliest years, Noah was a frequenter of the stage. At the age of eleven Noah became part of a group of boys that haunted the back alleys of the John Street theater in New York hoping for a free pass (Sarna 4). Later in Philadelphia he became a member and contributing writer to a young troupe of actors and was given his first opportunity to publicly express feelings for country that were to mature in future productions. As he explained in reminiscences written at age forty-seven, "I had an early hankering for the national drama, a kind of juvenile patriotism, which burst forth, for the first time, in a few sorry doggerels in the form of a prologue to a play" (Dunlap 317). The idea of the new nation stirred Noah as a boy and would continue to stir him in his later life to write for a "national drama" and a "national literature."

By 1807 the twenty-two-year-old Noah was finished with his education, and, after spending a few years traveling the country as a salesman, he was ready to settle down and begin a career. He joined the Democratic-Republican Party, perhaps in part because of the Federalists' reputation for anti-Semitism, and became actively involved in the Pennsylvania gubernatorial campaign of Simon Snyder in 1808.

Noah's early exposure to the theater might have been one reason why Noah was attracted to a career in politics. In 1832 Noah wrote to William Dunlap, who was at that time preparing his history of the American theater and had already had a number of plays successfully produced, that his "line" was actually "in the more rugged paths of politics." But even so the character of politics for Noah was shaped, like the rest of life, by the metaphor of theater. Like theater, Noah would suggest, a life in politics had its "'exits and entrances'—where the 'prompter's whistle' is constantly heard in the voice of the people . . ." (Dunlap 317).

Noah wrote his first drama, the youthful play, *The Fortress of Sorrento,* in 1808, for which he received in pay copies of other dramatic pieces printed by his publisher Longworth. *The Fortress of Sorrento* was never produced, and like Noah's next play, *Paul and Alexis* (1812), it did not present—as Noah's later plays would—the theme of America. Noah wrote for a stage still dominated by the English classics, and in these early years Noah's drama was highly imitative. It was not until his return from his excursion abroad as consul to Tunis that Noah would take up the theme and the vernacular of America.

Like many American Jews, Noah was also a journalist, working at his uncle's paper, the *Public Advertiser,* and writing a series of articles for the *Charleston Times* under the pseudonym Muly Mulak. Through these writings he was first able to communicate, and thus begin to create, his image of the American. In the Muly Mulak articles, supposedly written by a Turkish traveler in the United States, Noah used a breezy, comic style for his mild, satiric pokes at American customs and fashions. In later articles, he turned to serious political issues, resulting in two men challenging Noah to duels (Noah was known to be Mulak). Through Mulak, Noah was able both to celebrate and shape the daily life of Americans; he would criticize what he disliked about American society, although always in a conciliatory tone.

Despite his successes in theater and journalism, neither was sufficiently lucrative and Noah set his sights elsewhere. Making use of family connections, he applied to the government for a consular position. Once again, he was concerned with what his appointment would imply about America; in his petition to the secretary of state, he wrote, "I wish to prove to foreign powers that our Government is not regulated in the appointment of their officers by religious distinction. . . . I know of no measure which can so promptly lead members of the Hebrew Nation to emigrate to this country with their capitals, than to see one of their persuasion appointed to an honourable office" (Sarna 8). With a consular post, Noah hoped to serve as an example to Jews all over the world; he would be living proof of America's religious tolerance. Unfortunately, the outcome was not what Noah expected.

Having been appointed consul to Tunis, Noah bungled his first secret mission and was recalled, ostensibly because his religion was "an obstacle to the exercise of your consular functions." Although Noah knew that his religion was not the real reason for his dismissal—admitting in a letter of September 5, 1820, that "the real ground for disapprobation was probably a just one"—he was extremely concerned with the message his letter of dismissal (a letter that was recorded on government files) would send to the world, and the precedent it would set, since it indicated that the United States was willing to fire a man because of his religion. He spent years trying to clear his name, resulting, in 1819, in one of his most important works, *Travels in England, France, Spain, and the Barbary States in the Years 1813–1814 and 15*, which included, along with various anecdotes, a long section regarding his actions in Tunis. *Travels'* entertaining style made it extremely popular; to this day, it makes intriguing reading and is the best source on early nineteenth-century Tunisian Jewry. It was also upon his return from Tunis, having like many a later writer acquired some relative understanding of the character of the American from having been abroad, that Noah produced his most important drama, those plays that would establish him as one of the dramatists who had done most to give shape to the identity of America and the American. Between the years 1819 and 1823 Noah wrote four full-length plays in which Americans appeared prominently: *She Would Be a Soldier, or the Plains of Chippewa* (1819) set during the War of 1812; *Yusef Caramalli, or the Siege of Tripoli,* which is no longer extant but was first produced in 1820 and apparently drew upon the American naval engagements in the Barbary region; *Marion, or the Hero of Lake George* (1822) about a family divided between patriots and Tories during the American revolution; and *The Grecian Captive, or the Fall of Athens* (1822) in which Greek struggle for independence is aided by the frigate *United States*. Noah also wrote several shorter interludes, *Oh Yes! or, the New Constitution, The Siege of Yorktown, The Great Canal,* and later co-authored along with his cousin Jonas B. Phillips *Nathalie* or *the Frontier Maid* (1840). None of these works are any longer extant, yet it is obvious from what does exist that Noah's best energies and talents were spent in the service of an American drama and national literature.

But the stage was not as reliable a source of income as journalism. Noah became editor of the *National Advocate* and, by introducing satires, caricatures, scandal, and articles on domestic economy, made the *Advocate* the most popular paper in New York. Sponsored by the Bucktail Party (a faction of the Tammany Hall Democratic–Republican Party), The *Advocate* served as the party's voice, clarifying both the party's policy and that of its enemies. But Noah was not content to be a mouthpiece for the party. Instead, through angry attacks on De Witt Clinton, he worked to define the Bucktails.

In 1820 Noah ran for the position of sheriff, hoping for the status and stability that the position would offer him. In the election, there was some talk of whether a "Shylock" should have the power of the law; but, nonetheless, the Council of Appointments elected Noah. During his term as sheriff, Noah proved himself to be a dedicated humanitarian, trying unceasingly to improve the conditions of prisoners, particularly debtors. During the yellow fever epidemic, when people fled New York to escape the plague, Noah opened the jails, let the prisoners out, and, if they didn't come back, he himself became obliged to the creditors. But such benevolence proved no protection in the brutal, vicious elections of 1822. Knowing that the new constitution made the sheriff's post elective by the people, the anti-Noah clique of Tammany Hall launched into one of the most virulently anti-Semitic campaigns in American history. They accused Noah of writing a pamphlet that called the New Testament forged, and spoke of the "venomous satisfaction" Noah would find in "hanging Christians"—although to that Noah replied, "Pretty Christians to require hanging at all." Noah lost the election and was forcibly taught that beneath American tolerance lurked virulent anti-Semitism.

Noah had long been a prominent public figure. Unlike most American Jews in public positions, however, Noah did not try to hide or ignore his religion but instead proclaimed it boldly. There were dangers in this approach; throughout his career, he was often referred to as "Noah the Jew" or "Shylock." Nevertheless, his status as a leading American Jew proved useful while he worked to solidify his connections with the Jewish community and helped him to create a public image of himself as a man who was a patriot because of, rather than despite, his loyalty to the Jewish people. He proclaimed, "Until the Jews can recover their ancient rights and dominions, and take their rank among the governments of the earth, this is their chosen country" (*Discourse* 19). This patriotic image, together with the connections he had made with other leading Jews, were to be brought into play as Noah embarked on his most ambitious project, Ararat.

Noah had always believed that the Jews were to return to Zion, but unlike many of his contemporaries, he did not believe that the Jews should wait for God to restore them. In 1818 he would have been content to remain in the America created by his forebears, secure in the belief that anti-Semitism would fade away in the New World. But as the anti-Semitic campaign directed against him had shown, prejudice flourished even among the educated class of America. Just as Theodore Herzl, the founder of modern Zionism, was to learn eighty years later, progress was no guarantee of tolerance. Between the violent prejudice Noah had seen in America and the difficulty of maintaining such Jewish customs as the Saturday Sabbath in a Christian nation, Noah decided that the best way to preserve Judaism was to form a Jewish colony on Grand Island in upstate New York. This colony would be called Ararat after the hill where the biblical Noah's ark rested after the flood.

Despite Noah's problems with anti-Semitism, he still was a patriot, loyal to America, certain that, as he explained in a letter of October 22, 1825, "this is the country which the Almighty has blessed, and in which Israel and Judah may repose in safety and happiness." Noah conceived of Ararat as an American colony, benefiting both the Jewish people and the American nation, not to mention himself. Noah petitioned the state legislature to sell him Grand Island in 1820 and was finally given the chance to purchase the island in 1824. Noah wrote to numerous New York investors and eventually convinced eleven investors to put up money to purchase Grand Island. This accomplished, he wrote to prominent European Jews, inviting them to come to Ararat. After a theatrical dedication ceremony in which Noah, assuming the role of "Judge of Israel" and dressed in a Richard III costume borrowed from a local theater, set forth the decrees of Ararat, Noah went home and waited for the Europeans. But the Europeans never came. Today, all that remains of Ararat is the three-hundred-pound cornerstone, a memorial both to the idealism and naïveté with which Noah began the Ararat project.

But Ararat's failure did not seem to set Noah back in the least. It was as though he were content simply to transmit the message of Jewish nationalism. He returned to his political and journalistic careers. He began his own paper, the *New York National Advocate,* which was brought down by his partner's gambling, and then, undaunted, created another paper, the *New York Enquirer,* and still later seems to have repurchased the *New York National Advocate.* Both became successful, pioneering newspapers in New York, beginning the trend toward "muckraking" pieces and contributing to the mood of popular dissatisfaction which helped Andrew Jackson reach the presidency (Sarna 79). Noah cast his lot with Andrew Jackson, formed an alliance with his former enemy, De Witt Clinton, and married Rebecca Jackson (no relation to Andrew Jackson). For his support of Jackson Noah received in 1829 the position of surveyor of New York harbor, a post which was accompanied by the fairly sizable salary of $5,000 plus fees per annum (Sarna 87) at a time when a carpenter's salary in the same city might be a dollar a day. At that period of his life, Noah could look with some comfort to his career in politics, however "rugged" his start in politics might have been; writing plays could never have brought him even a livable income. But politics was still a precarious occupation. In 1833, due to accusations of conflict of interest between his editorial work and his post as Surveyor—as well as political opponents within Jackson's party—Noah was not renominated by Jackson to the Surveyorship. Noah returned once again to journalism, creating the *New York Evening Star.* The *Star* dedicated itself to uplifting morals (Sarna 98), refusing to fall into the sensationalism and scandal mongering of the "penny-papers." Noah's attacks on political opponents who were advisors of Jackson's eventually led to Noah's alliance with the anti-Jacksonians, and ultimately to leaving the party entirely to join the Whigs who welcomed his skilled writing and journalistic power. His increasing conservatism often led him to morally shaky positions, including a nativist stance.

The issue which always remained foremost in Noah's mind, however, was the place of Jews in America. Spurred on by the violent anti-Semitism of newspaper editor James Gordon Bennett, Noah continued to lead American Jews—delivering speeches, answering questions, and giving advice to Jews trying to adapt to America. Noah led the protest against the government of Damascus for its torture of Jewish prisoners, and worked to strengthen the Jewish community internally, especially through education. He worked with the Society for the Education of Poor Children and Relief of Indigent Persons of the Jewish Persuasion, helping with fund-raising, and served as examiner at three different Jewish boarding schools. As Noah entered the last years of his life, he returned to the political arena, and was granted a judgeship on the New York Court of Sessions where, despite attacks by James Gordon Bennett, he gained a reputation as a fair and compassionate judge.

Despite the failure of Ararat, Noah had not given up on the idea of Zion. And political events in the 1830s and 1840s gave Noah a chance to put his ideas into effect. In 1845 Noah published his *Discourse on the Restoration of the Jews;* and we know because of Jonathan Sarna's recent researches that Noah also published in 1849, an *Address Delivered at the Hebrew Synagogue in Crosby-Street, New York, on Thanksgiving Day, to Aid the Erection of the Temple at Jerusalem.* Noah now argued not for a colony in America but rather for return to the original land of Israel. Israel was to be Noah's last cause. In February 1851, Noah suffered a stroke. He remained alert and continued to write a correspondence column, but on March 16, 1851, he had a second stoke, leaving him crippled. On March 22, at the age of sixty-five, he died.

Mordecai Manuel Noah's life was one filled with disappointments. Despite his talents and successes as a playwright, essayist, and newspaperman, his soft-heartedness and recklessness left him in financial straits a good portion of his life; and his political career, which ranged from New York sheriff to U.S. consul at Tunis and back again to Surveyor of the Port of New York, was constantly derailed as much by his own naïveté and bad decisions as by the anti-Semitism which he sometimes blamed for the failures and which, at times, was partly responsible for them. But despite all of this, his central mission was a success—Noah helped solidify the identity of America as a nation of immigrants—Jewish, no less than Swedish, German, French, or English. Noah was, in Abraham Karp's words, the "first American Jew." Through his dramatic writings, essays, travel writings, newspaper columns, speeches, as well as by the example of his career, he spread his ideas about America and Judaism to the world. Motivating Noah was a strong sense of history—the past history of the Jews and the yet to be made history of the new nation—and it was that sense of history from which Noah's sense of himself and his sense of the American character emerged.

The Historical Drama of Mordecai Noah's *She Would Be a Soldier*

Michael Schuldiner

As a boy, Noah regularly attended the Chestnut Street theater where a season's ticket cost $18, a sum of money which, as Noah put it, required "great efforts to compass." But the shows were well worth the cost, said Noah. As he later explained,

> Our habits through life are frequently directed by our early steps. I seldom missed a night [of theater]; and always retired to bed, after witnessing a good play, gratified and improved. (Dunlap, *History* 318–13)

One might suggest that the "idea" of theater in Noah's time—its drama and spectacle—was the context in which Noah's image of himself developed. In later years, even as he assumed the careers of statesman and politician, Noah still carried the theater with him into the domain of the political, where the "theatrical"—the melodramatic and flamboyant—became in Noah's hands a tool with which he attempted to shape reality, and sometimes succeeded.

Noah was not above recognizing that distinctions had to be made between reality and illusion, between politics itself, which required a good sense of the character of the times, and theater which might present a people's idealized version of what they imagined themselves to be. Indeed, Noah could caution that in politics "there is more fact than poetry, more feeling than fiction" (Dunlap, *History* 317). But having distinguished between the "fiction" and the "fact," Noah the politician was not above indulging what must have seemed to many during his time as the whim or fancy of a "poet." The grand gesture of Sheriff Noah wholesalely freeing the inmates of New York's debtor's prisons when the yellow fever struck in 1822 was one such bit of theatrics. Less successful was the "Ararat" venture of 1825 in which Noah proposed to gather the persecuted Jews of Europe on Grand Island in New York. One need only be reminded that full-scale processions—complete with marching band—of the sort that were brought out for the consecration of the "new Jewish homeland" were commonly found on the stage of the period (indeed, might have appeared in Noah's own plays) to realize that what was going on near Grand Island was as much living theater as public relations and social project. Whether in the role of statesman or proto-Zionist, or, as we shall see, whether writing drama or biography, Noah was always on stage.

Noah's sense of theater and of himself as politician and statesman was in large measure an extension of his sense of history, the history that Noah, as a prominent voice in that new nation, might himself take part in. If, therefore, Noah sometimes indulged the melodramatic in the service of nationalism in his writings, it should not be surprising. Moreover, it is from Noah's desire to participate in the making of history that one can account not only for much of his visionary activity but also his ambitions for American literature, and the American theater in particular. "National plays should be encouraged," insisted Noah.

> They have done everything for the British nation, and can do much for us; they keep alive the recollection of important events, by representing them in a manner at once natural and alluring. We have a fine scope, and abundant material to work with, and a noble country to justify the attempt. (Preface, *She Would Be a Soldier*)

Noah realized that culture and myth were the binding agents that held peoples together in communities and nations. The writing of American literature was in itself, quite literally, the making of the American identity. Like many another individual, most notably Ralph Waldo Emerson some years later, Noah called for a distinctively American literature and theater, and wrote some of it himself.

Noah's apprenticeship as a dramatist was in part practical. Apart from regularly attending the theater, Noah was also as a young man a member of an amateur troupe of players that performed in Philadelphia. It was for this troupe that Noah also wrote his first lines, a prologue to a play the troupe was producing (Dunlap, *History 317*). But it is also clear that Noah had access to and read a good deal of dramatic literature. Noah's first, fledgling effort, *The Fortress of Sorrento,* was published in 1808 by David Longworth, who provided Noah as payment a copy of every play Longworth had published up to that point. This, in Noah's words, "at once furnished me with a tolerably large dramatic collection" (Dunlap, *History* 319–20). Included in that collection were a number of prominent British plays, all published in New York by David Longworth: Beaumont and Fletcher's *Rule a Wife and Have a Wife* (1806), Oliver Goldsmith's *She Stoops to Conquer* (1806), Richard Sheridan's *The Critic* (1807) and *The Rivals* (1807), Shakespeare's *Othello*

(1807), Edward Young's *The Revenge* (1806), as well as a number of adaptations, such as David Garrick's *The Country Girl* (1806) based on William Wycherly's *The Country Wife,* and Sheridan's *A Trip to Scarborough* (1807), an altered version of Sir John Vanbrugh's *The Relapse.* Included in Noah's new library were, of course, a number of American productions; and among the Americans perhaps the best represented was William Dunlap. But there were others as well. In particular, Charles Breck's *The Fox Chase* (1808) was an item on Longworth's list that, as will be pointed out below, no doubt influenced to some extent one of the thematic strands in Noah's *She Would Be a Soldier.* The general advantage of having such a collection, of course, is that Noah now could easily study the craft of the playwright from the texts he had at hand.

In fact, Noah enjoyed more success and prominence as a playwright than most. The *New York Mirror* for September 24, 1836, listed Noah as one of the outstanding American writers of the time—along with James Fenimore Cooper and Washington Irving (Williams 2:51). And it was no doubt on the basis of such plays as Noah's *She Would Be a Soldier* (1819) that the assessment was made. *She Would Be a Soldier* was by monetary standards alone among the more successful productions of the period. While even the more standard English plays, such as Richard Sheridan's *School for Scandal,* and even productions of Shakespeare were averaging receipts of two to three hundred dollars per night, *She Would Be a Soldier* brought from $435 on a rainy night to $811.50 on a fine one (Quinn 152n). The receipts were even larger when it played on Washington's birthday in 1820. That evening the play brought in a cash house of $1,178.50, the most brought in for a single performance during that season (Friedman, *Pilgrims* 223). Moreover, not only was it especially well attended when it played, it continued to be produced, on and off, until 1848—for nearly thirty years. *She Would Be a Soldier* was worthy of the patronage it received. As Arthur Hobson Quinn pointed out as late as 1943, Noah was one of the two most important dramatists of American nationality of that period. Indeed, there are not many plays of the period that are of equal historical depth.[1] *She Would Be a Soldier* is remarkable for its presentation and analysis of the character types of the period, types, by the way, with which its audiences would have been familiar and must certainly have enjoyed seeing appear on stage. These vibrant and comic characters offer us today an invaluable and entertaining glimpse into the character of early nineteenth-century America.

There was little original about the plot of *She Would Be a Soldier.* But original plot structure was not a priority for dramatists of the period in general nor was it important for Noah in particular. As David Grimsted explained in *Melodrama Unveiled,* the best study to date of the drama of the period, plot structures became standardized very quickly in those times; dramatists would exercise their ingenuity in the creation of the particular incidents of plot (16). Moreover, originality of plot would not have been a priority for Noah. As Noah would later demonstrate for his readership in his extensive presentation of Shakespeare's sources, there was little original about Shakespeare's plots either.[2] In fact, the plot of *She Would Be a Soldier* revolved around a popular theme of Noah's period, "the woman in man's britches." As early as 1798 the theme had been presented in New York in

John Daly Burk's play *Female Patriotism: or, The Death of Joan of Arc.* At about the same time the theme had been presented in France in an opera by Pierre Leveaux entitled *Leonore, or L'Amour Conjugal*; and it is in all likelihood that this play by Leveaux was the basis for Noah's own first attempt at the theme of woman in man's britches in *The Fortress of Sorrento.* After Noah's early effort, Charles E. Grice would in 1816 again briefly present the woman in man's britches in his play *The Battle of New Orleans.*

But *She Would Be a Soldier* (1819) differed in its presentation of the heroine. In a play such as John Daly Burk's *Female Patriotism; or, The Death of Joan of Arc* the woman puts on man's clothing in order to join the army and fight for the glory of country. More often, as in the case of Noah's *Fortress of Sorrento* and Grice's *Battle of New Orleans* the dramatic significance of the heroine is that, disguised as a man, she is able to save the hero from his enemies. In Noah's play the heroine, Christine, dons a soldier's uniform to escape from an unwanted suitor. In all likelihood this particular twist on the motif was suggested to Noah by the life of the Revolutionary War heroine Deborah Sampson Gannett upon whom Noah no doubt based his portrait of his heroine, Christine.

Having been indentured at an early age to a Middleboro family, Deborah Sampson, in 1782 at the age of twenty-one, purchased a suit of men's clothes, and successfully enlisted in the army, eventually joining up with the 4th Massachusetts Regiment. She received a number of battle wounds, but it was only when she fell ill with a fever in Philadelphia that an attending physician discovered her secret. Deborah Sampson was honorably discharged in 1783, the first woman ever to serve—and serve with distinction—as a combat soldier in the U.S. armed forces. The year after her discharge she married Ben Gannett, a farmer, and as their family grew it became increasingly difficult to make ends meet. Deborah tried to supplement their income with speaking tours around the country about her life as a soldier. Unfortunately, her family was never able to establish itself financially, and Deborah Sampson Gannett died in poverty in 1827 at the age of sixty-seven. The similarities between Deborah Sampson and Noah's Christine are fairly obvious, and the evidence for Deborah Sampson serving as the model for the characterization of Christine is very convincing.[3]

For one thing the Christine of *She Would Be a Soldier*, like Deborah Sampson, runs away to join the army largely to avoid marriage with a man chosen for her by her parent. In Deborah Sampson's case it was her mother who decided on the well-to-do individual who was to marry her daughter; and Deborah, finding the individual entirely disagreeable, decided to leave home and join the service. In the case of Noah's Christine, it is her immigrant father, Jasper, who gives the hand of his daughter (albeit begrudgingly) to Jerry Mayflower, a farmer of an old and established name. But as in the case of Deborah Sampson, Christine finds the thought of marriage to her intended so disagreeable that she puts on men's clothing, goes off, and turns out joining the army. There are of course differences in the situations of the two. Christine is not just escaping from one suitor; she is also fleeing to another, her beloved Lieutenant Lenox, an officer with the neighboring encampment where the Battle of Chippewa will be fought. Christine enlists when she gets to the camp, and she is willing to die for her country only because she there finds Lieutenant Lenox with another woman and thinks that Lenox has betrayed her love. Noah's plot is more complex, so far as we know, than the particular segment of Deborah Sampson's life that it is based on; Noah has added more motivation for Christine's joining the army. Christine is not only joining the army to escape from an unwanted match but also to escape from a life that offers no happy alternative.

Deborah Sampson became the nineteenth-century "type" of the frontierswoman, which emphasized accomplishments of both brain and brawn, "school learning" as well as frontier survival skills, a combination that to the modern eye might appear incongruous, but perhaps was taken more seriously in the days when an American frontier existed. Actually, Deborah Sampson herself was not especially well educated. As an indentured servant during her formative years the opportunities for intellectual improvement were minimal; she largely had to teach herself. It is clear, however, that she could hold her own on the battlefield and was quite capable of handling a firearm. Her performances on the road began with stories of her life in the army, and always ended with her in uniform performing a rifle drill to a patriotic aire in the background. It was to this type of the educated frontierswoman that Noah's Christine conformed. In the opening scenes where Major Lenox is sketching a portrait of Christine before he is called back to army headquarters (and the beginning of the Battle of Chippewa) Christine's relative sophistication is revealed. The audience learns that Christine speaks French, has read enough and is sufficiently musical to be able to sing her Lenox a ballad by the Queen of Holland, and knows enough about art history to pay Lenox the backhanded compliment that his portrait of her better resembles the *Venus de Medici*. But besides these more civilized and traditionally feminine accomplishments, Christine is a superb marksman. As her father tries to explain to Jerry Mayflower, Christine's bumpkin suitor, his daughter's accomplishments might be too much for Jerry. Christine, says Jasper, can "crack a bottle at twelve paces with a pistol" and "bring down a buck, at any distance." (Jerry confesses that he has "cracked" a bottle or two himself, but the bottle was never quite so far off; and as for bucks, he's not really sure he'd like a wife that meddles with the "bucks.") The literary type of the civilized frontierswoman is of course one that has survived, having perhaps most recently appeared as the Alaskan heroine in Jack London's *Daughter of the Snows*. Equally important, however, is the fact that Christine is the first character in American fiction to be based on Deborah Sampson Gannett, America's first woman combat soldier. Certainly, Deborah Sampson Gannett would have been in the back of the mind of each member of Noah's audience as Christine's trials were presented on stage. And Christine, in turn, might have lent some further sustenance to the myth of Deborah Sampson Gannett that was maturing during the time Noah's play was being produced. It is difficult to say. It seems generally to be the case, however, that in modern times Deborah Sampson has been replaced by the more passive figure of Betsy Ross as the heroine of the American revolution.

Much more clearly delineated in Noah's play is his portrait of immigrants, which takes on a decidedly political tone. Noah's characterization of French immigrants in Mordecai Manuel Noah, *She Would Be a Soldier* is clearly more favorable than his characterization of the British, which is what one might expect from Noah, a Democratic-Republican and Madison supporter. Noah's view of immigrants generally was expressed in his *Essays of Howard,* a collection of certain of his newspaper writings. As he looked around himself and saw the immigrant Swiss, French, Dutch, English, and Irish immigrants, the persona of Noah's *Essays* asked, "What is this combination of foreign habits and strange customs to produce to our country—good or evil?" Noah's answer is that "an industrious and increasing population" is absolutely necessary to a young country. As for the social and cultural impact that these immigrants of different nations will have on America, Noah is optimistic:

> This association of foreigners, this blending of habits, manners and language, will temper the genius and national disposition of the people, and give a softness, harmony, and judicious character to the American community.

Noah, for all his chauvinism (he would later adopt a nativist political philosophy), realized at this stage of his life that forging the American character meant tempering the rugged "genius and national disposition" of Americans with those habits from abroad that give a "softness" or sophistication, as well as judicious character and harmony to a people.

What Noah was suggesting in 1820 is that, more so than any other consideration, the contact that the American would have with foreign cultures would have a salutary effect on the development of the American character; and of course the most pervasive form of contact with different languages and peoples would come from the immigrants who were settling America at that time and continue to settle America today. This is not to say that the American character would not in turn make its impact on the habits and way of life of those who migrated to U.S. shores, as well as on the culture of far-away Europe. It is to say, however, that the vitality of American culture depended then, as it does today, on the interaction between the different cultures or peoples of America and the middle-American male and female.

In *She Would Be a Soldier*, Jasper, Christine's father and a French immigrant, provides for his American-born daughter precisely that acculturation, that "softness" or sophistication of which Noah speaks in his *Essays.* In *She Would Be a Soldier* it is that French influence of Jasper on his daughter which contributes to the evolution of a distinctly American character type, the civil frontierswoman. Although Jasper himself is the son of a peasant and has had the benefit of only the local parish school, Jasper has apparently educated himself to some degree, much as Noah had. His concern for his daughter has been "in cultivating her mind, and advancing her happiness." Certainly, Christine's ability to speak French is due to her father's tutelage; and one can assume that her knowledge of music and art is as well. Indeed, it is Jasper who provides his daughter with the education and cultivation that she exhibits. Natural genius has been tempered by an acquired foreign culture. The immigrant has produced an American of a decidedly different and distinctive hue.

As for the process by which the immigrant Jasper becomes "American," or "naturalized" as it were, that seems to have involved two rituals, war and marriage. Jasper left France, not because of poverty or misfortune at home, but for the adventure of following the Marquis de Lafayette into battle against the British in America. He was wounded at Yorktown, saw the United States acknowledged a sovereign country, and was promoted to sergeant by Washington. When the army was disbanded, Jasper traveled on foot to see the country he had helped liberate, and purchased a piece of land, which he proceeded to clear and cultivate. He built his cottage and his land flourished, but he grew lonely. Soon thereafter he took to wife the Miller's daughter, Kate, who, after several years bore him a daughter Christine, but died in delivery. Despite Jasper's trials, there are suggestions that the naturalization process has not really been completed. Jasper, having grown up in poverty is understandably impressed when the wealthy farmer Jerry Mayflower offers to marry Christine. But Jasper, after recognizing that Jerry is no match for the cultivated Christine and even after finding Jerry out for a coward, still consents to the match with his daughter. Jasper remains deferential to the wealthy farmer of old "Mayflower" stock, suggesting that he does not feel that he entirely belongs to his new country, or at least not as much as Jerry belongs to it.

The other case of a "naturalization" ongoing in the course of the play is that of the British captain Pendragon. Like Jasper he has come to America as a soldier for the adventure, and like Jasper he meets an American woman who, the implication is, will complete his naturalization. The portrait drawn of the British captain by Noah, however, is quite comic and not very flattering, much what one might expect of Noah who endorsed the War of 1812, although the portrait drawn of Pendragon is by no means totally disparaging. Unlike Jasper, the French immigrant who leaves his mark on the American character in his daughter Christine, in Captain Pendragon's case it is he who must undergo socialization in order to survive in America, and the nature of that socialization process is described by Noah in comic terms.

The naturalization of Pendragon begins as he makes his first entrance on stage. The Battle of Chippewa will soon take place (offstage), and Pendragon and his valet, Parole, enter a country inn where they will await their orders and pass the time. Pendragon calls over the waiter and asks for something to eat: "an anchovey, a toast, and a bottle of port" (Act 2, Sc. 1). The waiter has no idea what an anchovy is, but realizes that the British officer is asking for something out of the ordinary and so offers him bear meat in lieu of the inn's regular fare of "possum fat and hominy." Pendragon's consternation grows as an Indian chief arrives at the inn to tell Pendragon that at the upcoming Battle of Chippewa, Pendragon will serve under the chief, whose tribe will be fighting alongside the British. Pendragon is taken aback, but he positively reels when he is told by the Indian that not only must Pendragon fight under his command but dress as the Indian does. "Harkee, sir," returns Pendragon, having regained his composure,

> I'd have you to know, that I am a man of fashion, and one of the fancy—formerly of the buffs, nephew of a peer of the realm, and will be a member of parliament, in time; and officer of great merit and great services, Mr.—Red Jacket. Paint my face, and fight without clothes? I desire, sir, that you will please to take notice, that I fought at Badahoz with the immortal Wellington, and had the honour to be wounded, and promoted, and had a medal for my services in that affair, Mr.—Split-log. Put rings in my nose? a man of taste, and the *ne plus ultra* of Bond-street, the very mirror of fashion and elegance? Sir, I beg you to observe, that I am not to be treated in this manner—I shall resent this insult.

The Indian, of course, is not impressed by Pendragon's outburst and offers to skewer him over a slow fire—after the battle—if Pendragon does not comply with his commands. When Pendragon next appears on stage, it is as Noah's version of the "noble" savage—half-naked and smeared with war paint, but still the nephew of a peer of the realm, his opera glass dangling from his hand.

Happily Pendragon is taken captive by the Americans and is arraigned before the American general where Pendragon meets the general's spirited daughter, Adela, who it appears will complete Pendragon's naturalization. Adela and Pendragon have in common their love of battle. Pendragon has been fighting in America for the adventure of it and for the stories that he will be able to bring back to England and tell his friends. Adela likewise enjoys life with her general-father because it makes for adventure. Adela recounts the story to Lieutenant Lenox, her old teacher whom she meets at the army encampment, of how she adeptly handled herself when caught in the middle of a skirmish one day while out riding with her father's detachment. She wishes she had done something heroic so that "my name would have been immortalized like Joan of Arc's." When Pendragon meets Adela while he is being arraigned before the general, he is immediately taken by her beauty, and she is taken by the fact that a British dandy stands before her in war-paint, half-naked with a monocle in his hand. Pendragon complains to her of the "kind of helter-skelter warfare" in America, and Adela humors him. After the arraignment, the general invites Captain Pendragon to his tent for refreshment. Pendragon asks Adela for "the felicity of your little finger" as he exits, and as the two walk off stage together the audience is left with the impression that curiously these opposites—the American bred and spirited daughter of the general and this British fop of an officer—are a pair. Thus, curiously, war for Pendragon, as in Jasper's case, forms part of the naturalization process, even though his fighting was done on the enemy side. And as in Jasper's case the other integral element in the Americanization of Pendragon promises to be love.

Having just described perhaps one of the more unusual characters to appear on the American stage of the period, one might wonder whether the character of Pendragon or the circumstances of the Battle of Chippewa described by Noah bear any resemblance to reality. In fact, Indians did fight alongside the British against the Americans in the Battle of Chippewa. Moreover, there really was a British peer of the realm in that battle, who had formerly fought under Wellington, as Pendragon had, and was known for his delicate palette, which Pendragon also exhibits—and known especially for his eccentric habit of bringing his own Champagne into battle with him (Berton 322, 325–26). That was George Hay, the eighth Earl of Tweeddale who first became prominent when a military dispatch of his was intercepted by the American army and found to contain a complimentary account of the valor of the American soldier. The letter was published in the American newspapers and after that, legends grew up around him ("Document" 77). Noah, who was a newspaperman himself, could not have failed to read or hear of the stories of Tweeddale, and used the eighth Earl of Tweeddale as his model for the character of Pendragon. Noah's audience would have been aware of the person of Tweeddale in the character of Pendragon, and Noah's portrait of the British soldier-fop would have conveyed, apart from a good deal of hilarity, a ring of truth. Moreover, that truth would have been especially appealing to the Democratic-Republican audience of New York before which *She Would Be a Soldier* played. But the point here is that, as in the case of Christine, Noah is again presenting in Pendragon a type of character that existed or was thought to exist at the time.

The least flattering but nonetheless historically based portrait is that of the young American rustic of Mayflower lineage, Jerry. But while the portrait of Jerry is the most unflattering, it is also true that no figure in Noah's play is more politically motivated. Jerry for Noah and his audience is the epitome of the Federalist who opposed the War of 1812 and for whom Democratic-Republicans felt a particular disdain. In order to fully understand Noah's portrait of Jerry it is necessary to understand also that Jerry Mayflower is a true "Jonathan" figure, the countrified son of the British caricature, "John Bull," and a genuine chip off the British block. In fact, Noah's Jerry is especially likened to his British father "John Bull." Like John Bull, for example, Jerry is a country squire.[4] And like his British forebears, Jerry enjoys, indeed glories, in the foxhunt.

The foxhunt had earlier appeared as a prominent theme in Charles Breck's *The Fox Chase: A Comedy*. In Breck's play the fox chase serves as a metaphor for the way in which debtors were hounded by the police in Noah's day (7) and man's inhumanity to his fellow creatures and other men in general (12). Henry Lunewell, who is one of those being hounded for debt, complains when he thinks the police have found him at his father's home in the woods,

> What, still the buckskin trailed about the country for these greyhounds of usury—over hills and vallies, plains and rivers—and at length traced to the middle of a forest! (Act I, sc. 1)

The Fox Chase played in Philadelphia and Baltimore; and since it was published by David Longworth in early 1808, it would have been among those plays that Noah received as payment for his *The Fortress of Sorrento*. As in Breck's play, the metaphor of the British foxhunt informs the conduct of the characters in Noah's play. In Noah's play, it is the conduct of Jerry Mayflower that is informed by the sport, specifically Jerry's conduct in love and war, those two activities in terms of which the identity of the American male seems to be defined for Noah. That a British sport is the central metaphor guiding Jerry's conduct does not bode well for Jerry or his identity, as we shall see.

In particular, Jerry's conduct in his pursuit of glory at the battle for Queenstown Heights and his conduct in pursuit of Christine are both informed by the metaphor of the foxhunt, and in both situations an unflattering portrait emerges. Jerry's character as a soldier is made explicit toward the very beginning of the play when Jerry is trying to persuade Christine's father, Jasper, a former soldier, that Jerry is worthy of the accomplished Christine. Jerry uses the argument that he, like Jasper, is a veteran, has "been to the wars . . . got experience, laurels and lilies, and all them there things" (Act 1, Sc. 1). But when Jasper, somewhat taken, asks Jerry whether he really shared in the "glory" of the Battle of Queenstown, Jerry replies, "O yes, I shared in *all* the glory—that is—I didn't fight." And Jerry goes on to explain that so far as he could tell the glory, the fun of it, consisted in the preparations for the battle, not the actual battle itself. "I'll tell you how it was," says Jerry.

> I marched at the head of my village sogers, straight as the peacock in my farm yard, and I had some of the finest lads in our country, with rifles—well, we march'd and camp'd, and camp'd and march'd, and were as merry as grigs until we arrived at the river: hall the troops had cross'd and were fighting away like young devils: ods life, what a smoke! what a popping of small arms, and roaring of big ones! and what a power of red coats!

"Well," says Jasper, urging him to complete his story, "and you panted to be at them? clubb'd your rifles, and dashed over?" "Oh no, I didn't," replies Jerry. "I was afear'd that in such a crowd, nobody would see how I fought."

The glory of war, for Jerry, comically consists in "appearances"—the pomp that attends military engagements—the little pomp he can muster from among his small, comic band of farmers. He had marched at their head, erect as a peacock, he tells us, a group of the finest lads in the county—with rifles. There would be no glory, in Jerry's view, in the actual engagement itself. There was simply no point to going into a battle that was all smoke—where the glorious figure he and his rifle cut at the head of the troops would not be seen by others.

But while Jerry had gone to Queenstown for the glory, he had also enjoyed the "chase" that he was involved in, the military preparations prior to the battle. He and his soldiers had "march'd and camp'd, and camp'd and march'd," and had been "merry as grigs." There was simply no reason to go into a battle that offered nothing further in the way of sport or amusement—that was all popping and roaring. True to the sport of the fox hunt, Jerry had had a time of it stalking the prey; he could just as well let the hounds go in for the kill.

Jerry's pursuit of Christine is similarly informed by a desire for "glory" and the conventions of the fox hunt. Jerry's intention to marry Christine is motivated by his sense of what would "appear" well to others, although even at the outset he seems to have some sense that the reality of such a marriage might not be an entirely pleasant one. He wants to marry Christine largely because of her talents. In Jerry's words, she can "parlyvoo," and as her father tells him, she can crack a bottle with a pistol at twelve paces. But Jerry, even at the outset, reveals that marriage to Christine might prove worrisome; he is not really certain that he will be able to control Christine. And he is clever enough to know that a willful and dominant wife would do nothing for his esteem among his neighbors and friends. Anticipating a troublesome willfulness in Christine's character that might, in his view, plague any man, he offers, in his efforts to woo Christine, not to flog her when she gets out of hand (Act 1, Sc. 1). It is not entirely surprising that, at the end of the play when Jerry finds her with Lenox and she is in disguise as a soldier, he decides that he could just as well do without a woman who wears the pants in the family even before she is married, and lets Lenox have her. He had already been concerned about the length of her inseam for some time.

The character of Jerry here, as at the battle of Queenstown, is informed by that of the country squire in chase of his quarry. As does the hunter, Jerry in his pursuit of Christine experiences the excitement of the chase. He has been accompanied in his pursuit of Christine by his villager friends (his pack of hounds). The chase has been eventful. For example, while searching for Christine, he indulged in a drunken binge at the army canteen, got into a row with the soldiers, and was confined to close quarters within earshot of enemy canon. Moreover, Jerry does not actually corner Christine. Lieutenant Lenox, Christine's true beloved, is the one who identifies the woman in boy's trousers. Lenox discovers the quarry first. Given the conventions of the hunt as they existed in the 1820s, the trophy—usually the tail, or "brush"—was given to the first individual to arrive at the kill.[5] Christine, in Jerry's view, would rightfully have belonged to Lenox by virtue of his having first discovered her.

Jerry is in one sense the American equivalent of Fielding's Squire Weston, the more comic for having been transplanted, and like the country he has been transplanted to, much younger. But Jerry's conduct in both love and war more largely partake of the image of his British father, John Bull, at hunt with his hounds. In matters of both love and war, the matters which for Noah seem to define the American male, Jerry fares especially badly when compared to Jasper and even the British captain Pendragon. Like Pendragon, Jerry enjoys the flourish of battle; unlike Pendragon Jerry is unwilling to fight when the flourish ends.

One recent critic has expressed the reservation that the character of Jerry Mayflower does not exhibit "the usual fundamental moral goodness inherent in most stage Yankees" (Havens 111). In fact, an American soldier that Jerry meets with in his pursuit of Christine recognizes him as a coward who refused to fight at the Battle of Queenstown (Act 2, Sc. 3). But Noah, in his identification of Jerry as one unwilling to fight, has once again incorporated historical circumstance into his presentation of character.

During the War of 1812, much of which was fought in Canada, there arose the constitutional question of the nature and extent of federal power over state militia.

Massachusetts and Connecticut—dominated by Federalist, anti-Madison politicians—had from the very first refused to commit their militia, Connecticut arguing that the Constitution did not authorize the use of state militia to prosecute an offensive war (Kelly 244–45). At the Battle of Queenstown, New York State militiamen—to which Jerry Mayflower's fictional party of soldiers belonged—were employed as reinforcements for the regular army. But in the heat of battle, when called upon to provide support for the regulars who had already captured Queenstown, they all and one refused to fight, claiming "constitutional privilege" (Brackenridge 70; *War* 87, col. 2). Of the conduct of these militia, general Winfield Scott would later write, "These vermin who infest all republics, boastful enough at home, no sooner found themselves in the sight of the enemy than they discovered that the militia of the United States could not be constitutionally marched into a foreign country!" (*Memoirs* 63). Clearly, there existed some sentiment to the effect that these militia had only used the Constitution as an excuse to hide their cowardice; and it is this sentiment that Noah expresses through the character of Jerry Mayflower. In fact, Jerry too uses the excuse of "constitutional privilege" when explaining to Jasper his conduct at Queenstown. "Some one said," explains Jerry, "it were contrary to law and the constitution, to go into the enemy's country, but if they com'd into our country, it were perfectly lawful to flog 'em" (Act 1, Sc. 1). Obviously, Noah's Democratic-Republican sympathies were not with those who hid behind the Constitution and refused to follow Madison's orders, or with the Federalist States of Massachusetts and Connecticut which disparaged the language of the Constitution by, in his view, knowingly misconstruing its intended meaning.

But quite aside from the fairly obvious manner in which Noah used the character of Jerry to express his party loyalty, the idea that Jerry's character is flawed because it does not reveal those qualities that appeared in other Jonathans of the period is curious criticism coming from modern critics. Can one really insist that certain traits ought to have appeared in a given fictional character? Can one fault a character in a play because he does not reveal "fundamental moral goodness" and is thought a coward?

Jerry Mayflower, apart from being the American son of "John Bull," is, as has been pointed out, also one in a long line of Jonathans or stage yankees that first appeared in America in Royall Tyler's *The Contrast*. He was the naive bumpkin comically trying to make his way in a more sophisticated cultural setting. He was good natured and, indeed, a product of a moral, if not entirely religious, New England upbringing. And by 1850 he would usually come out on stage wearing a blue coat with tails and eccentric looking red and white striped trousers. That is, Jonathan—and Jerry—are important figures in American literature because they have come down to us in the more modern-day figure, Uncle Sam—the very personification of all that is American![6] The problems that recent literary historians of early America have had with Jerry seem to be due to, in effect, their unwillingness to face the fact that there might have been a "coward" somewhere in the Uncle Sam's ancestry. Jerry Mayflower's apparent "shyness" in love and war is, in effect, a flaw in Uncle Sam's character—that same Uncle Sam who is still perhaps best known for wanting you in his army.[7]

Noah, of course, was not the first dramatist to portray the Federalists in an unfavorable light. Indeed, far more virulent and scurrilous attacks on the Federalists had appeared on the American stage. J. Horatio Nichols had in several efforts blasted the Federalists, portraying them as monarchical, avaricious, unethical, and generally villainous. In Nichols' *The Essex Junto,* for example, Adams appears in the character of the "Duke of Braintree" and becomes the melodramatic arch-villain who attempts to force the heroine, Virginia, to marry him by threatening to brutalize her. Nichols did little more than his fellow dramatists and retell the tale of Snidely Whiplash and Little Nell when presenting the Federalists. By contrast, it was nothing short of a stroke of genius when Noah recognized the potential for comic abuse of Federalists in the stage yankee, the "Jonathan" character that Noah gave historical substance to in Jerry Mayflower.

NOTES

1. In the two books written within the last twenty years that discuss in some detail the drama of this period and include Mordecai Noah—Daniel F. Havens' *The Columbian Muse of Comedy* and Walter J. Meserve's *An Emerging Entertainment*—Noah seems to have been relegated to the status of a minor dramatist (Havens 101)—as good as anyone writing in England at the time (Meserve 307). Both Havens and Meserve discuss *She Would Be a Soldier* (Havens at some length) and, it should be noted, do speak well of certain of the characterizations. Havens and Meserve agree that Christine is an important character in drama, the independent American woman of action (Havens 112; Meserve 254). Further, Havens identifies the new ground broken by other characters in the play, such as the British Captain Pendragon and Jerry Mayflower.

For an excellent biography of Noah describing the significance of Noah's life, see Sarna's *Jacksonian Jew: The Two Worlds of Mordecai Noah.*

2. See Noah's commentary in *Shakespeare Illustrated; or the Novels and histories on Which the Plays of Shakespeare are Founded.*

3. "Fictive Treatments of Deborah Sampson Gannet, America's Revolutionary War Heroine." Circulating manuscript.

4. Paulding (*Diverting History* [1812] 4–5) identifies Jonathan as the son of John Bull, an English country squire. It is likely that Noah was familiar with this work. It is a thinly veiled allegory for the War of 1812 between Jonathan and his British father, John Bull. Also, it presents a view of the war with which Noah would have been sympathetic.

In the 1835 edition Paulding makes it clear that John Bull and Brother Jonathan were very much alike; in fact, says Paulding, "Squire Bull and Brother Jonathan were too much alike ever to be right-down good friends" (174).

5. For a concise description of the foxhunt in the 1820s, see Itzkowitz (3–4).

6. Rourke (16–17) makes this point. The point, however, had been made earlier and in an amusing fashion by Paulding in his *History of Uncle Sam* (1835): "John Bull had christened this son of his by the name of Jonathan; but by-and-by, when he became a man grown, being a good hearty fellow, about half horse half alligator, his friends and neighbors gave him the nickname of Uncle Sam" (178).

7. It is perhaps worth noting that Jerry Mayflower is not the only "low" Jonathan to have appeared on the American stage during this period. William Dunlap in *A Trip to Niagara* (1830) created a Jonathan who was a merchant and a cheat—who made nutmegs out of pine plank and sold them to grocers in New York. Still later Hiram Dodge, a peddler and another Jonathan type in *The Yankee Peddler* (1841) by Morris Barnett, was depicted as underhanded in his transactions, without any sentimental attachment to independence or liberty, and a parasite (Moody, *America Takes the Stage* 121, 124).

Nor should Noah's depiction of Jerry Mayflower be taken as suggesting an anti-yankee sentiment on Noah's part. Rather, Noah's view of Jerry should be understood as the product of his politics. He strongly supported "Mr. Madison's War" with the British in 1812 against the criticism of its detractors (Sarna 11), which would have included the "yankee" states of Massachusetts and Connecticut, as well as certain elements within the state of New York; and in 1819 when *She Would Be a Soldier* was written, Noah apparently still felt that the conduct of Massachusetts, Connecticut, and particularly the New York State militia in the battle at Queenstown had been less than honorable.

She Would Be a Soldier,

or The Plains of Chippewa;
An Historical Drama, in Three Acts

By **M. M. Noah**

Performed For The First Time On The 21st Of June, 1819.

New-York:
Published At Longworth's Dramatic Repository,
Shakspeare Gallery.

G. L. Birch & Co. Printers.

1819.

Preface

The following dramatic *bagatelle* was written in a few days, and its reception, under every circumstance, far exceeded its merits. I had no idea of printing it, until urged to do so by some friends connected with theatres, who, probably, were desirous of using it without incurring the expense of transcribing from the original manuscript. Writing plays is not my "vocation;" and even if the mania was to seize me, I should have to contend with powerful obstacles, and very stubborn prejudices; to be sure, these, in time, might be removed, but I have no idea of being the first to descend into the arena, and become a gladiator for the American Drama. These prejudices against native productions, however they may be deplored as impugning native genius, are nevertheless very natural. An American audience, I have no doubt, would be highly pleased with an American play, if the performance afforded as much gratification as a good English one; but they pay their money to be pleased, and if we cannot afford pleasure, we have no prescriptive right to ask for approbation. In England, writing of plays is a profession, by which much money is made if the plays succeed; hence a dramatic author goes to work, *secundum artem.*—He employs all his faculties, exhausts all his resources, devotes his whole time, capacity and ingenuity to the work in hand; the hope of reward stimulates him—the love of fame urges him on—the opposition of rivals animates his exertions—and the expectation of applause sweetens his labours—and yet, nine times out of ten, he fails. Mr. Dunlap, of this city, has written volumes of plays, and written well, "excellent well," but he made nothing; nay, he hardly obtained the civic wreath which he fairly earned. Barker, of Philadelphia, whose muse is the most delicate and enticing, has hung up his harp, which, I dare say, is covered with dust and cobwebs; and even Harby, of Charleston, whose talents are of the finest order, and who is a bold yet chaste poet, gained but little profit and applause from his labours. We must not expect, therefore, more encouragement for the American Drama than may be sufficient to urge us on. We will succeed in time, as well as the English, because we have the same language, and equal intellect; but there must be system and discipline in writing plays—a knowledge of stage effect—of sound, cadences, fitness of time and place, interest of plot, spirit of delineation, nature, poetry, and a hundred *et ceteras*, which are required, to constitute a good dramatic poet, who cannot, in this country, and while occupied in other pursuits, spring up over night like asparagus, or be watered and put in the sun, like a geranium in a flower pot.

I wrote this play in order to promote the benefit of a performer who possesses talent, and I have no objections to write another for any deserving object. New plays, in this country, are generally performed, for the first time, as anonymous productions: I did not withhold my name from this, because I knew that my friends would go and see it performed, with the hope of being pleased, and my opponents would go with other motives, so that between the two parties a good house would be the result. This was actually the case, and two performances produced nearly $2,400; I hope this may encourage Americans of more talent to attempt something.

National plays should be encouraged. They have done everything for the British nation, and can do much for us; they keep alive the recollection of important events, by representing them in a manner at once natural and alluring. We have a fine scope, and abundant materials to work with, and a noble country to justify the attempt. The "Battle of Chippewa" was selected, because it was the most neat and spirited battle fought during the late war, and I wish I was able to do it more justice.

New-York, July, 1819.

DRAMATIS PERSONAE[1]

GENERAL	Mr. Graham
JASPER	Mr. Robertson
LENOX	Mr. Pritchard
HON. CAPTAIN PENDRAGON	Mr. Simpson
JERRY	Mr. Barnes
LAROLE	Mr. Spiller
JENKINS	Mr. Johnson
INDIAN CHIEF	Mr. Maywood
1ST. OFFICER	Mr. Bancker
SOLDIER	Mr. Nexsen
WAITER	Mr. Oliff
JAILOR	Mr. Baldwin
Soldiers, Peasants, Indians, &c.	
CHRISTINE	Miss Leesugg
ADELA	Miss Johnson
MAID	Mrs. Wheatley
Peasant Women, &c.	

1. In Dr. Atkinson's copy of this play, the following cast is given: as a note, in the handwriting of Henry Wallack:

PHILADELPHIA, 1819.

GENERAL	Hughes
JASPER	———
LENOX	Darley, John, Jr.
PENDRAGON	Wood, William
JERRY	Jefferson, Joseph
LAROLE	Blissett, Francis
CHIEF	Wallack, Henry
CHRISTINE	Darley, Mrs. John (Miss E. Westray)
ADELA	Wood, Mrs. Wm. (Miss J. Westray

She Would Be a Soldier, or The Plains of Chippewa

ACT I.

Scene I. *A Valley with a neat Cottage on the right, an Arbour on the left, and picturesque Mountains at a distance. Enter from the cottage,* JASPER *and* JENKINS.

JENKINS: And so, neighbour, you are not then a native of this village?

JASPER: I am not, my friend; my story is short, and you shall hear it. It was my luck, call it bad or good, to be born in France, in the town of Castlenaudary, where my parents, good honest peasants, cultivated a small farm on the borders of the canal of Midi. I was useful, though young; we were well enough to live, and I received from the parish school a good education, was taught to love my country, my parents, and my friends; a happy temper, a common advantage in my country, made all things easy to me; I never looked for to-morrow to bring me more joy than I experienced to-day.

JENKINS: Pardon my curiosity, friend Jasper: how came you to leave your country, when neither want nor misfortune visited your humble dwelling?

JASPER: Novelty, a desire for change, an ardent disposition to visit foreign countries. Passing through the streets of Toulouse one bright morning in spring, the lively drum and fife broke on my ear, as I was counting my gains from a day's marketing. A company of soldiers neatly dressed, with white cockades, passed me with a brisk step; I followed them through instinct—the sergeant informed me that they were on their way to Bordeaux, from thence to embark for America, to aid the cause of liberty in the new world, and were commanded by the Marquis de la Fayette. That name was familiar to me; La Fayette was a patriot—I felt like a patriot, and joined the ranks immediately.

JENKINS: Well, you enlisted and left your country?

JASPER: I did. We had a boisterous passage to America, and endured many hardships during the revolution. I was wounded at Yorktown, which long disabled me, but what then? I served under great men, and for a great cause; I saw the independence of the thirteen states acknowledged, I was promoted to a sergeancy by the great Washington, and I sheathed my sword, with the honest pride of knowing, that I had aided in establishing a powerful and happy republic.

JENKINS: You did well, honest Jasper, you did well; and now you have the satisfaction of seeing your country still free and happy.

JASPER: I have, indeed. When the army was disbanded, I travelled on foot to explore the uncultivated territory which I had assisted in liberating. I purchased a piece of land near the great lakes, and with my axe levelled the mighty oaks, cleared my meadows, burnt out the wolves and bears, and then built that cottage there.

JENKINS: And thus became a settler and my neighbour; thanks to the drum and fife and the white cockade, that lured you from your home.

JASPER: In a short time, Jenkins, everything flourished; my cottage was neat, my cattle thriving, still I wanted something—it was a wife. I was tired of a solitary life, and married Kate, the miller's daughter; you knew her.

JENKINS: Ay, that I did; she was a pretty lass.

JASPER: She was a good wife—ever cheerful and industrious, and made me happy: poor Kate! I was without children for several years; at length my Christine was born, and I have endeavoured, in cultivating her mind, and advancing her happiness, to console myself for the loss of her mother.

JENKINS: Where is Christine? where is your daughter, neighbour Jasper?

JASPER: She left the cottage early this morning with Lenox, to climb the mountains and see the sun rise; it is time for them to return to breakfast.

JENKINS: Who is this Mr. Lenox?

JASPER: An honest lieutenant of infantry, with a gallant spirit and a warm heart. He was wounded at Niagara, and one stormy night, he presented himself at our cottage door, pale and haggard. His arm had been shattered by a ball, and he had received a flesh wound from a bayonet: we took him in—for an old soldier never closes his door on a wounded comrade—Christine nursed him, and he soon recovered. But I wish they were here—it is growing late: besides, this is a busy day, friend Jenkins.

JENKINS: Ah, how so?

JASPER: You know Jerry Mayflower, the wealthy farmer; he has offered to marry my Christine. Girls must not remain single if they can get husbands, and I have consented to the match, and he will be here to-day to claim her hand.

JENKINS: But will Christine marry Jerry? She has been too well educated for the honest farmer.

Jasper: Oh, she may make a few wry faces, as she does when swallowing magnesia, but the dose will go down. There is some credit due to a wife who improves the intellect of her husband; aye, and there is some pride in it also. Girls should marry. Matrimony is like an old oak; age gives durability to the trunk, skill trims the branches, and affection keeps the foliage ever green. But come, let us in. [Jasper *and* Jenkins *enter the cottage.*

*Pastoral Music.—*Lenox *and* Christine *are seen winding down the mountains—his left arm is in a sling.*

Christine: At last we are at home.—O my breath is nearly gone. You soldiers are so accustomed to marching and counter-marching, that you drag me over hedge and briar, like an empty baggage-wagon. Look at my arm, young Mars, you've made it as red as pink, and as rough as—then my hand—don't attempt to kiss it, you—wild man of the woods.

Lenox: Nay, dear Christine, be not offended; if I have passed rapidly over rocks and mountains, it is because you were with me. My heart ever feels light and happy when I am permitted to walk with you; even the air seems newly perfumed, and the birds chaunt more melodiously; and see, I can take my arm out of confinement—your care has done this; your voice administered comfort, and your eyes affection. What do I not owe you?

Christine: Owe me? Nothing, only one of your best bows, and your prettiest compliments. But I do suspect, my serious cavalier, that your wounds were never as bad as you would have me think. Of late you have taken your recipes with so much grace, have swallowed so many bitter tinctures with a playful smile, that I believe you've been playing the invalid, and would make me your nurse for life—O sinner as you are, what have you to say for yourself?

Lenox: Why, I confess, dear Christine, that my time has passed with so much delight, that even the call of duty will find me reluctant to quit these scenes, so dear to memory, hospitality, and, let me add, to love. Be serious, then, dear Christine, and tell me what I have to hope; even now I expect orders from my commanding officer, requiring my immediate presence at the camp; we are on the eve of a battle—Speak!

Christine: Why, you soldiers are such fickle game, that if we once entangle you in the net, 'tis ten to one but the sight of a new face will be sufficiently tempting to break the mesh—you're just as true as the smoke of your cannon, and you fly off at the sight of novelty in petticoats, like one of your Congreve rockets—No, I won't love a soldier—that's certain.

Lenox: Nay, where is our reward then for deserving well of our country? Gratitude may wreath a chaplet of laurel, but trust me, Christine, it withers unless consecrated by beauty.

CHRISTINE: Well, that's a very pretty speech, and deserves one of my best courtesies. Now suppose I should marry you, my "dear ally Croaker," I shall expect to see myself placed on the summit of a baggage-wagon, with soldiers' wives and a few dear squalling brats, whose musical tones drown e'en the "squeaking of the wry-neck'd fife;" and if I should escape from the enemy at the close of a battle, I should be compelled to be ever ready, and "pack up my tatters and follow the drum." —No, no, I can't think of it.

LENOX: Prithee, be serious, dear Christine, your gaiety alarms me. Can you permit me to leave you without a sigh? Can I depart from that dear cottage and rush to battle without having the assurance that there is a heart within which beats in unison with mine? a heart which can participate in my glory, and sympathize in my misfortunes?

CHRISTINE: No—not so, Lenox; your glory is dear to me, your happiness my anxious wish. I have seen you bear pain like a soldier, and misfortune like a man. I am myself a soldier's daughter, and believe me, when I tell you, that under the appearance of gaiety, my spirits are deeply depressed at your approaching departure. I have been taught, by a brave father, to love glory when combined with virtue. There is my hand;—be constant, and I am ever your friend; be true, and you shall find me ever faithful.

LENOX: Thanks—a thousand thanks, beloved Christine; you have removed a mountain of doubts and anxious wishes from my heart: I did hope for this reward, though it was a daring one. Love and honour must now inspire me, and should we again be triumphant in battle, I shall return to claim the reward of constancy—a reward dearer than thrones—the heart of a lovely and virtuous woman.

CHRISTINE: Enough, dear Lenox; I shall never doubt your faith. But come, let us in to breakfast—stay—my knight of the rueful countenance, where is the portrait which you have been sketching of me? Let me look at your progress.

LENOX: 'Tis here. [*Gives a small drawing book.*

CHRISTINE: [*Opening it.*] Heavens, how unlike! Why Lenox, you were dreaming of the *Venus de Medici* when you drew this—Oh, you flatterer!

LENOX: Nay, 'tis not finished; now stand there, while I sketch the drapery.—[*Places her at a distance, takes out a pencil, and works at the drawing.*]

CHRISTINE: Why, what a statue you are making of me. Pray, why not make a picture of it at once? Place me in that bower, with a lute and a lap dog, sighing for your return; then draw a soldier disguised as a pilgrim, leaning on his staff, and his cowl thrown back; let that pilgrim resemble thee, and then let the little dog bark, and I fainting, and there's a subject for the pencil and pallet.

Lenox: Sing, dear Christine, while I finish the drawing—it may be the last time I shall ever hear you.

Christine: Oh, do not say so, my gloomy cavalier; a soldier, and despair?

The Knight Errant
Written by the late Queen of Holland.

It was Dunois, the young and brave, was bound to Palestine,
But first he made his orisons before St. Mary's shrine:
And grant, immortal Queen of Heav'n, was still the soldier's prayer,
That I may prove the bravest knight, and love the fairest fair.

His oath of honour on the shrine he grav'd it with his sword,
And follow'd to the Holy Land the banner of his Lord;
Where, faithful to his noble vow, his war-cry fill'd the air—
Be honour'd, aye, the bravest knight, beloved the fairest fair.

They ow'd the conquest to his arm, and then his liege lord said,
The heart that has for honour beat must be by bliss repaid:
My daughter Isabel and thou shall be a wedded pair,
For thou art bravest of the brave, she fairest of the fair.

And then they bound the holy knot before St. Mary's shrine,
Which makes a paradise on earth when hearts and hands combine;
And every lord and lady bright that was in chapel there,
Cry'd, Honour'd be the bravest knight, belov'd the fairest fair.

Lenox: There, 'tis finished—how do you like it?

Christine: Why, so, so—if you wish something to remind you of me, it will do.

Lenox: No, not so; your image is too forcibly impressed here to need so dull a monitor. But I ask it to reciprocate—wear this for my sake [*Gives a miniature.*], and think of him who, even in the battle's rage, will not forget thee. [*Bugle sounds at a distance.*] Hark! 'tis a bugle of our army. [*Enter a* Soldier, *who delivers a letter to* Lenox *and retires*—Lenox *opens and reads it.*

The enemy, in force, has thrown up entrenchments near Chippewa; if your wounds will permit, join your corps without delay—a battle is unavoidable, and I wish you to share the glory of a victory. You have been promoted as an aid to the general for your gallantry in the last affair. It gives me pleasure to be the first who announces this grateful reward—lose not a moment. Your friend, Mandeville."

I must be gone immediately.

Enter JASPER *and* JENKINS *from the cottage.*

JASPER: Ah! Lenox, my boy, good morning to you. Why, Christine, you have had a long ramble with the invalid.

CHRISTINE: Lenox leaves us immediately, dear father; the army is on the march.

JASPER: Well, he goes in good time, and may success attend him. Ods my life, when I was young, the sound of the drum and fife was like the music of the spheres, and the noise and bustle of a battle was more cheering to me, than "the hunter's horn in the morning." You will not forget us, Lenox, will you?

LENOX: Forget ye? Never—I should be the most ungrateful of men, could I forget that endearing attention which poured oil into my wounds, and comforted the heart of a desponding and mutilated soldier. No, Jasper, no; while life remains, yourself and daughter shall never cease to live in my grateful remembrance. [Christine *and* Lenox *enter the cottage.*

Pastoral Music.—Peasants are seen winding down the mountains, headed by JERRY, *dressed for a festive occasion, with white favours, nosegays, &c.*

JERRY: Here I am, farmer Jasper—come to claim Miss Crissy as my wife, according to your promise, and have brought all my neighbours. How do you do?

JASPER: Well—quite well—and these are all your neighbours?

JERRY: Yes—there's Bob Short, the tanner; Nick Anvil, the blacksmith; Patty, the weaver's daughter—and the rest of 'em; come here, Patty, make a curtchey to the old soger—[PATTY *comes forward.*]—a pretty girl!
I could have had her, but she wanted edication—she wanted the airs and graces, as our schoolmaster says.

JASPER: Well, farmer, you are an honest man, but I fear my Christine will not approve this match, commenced without her advice, and concluded without her consent. Then her education has been so different from—

JERRY: O, fiddle-de-dee, I don't mind how larned she is, so much the better—she can teach me to parlyvoo, and dance solos and duets, and such elegant things, when I've done ploughing.

JASPER: But I'm not sure that she will like you.

Jerry: Not like me? Come, that's a good one; only look at my movements—why she can't resist me. I'm the boy for a race, for an apple-paring or quilting frolic—fight a cock, hunt an opossum, or snare a partridge with any one.—Then I'm a squire, and a county judge, and a *brevet* ossifer in the militia besides; and a devil of a fellow at an election to boot. Not have me? damme, that's an insult. Besides, sergeant Jasper, I've been to the wars since I've seen ye—got experience, laurels and lilies, and all them there things.

Jasper: Indeed!

Jerry: Yes—sarved a campaign, and was at the battle of Queenstown. What do you think of that?

Jasper: And did you share in the glory of that spirited battle?

Jerry: O yes, I shared in all the glory—that is—I didn't fight. I'll tell you how it was: I marched at the head of my village sogers, straight as the peacock in my farm yard, and I had some of the finest lads in our county, with rifles—well, we march'd and camp'd, and camp'd and march'd, and were as merry as grigs until we arrived at the river: half the troops had cross'd and were fighting away like young devils: ods life, what a smoke! what a popping of small arms, and roaring of big ones! and what a power of red coats!

Jasper: Well, and you panted to be at them? clubb'd your rifles, and dashed over?

Jerry: Oh no, I didn't—I was afear'd that in such a crowd, nobody would see how I fought, so I didn't cross at all. Besides, some one said, it were contrary to law and the constitution, to go into the enemy's country, but if they com'd into our country, it were perfectly lawful to flog 'em.

Jasper: And you did not cross?

Jerry: Oh no, I stood still and look'd on: it were contrary to the constitution of my country, and my own constitution to boot—so I took my post out of good gun shot, and felt no more fear nor you do now.

Jasper: No doubt. Admirable sophistry, that can shield cowards and traitors, under a mistaken principle of civil government! I've heard of those scruples, which your division felt when in sight of the enemy. Was that a time to talk of constitutions—when part of our gallant army was engaged with unequal numbers? Could you calmly behold your fellow citizens falling on all sides, and not avenge their death? Could you, with arms in your hands, the enemy in view, with the roar of cannon thundering on your ear, and the flag of your country waving amidst fire and smoke—could you find a moment to think of constitutions? Was that a time to pause and suffer coward scruples to unnerve the arm of freemen?

JERRY: Bravo! bravo! sergeant Jasper; that's a very fine speech—I'll vote for you for our assemblyman; now just go that over again, that I may get it by heart for our next town meeting—blazing flags—fiery cannon—smoking constitutions—

JASPER: I pray you pardon me. I am an old soldier, and fought for the liberty which you enjoy, and, therefore, claim some privilege in expressing my opinion. But come, your friends are idle, let us have breakfast before our cottage door.—Ah, Jerry, my Crissy would make a fine soldier's wife: do you know that I have given her a military education?

JERRY: No, surely—

JASPER: Aye, she can crack a bottle at twelve paces with a pistol.

JERRY: Crack a bottle! Come, that's a good one; I can crack a bottle, too, but not so far off.

JASPER: And then she can bring down a buck, at any distance.

JERRY: Bring down a buck? I don't like that—can't say as how I like my wife to meddle with bucks. Can she milk—knit garters—make apple butter and maple sugar—dance a reel after midnight, and ride behind her husband on a pony, to see the trainings of our sogers—that's the wife for my money. Oh, here she comes.

Enter CHRISTINE *and* LENOX *from the cottage.*

JASPER: Christine, here is farmer Mayflower and his friends, who have come to visit our cottage, and you in particular.

CHRISTINE: They are all welcome. Good morning, Jerry—how is it with you?

JERRY: Purely, Miss Crissy, I'm stout and hearty, and you look as pretty and as rosy as a field of pinks on a sunshiny morning.

JASPER: Come here, farmer—give me your hand—Christine, yours—[*Joins them.*]—there; may you live long and happy, and my blessings ever go with you.

CHRISTINE: [*Aside in amazement.*] Heavens! what can this mean? [LENOX *is agitated—pause—*JASPER *and group retire—* LENOX *remains at a distance.*

JERRY: Why, Miss Crissy, your father has consented that I shall marry you, and

I've come with my neighbours to have a little frolic, and carry you home with me.

CHRISTINE: And am I of so little moment as not to be consulted? Am I thus to be given away by my father without one anxious question? [*With decision.*] Farmer, pardon my frankness; on this occasion, sincerity alone is required—I do not like you, I will not marry you—nay, do not look surprised. I am a stranger to falsehood and dissimulation, and thus end at once all hopes of ever becoming my husband.

JERRY: Why, now, Miss Crissy, that's very cruel of you—I always had a sneaking kindness for you, and when your father gave his consent, I didn't dream as how you could refuse me.

CHRISTINE: My father has ever found me dutiful and obedient, but when he bestows my hand, without knowing whether my heart or inclinations accompany it, I feel myself bound to consult my own happiness. I cannot marry you, farmer.

LENOX: [*Advancing.*] All things are prepared, and I am now about to depart. Christine, farewell! Friends, good fortune await you! [*Aside.*] Dear Christine, remember me. [*Exit hastily.*

JERRY: Lack-a-daisy! What a disappointment to me, when I had put my house in such nice order—painted my walls—got a new chest upon chest—two new bed quilts, and a pair of pumps, and had the pig-sty and dairy whitewashed.—Hang me, after all, I believe, she is only a little shy. Oh, I see it now, she only wants a little coaxing—a little sparking or so—I've a great mind to kiss her. I will, too. [*Approaches* CHRISTINE, *who stands at a distance, buried in deep thought.*

CHRISTINE: Begone—dare not touch me! Heavens, am I reserved for this humiliation? Could my father be so cruel?

JERRY: Now, Crissy, don't be so shy—you know you like me—you know you said t' other day, when I were out training, that I held up my head more like a soger than anybody in the ranks; come now, let's make up; you'll always find me a dutiful husband, and if I ever flog you, then my name's not Jerry.

Enter JASPER *from the cottage, with a basket;* PEASANTS *following with fruit.*

JASPER: Come, let us have breakfast in the open air—help me to arrange the table.

JERRY: Breakfast! Oh, true, I've a powerful appetite. [*Assists.*

CHRISTINE: [*Aside.*] What is to be done? I have not a moment to lose; my father is stern and unyielding—I know his temper too well, to hope that my entreaties will prevail with him—the farmer is rich, and gold is a powerful tempter. I must be gone—follow Lenox, and in disguise, to avoid this hateful match. I'll in, whilst unobserved. [*Enters the cottage.*

Jasper: Come, sit down, farmer and neighbours; and you, my pretty lads and lasses, let's have a dance. Ah, here is a foraging party.

[*Enter* Soldiers.

Party dance—several pastoral and fancy dances—and as the whole company retires, Christine *comes from the cottage with cautious steps—she is dressed in a frock coat, pantaloons and hat.*

Christine: They are gone—now to escape. Scenes of my infancy—of many a happy hour, farewell! Oh, farewell, forever! [*Exit.*

Jasper *and* Jerry *return.*

Jerry: She refused me plumply.

Jasper: Impossible!

Jerry: No, it's quite possible. Farmer, said she, I will *not* marry you—and hang me if there's any joke in that.

Jasper: Refuse an honest man? A wealthy one, too? And one whom her father gives to her? Trifling girl! Insensible to her happiness and interest. What objections had she to you, farmer?

Jerry: Objections! Oh, none in the world, only she wouldn't marry me; she didn't seem struck at all with my person.

Jasper: Mere coyness—maiden bashfulness.

Jerry: So I thought, sergeant Jasper, and was going to give her a little kiss, when she gave me such a look, and such a push, as quite astounded me.

Jasper: I will seek and expostulate with the stubborn girl. Ah, Jerry, times have strangely altered, when young women choose husbands for themselves, with as much ease and indifference, as a ribbon for their bonnet. [*Enters the cottage.*

Jerry: So they do—the little independent creatures as they are—but what Miss Crissy could see in me to refuse, hang me if I can tell. I'm call'd as sprightly a fellow as any in our county, and up to everything—always ready for fun, and perfectly good-natured. [*Enter* Jasper *from the cottage, agitated.*

Jasper: She is nowhere to be found—she has gone off and left her poor old father. In her room, I found these lines scrawled with a pencil: "You have driven your daughter from you, by urging a match that was hateful to her. Was her happiness not worth consulting?" What's to be done? Where has she gone? Ah, a light breaks in upon me—to the camp—to the camp!

JERRY: Oho! I smell a rat too—she's gone after Mr. Lenox, the infantry ossifer. Oh, the young jade! But come along, old soger—get your hat and cane, and we'll go arter her—I'm a magistrate, and will bring her back by a habes corpus.

They enter the cottage.

Scene II. *A Wood.*

Enter CHRISTINE *in haste, looking back with fear.*

CHRISTINE: On, on, or I shall be pursued and o'ertaken—I have lost my way. Ah, yonder is the camp—I see the flags and tents—a short time and I shall be with you, dear Lenox. [*Exit.*

Enter JASPER; JERRY *and* PEASANTS.

JERRY: We're on the right track, farmer; I know all tracks—used to 'em when I hunt 'possums.

JASPER: Cruel girl! to desert her old father, who has ever been kind and affectionate.

JERRY: Cruel girl! to desert me, who intended to be so very affectionate, if she had given me a chance.

JASPER: We cannot be far from the outposts, let us continue our search. [*Exeunt.*

Scene III. *A Camp.*

A row of tents in the rear with camp flags at equal distances; on the right wing is a neat marquee, and directly opposite to it another. Sentinels on duty at each marquee.

Enter from the marquee, LENOX *and* ADELA

LENOX: I never was more surprised! just when I had brush'd up my arms, and prepared to meet the enemy, who should I find in camp but you, my old hoyden scholar. Why Adela, you have grown nearly as tall as a grenadier, and as pretty—zounds, I would kiss you, if I dare.

ADELA: I am delighted to see you, dear Lenox; you are still as gay and amiable as when you taught your little Adela to conjugate verbs, and murder French; I heard of your gallantry and wounds, and imagined I should see you limping on crutches, with a green patch over one eye, and a wreath of laurel around your head, a kind of limping, one-eyed cupid; but I find you recovered from your wounds, and ready for new ones, my soldier.

Lenox: Bravo! the little skipping girl, who was once so full of mischief, has grown a tall and beautiful woman. But what brings you to camp, Adela? What have you to do with "guns and drums? heaven save the mark!"

Adela: Why, my father wrote for me, expecting that the campaign was drawing to a close; but scarcely had I arrived here, when intelligence reached us that the enemy, in force, had occupied a position near Chippewa; it was too late to return, so I remained to see a little skirmishing.

Lenox: And are you prepared to endure the privations of a camp?

Adela: Oh, it is delightful! it is something out of the common order of things, something new—such echoing of bugles—glistening of fire-arms, and nodding of plumes—such marchings and countermarchings—and such pretty officers too, Lenox; but then a terrible accident happened to me the other day.

Lenox: Aye, what was it?

Adela: Why, you must know that I accompanied my father, who with his suite, and a small detachment, went out on a reconnoitering project.—Just as we *debouched* from the wood, according to the military phrase, we came suddenly and unexpectedly on a foraging party of the enemy, who began to fight and retreat at the same time.

Lenox: Well?

Adela: My horse happening to be an old trooper, the moment the bugles sounded, and he heard the prattle of the small arms, he dashed in amongst them, and there was I screaming in a most delightful style, which, by some, must have been mistaken for a war-whoop, and to mend the matter, a very polite and accomplished Indian took aim at me with his rifle, and actually shot away the plume from my hat, which, I dare say, was as valuable a prize to him as I should have been.

Lenox: And how did you escape from your perilous situation?

Adela: Oh, I soon recovered my fright, and reined in my old horse; my father and a few soldiers cut in before me, and covered my retreat, so that in the conclusion of this little affair, I gained a feather in my cap, though the enemy carried of the plume; and I found myself at last on the field of battle, as cool as any hero in the army.

Lenox: And so, my lively Adela, you have been fairly introduced to Mars and Bellona: how do you like them?

Adela: Prodigiously. I find, after all, that courage is something like a cold bath; take the first plunge, and all is over. Lord, Lenox, how delightful it would have been, had I been armed and fought gallantly in that affair; my name would have been immortalized like Joan of Arc's. Congress would have voted me a medal, I should have had a public dinner at Tammany-Hall, and his honour the mayor would have made me one of his prettiest speeches, in presenting me with the freedom of the great city in a gold box.

Lenox: And so, then, you admire a military life?

Adela: Oh, I'm in raptures with it! I am a perfect female Quixote, and would relinquish a thousand dandy beaux for one brave fellow; and therefore, Lenox, don't be surprised, if you should see me going about from tent to tent, chaunting the old songs of

"Soldier, soldier, marry me,
With your fife and drum."

Christine *suddenly appears in the background and surveys the party with astonishment.*

Christine: Heavens! what do I see? Lenox, and with a female so affectionately?

Lenox: Your spirits charm me, dear Adela, and revive those feelings for you, that time has impaired, but not destroyed. But come, let us in and see your worthy father. [*Leads her into the tent to the left.*

Christine: Cruel, unkind, false Lenox! Are these your vows of constancy? are these your protestations of love? Scarcely are you free from our cottage, when your vows and pledges are but air. Wretched Christine! what will become of you? I have deserted my father's house to avoid a hateful match, and seek the protection of the man I love; he is false, and I am lost. What's to be done? Return home a penitent, and meet the frowns of my father, and be wedded to the man I hate? Never. Seek out Lenox, and upbraid him with his falsehood? No, pride and wounded honour will not permit me. Let him go—he is a wretch who trifles with the affections of a woman. I care not what becomes of me, despair is all that I have left. Ha! a thought strikes me with the lightning's force—the army—I will enlist—this disguise is favourable, and in the battle's rage, seek that death which quickly awaits me—'tis resolved. [Corporal *passes over the stage.*] Hist, corporal.

Corporal: Well, my lad, what would ye?

Christine: I would enlist, good corporal, and serve my country.

Corporal: Enlist! As a drummer or fifer, I suppose.

Christine: No; in the ranks—and though small, you will find me capable. Give me your musket.

[Christine *takes the musket, shoulders, presents, and goes through a few motions.*

Corporal: Well done, my little fellow; you'll do, if it's only for a fugelman; come along to our sergeant, and receive the bounty. [*Exit.*

Christine: Now, Lenox, now am I fully revenged for your cruel desertion.[*Follows.*

End of the First Act.

ACT II.

Scene I. *York, in Upper Canada; a Tavern meanly furnished.*

Enter LaRole, *in pursuit of the chambermaid.*

LaRole: Come here, you littel demoiselle—you bootiful sauvage, vy you run vay from me—hay?

Maid: I wish you would let me alone, mounsure, you officers' gentlemen are very disagreeable things.

LaRole: Disagreeable? ma foi! I am one jòli garçon, one pretti batchelor; disagreeable? I vill tell you, ma belle grizette, I am maître de mode, I give de leçons for dance, to speake de English, and de Française aussi; I can fence, aha! or fight de duel, or de enemi, je suis un soldat.

Maid: Well, if you're a soldier, you have no business to be following me up and down the house like a pet lamb. Why don't you go to camp?

LaRole: Camp? vat is de camp? Oho, le champ de bataille; I shall tell you, mademoiselle, I did fight at the bataille de Vittoria, com un diable, like littel devil. I did kill beaucoup d'Anglais. Mai my maître, le capitain, he did give me a dam tump on my head wis his rapier, and did knock me down from on top of my horse, and make a me von prisonier.

MAID: Poor fellow! And so, mounsure, you were made prisoner?

LAROLE: Oui, ven I could not run avay, begar I surrender like von brave homme, and now I am jentiman to capitain Pendragoon; I do brus his coat, poudre his hair, and pull his corset tight, and ven he was order to come to Amerique, and fight wis de Yankee Doodel, begar me come too. I arrive ici, I am here, to make a littel de love to you.

MAID: Well now, once for all, I tell you not to be following me; I don't like Frenchmen—I can't parlyvoo.

LAROLE: You no like de Frenchiman? O quell barbare! vy you ave von abominable goût, mademoiselle, von shockin taste. I shall tell you, mademoiselle, en my contree, en France, de ladies are ver fond of me. O beaucoup, I am so charmant—so aimable, and so jentee, I have three five sweetheart, ami de coeur, mai for all dat I do love you ver mush, par example.

MAID: Let me go! [*Bell rings.*] There, your master calls you. [*Exit.*

LAROLE: Dam de littel bell, I vill not come; mon maitre he always interrupt me ven I make de love to the pretti ladi, he be jealous, begar I vill not come. [*Exit opposite side.*

Enter CAPTAIN PENDRAGON, *dressed in the British uniform, but in the extreme of fashion—throws himself into a chair.*

PENDRAGON: Oh, curse such roads! My bones are making their way out of their sockets—such vile, abominable, detestable—Waiter!—If my friends at Castle Joram only knew the excruciating fatigues which I am undergoing in this barbarous land—Why, waiter!—or if his highness the commander-in-chief was only sensible of my great sacrifices to—Why, waiter! where the devil are you?

Enter WAITER.

WAITER: Here I be, sir.

PENDRAGON: Why didn't you come when I first called? Do you think I've got lungs like a hunter? I'm fatigued and hungry. Get me an anchovy, a toast, and a bottle of old port.

WAITER: A what, sir? an ancho—

PENDRAGON: Yes, sir, an anchovy—small ones—delicate.

WAITER: Why, sir, we don't know what these are in this country.

PENDRAGON: The devil you don't! Then pray, sir, what have you to eat in this damn'd house fit for a gentleman?

WAITER: Why, sir, not much—the army eats us out of house and home. We have some very excellent fresh bear meat, sir.

PENDRAGON: Bear meat! Why, what the devil, fellow, do you take me for a Chickasaw, or an Esquimau? Bear meat! the honourable captain Pendragon, who never ate anything more gross than a cutlet at Molly's chop-house, and who lived on pigeons' livers at Very's, in Paris, offered bear meat in North America! I'll put that down in my travels.

WAITER: Why, sir, it is considered here a great delicacy.

PENDRAGON: The devil it is! Then pray, sir, what are your ordinary fares, if bear's meat is considered a delicacy?

WAITER: Why, truly, sir, this is but a young country, and we have to live upon what we can catch. Pray, would you fancy some 'possum fat and hominy?

PENDRAGON: Oh, shocking! begone, fellow—you'll throw me into a fever with your vile bill of fare. Get me a cup of tea—mix it, hyson and souchong, with cream and muffins.

WAITER: We can't give you any of those things, sir.—However, you can have an excellent cup of sage tea, sweetened with honey.

PENDRAGON: Sage tea! Why, you rascal, do you intend to throw me into a perspiration by way of curing my hunger? or do you take me for a goose or a duck, that you intend stuffing me with sage? Begone, get out, you little deformed fellow! [*Exit* WAITER.] I shall perish in this barbarous land—bear meat, 'possum fat, and sage tea! O dear St. James! I wish I was snug in my old quarters. LaRole! [*Enter* LAROLE.] Where the devil do you hide yourself in this damn'd house? Why, I shall starve—there's nothing to eat, fit for a gentleman.

LAROLE: Oui, monsieur, dis is von damn contree, I can find nosing to eat. I did look into all de pantri, mai parbleu, I find only a ver pretti demoiselle, mai, I could not eat her.

PENDRAGON: We must be off to the camp, LaRole, my quarters there will be infinitely more agreeable. I shall get the blue devils in this cursed place.

LAROLE: Vell, sair, I have all de devils ventre bleu, das you can imagine; dere is no politesse, no respect, nosing paid to me.

Pendragon: My fit of the blues is coming on me; sing me a song, LaRole.

LaRole: A chanson? Vell, sair, I shall sing to frighten avay de littel blue devil; vill you I shall sing de English or de Française?

Pendragon: Oh, English, by all means—curse your foreign lingo.

LaRole: Ahem! Ahem! you shall understand.

Vat is dis dull town to me,
Robin Hadair?
Vere is all de joys on earth, dat
Make dis town—

[*A bugle sounds without.*

Ha! what is dat? who de devil intrup me in my chanson?

Indian Chief: [*Speaks without.*] Have them all ready, with their rifles and tomahawks in order; [*Enters with another Indian.*] and you, Coosewatchie, tell our priests to take their stand on yonder hill, and as my warriors pass them, examine whether they have fire in their eyes. [*Exit* Indian.] How now, who have we here?

Pendragon: [*Examining him with his glass.*] Where the devil did this character come from? he's one of the fancy, I suppose.

Indian: Who and what are you?

Pendragon: Who am I? Why, sir, I am the honourable captain Pendragon, of his majesty's guards, formerly of the buffs.

Indian: [*Aside.*] The officer who is to be under my command. Well sir, you have lately arrived from across the great waters: How did you leave my father, the King of England?

Pendragon: How! call my most gracious sovereign your father? Why, sir, you are the most familiar—impertinent— 'sdeath! I shall choke—What the devil do you mean?

Indian: [*Coolly.*] What should I mean, young man, but to inquire after the health of my father, who commands my respect, who has honoured me with his favours, and in whose cause I am now fighting.

Pendragon: Well, sir, if you have the honour to hold a commission from his majesty, I desire that you will speak of him with proper awe, and not call him your father, but your gracious master.

Indian: Young man, the Indian warrior knows no master but the Great Spirit, whose voice is heard in thunder, and whose eye is seen in the lightning's flash; free as air, we bow the knee to no man; our forests are our home, our defence is our arms, our sustenance the deer and the elk, which we run down. White men encroach upon our borders, and drive us into war; we raise the tomahawk against your enemies, because your king has promised us protection and supplies. We fight for freedom, and in that cause, the great king and the poor Indian start upon equal terms.

Pendragon: A very clever spoken fellow, pon honour; I'll patronise him.

LaRole: Parbleu, he is von very sensible sauvage; vill you take von pinch snuff?

Indian: Pshaw!

LaRole: He say pshaw, I see he is born in de voods.

Pendragon: And are you prepared to fan these Yankees? We shall flog them without much fatigue, I understand.

Indian: Not so fast, young soldier; these pale-faced enemies of ours fight with obstinacy; accustomed to a hardy life, to liberty and laws, they are not willing to relinquish those blessings on easy terms; if we conquer them, it must be by no moderate exertions[;] it will demand force and cunning.

Pendragon: Oh, dry dogs, I suppose, not to be caught napping; well, I'm up to them, we'll fan them in high style; the ragged nabobs, I understand, are not far off, and our troops are in fine preservation.

Indian: True, preparation must be made to meet them. You are under my orders.

Pendragon: The devil I am!

Indian: Aye, sir; your general, at my request, has ordered you here to take command of a company of my warriors; but you must not appear in that dress: change it quickly, or they will not be commanded by you; they are men, and fight under the orders of men.

Pendragon: Change my dress! why what the devil do you mean, sir?

Indian: Mean? that you should appear in the ranks like a warrior, and not like a rabbit trussed for dressing—off with these garments, which give neither pleasure to the eye nor ease to the limbs—put on moccasins, wrap a blanket around you, put rings through your nose and ears, feathers in your head, and paint yourself like a soldier, with vermilion.

Pendragon: Why, this is the most impertinent and presuming savage in the wilds of North America. Harkee, sir, I'd have you to know, that I am a man of fashion, and one of the fancy—formerly of the buffs, nephew of a peer of the realm, and will be a member of parliament, in time; an officer of great merit and great services, Mr.—Red Jacket. Paint my face, and fight without clothes? I desire, sir, that you will please to take notice, that I fought at Badahoz with the immortal Wellington, and had the honour to be wounded, and promoted, and had a medal for my services in that affair, Mr.—Split-log. Put rings in my nose? a man of taste, and the *ne plus ultra* of Bond-street, the very mirror of fashion and elegance? Sir, I beg you to observe, that I am not to be treated in this manner—I shall resent this insult. Damme, I shall report you to the commander-in-chief at the Horse Guards, and have you courtmartialled for unfashionable deportment—Mr.— Walk-in-the-Water.

Indian: Come, come, sir, enough of this trifling; I do not understand it; you have heard my orders—obey them, or, after the battle, I'll roast you before a slow fire! [*Exit.*

LaRole: O le barbare! O de dam sauvage! dis is de most impertinent dog in de vorld. Roast before de fire! Parbleu, mon maître, ve are not de littel pig.

Pendragon: I'm horrified! lost in amazement! but I'll resent it. Damme, I'll caricature him.

LaRole: Oh, I vish I vas fight encore at Saragossa, vis mi lor Villainton; par example, I did get some hard tumps, mai I did get plenti to eat; but ici I ave nosing but de little bear to mange.

Pendragon: Come along—courage, LaRole. We'll fan the Yankee Doodles in our best style, and then get a furlough, and be off to White-Hall, and the rings in our noses will afford anecdotes for the bon-ton for a whole year. Allons. [Exeunt.

Scene II. *The American Camp at daybreak.*
The drum and fife plays the reveille. Sentinels on duty before the tents.

Lenox *enters from the tent on the right,* General *and* Adela *from the left.*

Lenox: Good morning, general; you are "stirring with the lark"—and you also, Adela.

General: The times require the utmost vigilance, Lenox: the enemy cannot escape a battle now, and we must be prepared at all points to meet him. Decision and energy cannot fail to promote success.

ADELA: And what is to become of me, father, in the battle? Am I to ride the old trooper again, and run the risk of having the tip of my nose carried away by a musket ball, and left on the field of battle in all my glory?

GENERAL: You shall be taken care of, dear Adela; we will place you in the rear, among the baggage-wagons.

ADELA: And if they should be captured, I become also a prisoner and probably a prize to some gallant Indian chief, who will make me his squaw, and teach me to kill deer. O delightful thought! [*Bugles sound.*

GENERAL: The troops are under arms, and approaching.

[*Quick march—the* GENERAL, LENOX *and* ADELA *pass to the left, and stand near the tent, the troops advance;* CHRISTINE *is among them, dressed in uniform; they pass round the stage in regular order, then form the line two deep;* CHRISTINE *is in front on the right, and keeps her eye fixed anxiously on* LENOX; *drum beats the roll; the troops come to an order, and then proceed through the manual by the tap of drum, and finally to a present; the* GENERAL, LENOX, *and other officers advance, and pass through the line in review; the flags wave, and the band strikes up "Hail Columbia."*

GENERAL: Well—everything is right. And now, soldiers, to your posts; remember, discipline, subordination, courage, and country, and victory will be ours. [GENERAL, LENOX *and* ADELA, *enter the tent to the left. The troops march off.* CHRISTINE *and a* SOLDIER, *headed by a* CORPORAL, *return to relieve guard at each tent. Port arms and whisper the countersign.* CHRISTINE *is placed before the tent on the right, her comrade on the left.* CORPORAL *retires with the two relieved sentries. After a pause, she beckons to her comrade.]*

CHRISTINE: Hist—comrade!

SOLDIER Well, what is it?

CHRISTINE: Will you exchange places? There is no difference—and the sun will be too powerful for me presently. Look, here is a dollar.

SOLDIER: With all my heart. [*They cross quickly, the* SOLDIER *receives the money—* CHRISTINE *now paces before the tent into which* LENOX, ADELA *and the* GENERAL *have retired.*]

CHRISTINE: Could I but see the false, perfidious Lenox, and upbraid him with his cruelty! [*She is in great uneasiness, pauses occasionally, and looks into the tent—her comrade is watching her.* LENOX *sings within.*]

Shall the pleasures of life unknown fade away,
In viewing those charms so lovely and gay?
Shall the heart which has breath'd forth rapturous flame,
Be hid from the world and unsought for by fame?

Thus spoke the fond Roscoe to Scylla the fair,
As he gaz'd on her charms, with a love-soothing care:
Hear now the last wish, that fondly I sigh,
I'll conquer in love, or in battle I'll die.

He girded his armour and flew to the field,
Determin'd while life flow'd never to yield;
The foe was subdued, but death's cruel dart
Was aim'd at the valiant and fond Roscoe's heart:

But the blow was defeated—he lived to enjoy
The sight of his Scylla, no longer so coy,
And his laurels fresh bloom'd, as she smil'd on the youth,
And gave her fair hand in reward for his truth.

CHRISTINE: Ha, that false voice! I can no longer bear it! [*Throws down her gun, and is about entering the tent, when her comrade, who has been attentively regarding her movements, rushes over and seizes her.*]

SOLDIER: Where are you going?

CHRISTINE: Unhand me this instant! [*Struggles.*

SOLDIER: Guards, there!

Enter an OFFICER *with* SOLDIERS, *who attempts to seize* CHRISTINE—*she draws her sword and stands on the defensive, and after some resistance, escapes.*

OFFICER: Pursue him quickly! [SOLDIERS *pursue.*

SOLDIER: He crosses the bridge.

OFFICER: The sentinels will reach him with their guns. [*Muskets discharged.*

SOLDIER: They have him—he is not hurt.

General, Adela, *and* Lenox *rush from the tent.*

General: What means this confusion?

2nd Officer: The sentinel who was placed here on duty, attempted, for some desperate purpose, to enter your tent; but being discovered, he refused to surrender, drew his sword on me and the guard, and, after some resistance, has been disarmed and secured.

Lenox: Good heavens! What object could he have had?

2nd Officer: I know not—but he is a new recruit, probably a spy from the enemy.

General: It must be so—see that a court martial be called to try him, and bring the result to me without delay. If he is guilty, a dreadful example shall be made of him. Begone. [*Exeunt* General, Soldiers, *&c.*

Scene III. *Another Part of the Camp.*

Enter Jasper, Jerry *and* Peasants.

Jasper: Nowhere to be found. I have asked everybody in the camp in vain—she is lost to me. Unhappy, cruel girl! to quit her old and fond father thus.

Jerry: Unhappy girl! to leave me in such an ungenteel manner too, run away from me on my wedding day! but I'll find her out.

Jasper: Impossible! we must return, dejected and disappointed.

Jerry: I'll peep into every tent, bribe the sogers—I've got a little money left. [Jasper *and* Peasants *retire.* Corporal *crosses the stage.*] Hist, corporal!

Corporal: Well, what would you?

Jerry: Why no, sure—it isn't—yes, it is—why Corporal Flash, how do you do? Don't you know me?

Corporal: Can't say I do, sir.

Jerry: Why, not know Jerry Mayflower? Don't you remember me at the battle of Queenstown, when you were in the boat and I on land, and you were crossing to fight Johnny Bull, and I didn't cross at all?

Corporal: Oh, I remember you now—I remember calling you a cowardly rascal at the time.

Jerry: So you did—how have you been? I am very glad to see you—you're not killed, I take it?

Corporal: No, not exactly killed—but I was wounded—an honour which you didn't seem to care much about.

Jerry: No, not much; I'm not very ambitious that way.

Corporal: What brings you to the camp, just when we are about having another brush with the enemy—do you want to run away again? Zounds! you deserve a round hundred at the halberts.

Jerry: Yes, I deserve many things that I don't get—but pray, corporal, mout you have seen a young woman in this here camp lately?

Corporal: Oh, plenty, among the suttlers.

Jerry: No, a kind of a pretty girl, a little lady-like, parlyvoos, and carries her head up straight.

Corporal: No—I've seen no such person.

Jerry: Well, Corporal Flash, I've a little cash, and what say you to a jug of whiskey punch? Brave men, you know, like you and I, should drink with one another.

Corporal: With all my heart; you're good for nothing else but to drink with.

Jerry: Then come along, my boy; we'll drown care, raise our spirits, and swallow the enemy in a bumper. [*Exeunt*.

Scene IV. *A Prison.*

Enter two Officers, Guards *and* Christine.

Officers *seat themselves at a table, with pens and ink.*

1st Officer: Young man, come forward. You have been charged with an act of mutiny, and with an attempt, for some unknown cause, to force your way, with arms in your hand, into the tent of the commanding general. We are convened for your trial—we have examined the testimony; and as you are a stranger in our ranks, no feelings of prejudice could have given a false colouring to that testimony. What have you to say?

CHRISTINE: Nothing.

OFFICER: Nothing?

CHRISTINE: Nothing! [*With firmness.*] I am guilty!

OFFICER: Have a care, pause before you make this avowal of your guilt.

CHRISTINE: [*With settled firmness.*] I have considered it well, and am ready to meet the consequences. I am guilty. [*With a burst of anguish.*] Oh, most guilty!

OFFICER: Unhappy young man, what could have tempted you to this act? Who set you on?

CHRISTINE: Seek not to know the cause, 'tis buried here. Do your duty—I am prepared for the result.

OFFICER: [*To the Board.*] The charge is fully admitted, and the rules of war prescribe the punishment. The object he had in view must yet be discovered; 'tis plain, however, that he is a spy, and has no hope of pardon. Record the verdict and sentence, for the inspection and concurrence of the general. [OFFICER *writes. The company rise from the table, and one approaches* CHRISTINE, *who appears buried in thought.*

OFFICER: Young man, I deeply commiserate your unhappy situation, but the rules of war are rigid, and must be enforced. You must prepare to die!

CHRISTINE: [*Starts, but recovers herself quickly.*] I am ready.

OFFICER: I would offer you hope, but acts of mutiny, and when covering such suspicious motives as yours, cannot be pardoned. You have but a day to live. I deeply regret it, for you appear to have qualities which, in time, would have made you a valuable citizen. You are cut off in youth, probably from the hopes of a fond parent.

CHRISTINE: [*In agony.*] Oh, no more—no more!

OFFICER: All the sympathy and indulgence which can be offered you shall be yours! Farewell. [*Exit* OFFICERS, GUARDS, *&c.*

CHRISTINE: At length 'tis concluded, and an ignominious death terminates my unmerited sufferings. Cruel father! and still more cruel Lenox! thus to have wounded the heart that loved you. Oh, what a situation is mine! separated from all know that death, alone, can tell my sad story. What's to be done? Discover all? No, no. Expose my weakness and folly—to see the false Lenox wedded to another, and I forced to accept the hand I loathe—to be pointed at for one who, lost to the delicacy of her sex, followed a perfidious lover in disguise, and, tortured by jealousy, enlisted, was mutinous, and sentenced to die; but who, to save a miserable life, avowed her situation, and recorded her disgrace at once? Never, never! let me die, and forever be forgotten—'tis but a blow, and it will end the pangs which torment me here. [*Enter a* Soldier, *who beckons.*] I am ready, lead the way. [*Exit.*

Scene V. *Another part of the Prison.*

Enter the Jailor, *driving* Jerry *before him.*

Jailor: In, in, you mutinous dog! do you come here to breed a riot in our camp?

Jerry: Now, my dear good-natured jailor, only have pity on me, and I'll tell you all about it.

Jailor: I won't hear you—didn't you breed a riot?

Jerry: Why no, it was not me. I am as innocent as a young lamb. I'll tell you how it was—come, sit down on this bench with me. [*They sit.*] You must know that I'm a farmer, pretty well off, as a body mout say, and I wanted a wife; hard by our village, there lived an old soger with a pretty daughter, so I courted the old man for his daughter, and he consented to the match.

Jailor: Well?

Jerry: And so I got together all my neighbours, and, with music, went to the old soger's to get my sweetheart, when, lo and behold! after all my trouble, she refused me plump.

Jailor: No, did she?

Jerry: Ay, indeed; she didn't seem stricken with the proposal—and for fear her father would force her to marry me, egad, she run away.

Jailor: And where did she go?

Jerry: I can't say, but her father and a whole *posse comitatus*, as we justices call 'em, went in search of her to the camp, and when I came here, I found some of my old comrades who fought with me at Queenstown; and so having a little money, we went to take a comfortable pitcher of whiskey punch together, and so, while over our cups, they doubted my valour, and hinted that I run away before the battle.

JAILOR: Well, and what did you do?

JERRY: Why, I offered to fight 'em single-handed all round, and we got into a dispute, and so when my money was all gone, they tweaked my nose, boxed my ears, and kick'd me out of the tent. So I then kick'd up a row, and—that's all.

JAILOR: A very pretty story, indeed! You look like a mutinous dog—so come, get into the black hole.

JERRY: Now, my dear jailor, do let me escape, and I'll give you the prettiest little pig in my farmyard.

JAILOR: What! bribe an honest and humane jailor, and with a pig? In with you.

JERRY: Well, but I've nothing to eat—I shall be half starved.

JAILOR: Oh no, you shall have something to employ your grinders on. [*Goes out, and returns with a black loaf, and a pitcher of water.*] There!

JERRY: O dear, nothing else but black bread and cold water? Can't you get me a pickle?

JAILOR: I think you're in a devil of a pickle already—come, get in! [*Removes a board from the scene, which discovers a small dark hole.* JERRY *supplicates.*

JERRY: How long am I to be here, Mr. Jailor, in company with myself?

JAILOR: That depends on your good behaviour. [*Cannon are heard.*] There! the battle has commenced.

JERRY: [*Putting his head out of the hole.*] O dear, what's that? The great guns are going off. Are you sure, my dear jailor, that this prison is bomb proof?

JAILOR: Take your head in, you great land turtle.

JERRY: Oh, what will become of me?

End of the Second Act.

Act III.

Scene in front of a pavilion tent; trumpets and drums sounding.

Enter General, Lenox, Soldiers, Officers, *&c.*

General: At length victory has crown'd our arms, and the result of this action will keep alive the spirits of our troops, and the hopes of our country. Hark! the bugles are sounding a retreat, and the enemy has abandoned the field and taken to his entrenchments. Lenox, your hand—your conduct this day has confirmed our hopes— allow me in the name of our country to thank you.

Lenox: Not a word, dear general, not a word; I have merely done my duty, and done no more than every soldier in our ranks.

General: What is the result of this day's action?

Lenox: The enemy has lost upwards of 500 in killed and wounded, and several principal officers have been taken prisoners.

General: In what position were they when the attack became general?

Lenox: The British commander, pressed by our artillery under Towson, issued in all his force from his entrenchments. It was a gallant sight, to see his solid columns and burnished arms advance on the margin of the river, and his cavalry, with lightning's force, dart on our flanks to turn and throw them into confusion; but they were met by the volunteers under the brave Porter, and gallantly repulsed.

General: Go on.

Lenox: The enemy then condensed his forces and crossed the bridge, and was encountered on the plains of Chippewa by Scott, with his brigade, when the action became severe and general. No ambuscade or masked batteries were held in reserve—the enemy was not a moment concealed from our view—no tangled thicket or umbrageous groves gave effect or facility to our rifles: the battle was fought on a plain—where man grappled man, force was opposed to force, skill to skill, and eye to eye, in regular, disciplined, and admirable order.

General: How near were you to the British general?

Lenox: In sight and hearing. Charge the Yankees! said a hoarse voice which I knew to be his. Charge away! said our ardent troops, as they advanced with fixed bayonets; the fire became dreadful, and our stars and stripes were seen waving in the blaze. Scott rode through the lines cheering the men, and gallantly leading them on; Jessup and his third battalion turned the right flank of the enemy after a dreadful conflict; Ketchum had kept up a cross and ruinous fire; and Towson, from his dread artillery, scattered grape like hail amongst them. On, on! cried Leavenworth, the day's our own, my boys! Just then a shot struck down my comrade, Harrison, and shattered his leg.

General Well?

Lenox: He grasped his sword and fought on his stump, clinging to the spot like fire-eyed Mars; the enemy, pressed on all sides, gave way; our troops pursued, and the flight become general. At length we drove them to their entrenchments, and remained masters of the field. Our trumpets sounded their retreat; victory perched on our eagles, and our bands struck up the soul-inspiring air of "Hail, Columbia, happy land!"

General: Well done, my brave fellows! This action will teach the enemy to respect that valour which they cannot subdue. See that the wounded prisoners are taken care of: give them all succor: victory loses half its value, when it is not tempered with mercy. [*Exit* General.

Lenox: Now to my dear Christine, to receive from her the reward which I hope I have fairly earned, and seek with her the joys of tranquillity and love.

Enter a Soldier.

Soldier: Towards the conclusion of the battle we made two Indian warriors prisoners, who were fighting desperately; we have them with us.

Lenox: Bring them in; I will examine them, touching the number and force of their tribe. [*Exit* Soldier, *who returns with* Pendragon *and* LaRole, *with a file of men; both are painted and dressed as Indians*; Pendragon *preserves his opera-glass, and* LaRole *his snuff box.*

Pendragon: What are we brought here for, fellow?

Lenox: Warriors, the fate of battle has placed you in our power; yet fear nothing, we shall treat you like men and soldiers. Deeply do we regret to see you take up arms against us, instigated by foreign influence, and bribed by foreign gold. How numerous is your tribe?

Pendragon: Why what the devil, sir, do you take us for Choctaws? Can't you tell a man of fashion in masquerade?

Lenox: Who and what are you?

PENDRAGON: I am the honourable Captain Pendragon, of his Majesty's Coldstream guards.

LENOX: The *honourable* Captain Pendragon, and taken prisoner fighting in the ranks with Indians, and in disguise? A man of rank and fashion, and a soldier, changing his complexion, his nature and his character—herding with savages—infuriating their horrid passions, and whetting their knives and tomahawks against their defenceless prisoners? Impossible! And who are you sir? [*To* LAROLE.

LAROLE: [*Taking snuff.*] Begar, sair, I am von man of fashion aussi, I am valet de sham to capitain Pendragoon; ve are in de masquerade, sair.

PENDRAGON: It's very true, sir, 'pon honour—we are in masquerade, though you look as if you doubt it. War, sir, is a kind of a—a singular science, and if you are to be knock'd on the head, 'tis of very little consequence whether your nose is tipped with blue or red, damme. I am in your power, sir, and a man of fashion, 'pon honour.

LENOX: Well, sir, if your example is to govern men of honour or men of fashion, I hope I am ignorant of the attributes of the one, or the eccentricities of the other. However, mercy to prisoners, even when they have forfeited mercy, may teach your nation lessons of toleration and humanity. Your life is safe, Sir.

PENDRAGON: Sir, you speak very like a gentleman, and I shall be happy to taste Burgundy with you at the Horse Guards.

LENOX: I thank you, sir.

LAROLE: Par example, dis Yankee Doodel is von very pretti spoken jeune gentiman, I will give him de encouragement. Sair, I vill be ver happy to serve you en my contree, to take un tasse de caffee at de Palais Royale en Paris wid you, to dress your hair, or pull your corset tight.

Enter GENERAL, ADELA *and* OFFICER.

GENERAL: Who have we here?

LENOX: Prisoners, sir, and in disguise.

ADELA: As I live, an Indian dandy!

PENDRAGON: A lady? [*With an air of fashion.*] Ma'am, your most devoted slave—inexpressibly happy to find a beautiful creature in this damn'd wilderness. You see, ma'am, I am a kind of a prisoner, but always at home, always at my ease, *à-la-mode* St. James—extremely rejoiced to have the honour of your acquaintance. A fine girl, LaRole, split me!

LaRole: Oh, oui, she is very fine, I like her ver mush.

Adela: Pray, Sir, may I ask how came you to fancy that disguise?

Pendragon: Oh, it's not my fancy, 'pon honour, though I am one of the fancy; a mere *russe de guerre*. We on the other side of the water, have a kind of floating idea that you North Americans are half savages, and we must fight you after your own fashion.

Adela: And have you discovered that any difference exists in the last affair in which you have been engaged?

Pendragon: Why, 'pon my soul, ma'am, this Yankee kind of warfare is inexpressibly inelegant, without flattery—no order—no military arrangement—no *deploying* in solid columns—but a kind of helter-skelter warfare, like a reel or a country-dance at a village inn, while the house is on fire.

Adela: Indeed?

Pendragon: All true, I assure you. Why, do you know, ma'am, that one of your common soldiers was amusing himself with shooting at me for several minutes, although he saw from my air, and my dodging, that I was a man of fashion? Monstrous assurance! wasn't it?

Adela: Why ay, it was rather impertinent for a common soldier to attempt to bring down a man of fashion.

LaRole: Oui—it is dam impertinent, mai par example, de littel bullet of von common soldat, he sometime kill von great general.

Pendragon: Pray, ma'am, will you permit me to ask, when you arrived from England, and what family has the honour to boast of so beautiful a representative?

Adela: Sir, I am not of England, I stand on my native soil.

Pendragon: Oh.

Adela: And much as I esteem English women for their many amiable qualities, I hope that worth and virtue are not wholly centered in that country.

Pendragon: Why, 'pon my soul, ma'am, though it is not fashionable this year to be prejudiced, yet were I to admit that I saw any beauty or elegance in America, my Bond-Street friends would cut me—split me!

ADELA: I cannot admire their candour. Merit is the exclusive property of no country, and to form a just estimate of our own advantages, we should be ever prepared to admit the advantages possessed by others.

Enter a SOLDIER.

SOLDIER: We have surprised and made captive the celebrated Indian chief, who fought so desperately against us.

GENERAL: Bring him before us. [*Exit* SOLDIER.] He has long been the terror of the neighbourhood, and the crafty foe of our country.

Enter SOLDIERS *with the* INDIAN CHIEF.

INDIAN: Who among you is the chief of these pale-faced enemies of our race?

GENERAL: I am he.

INDIAN: 'Tis well, sir; behold in me your captive, who has fallen into your power after a resistance becoming a warrior. I am ready to meet that death which I know awaits me.

GENERAL: Chief, your fears are groundless; we intend you no harm, but by our example, teach you the blessings of valour and mercy united.

INDIAN: Wherefore show me mercy? I ask it not of you.—Think you that I cannot bear the flames? that a warrior shrinks from the uplifted tomahawk? Try me—try how a great soul can smile on death. Or do you hope that I will meanly beg a life, which fate and evil fortune has thrown into your hands?

GENERAL: We ask no concessions of you, warrior; we wish to see you sensible of the delusions into which foreign nations have plunged you. We wish to see you our friend.

INDIAN: Your friend? Call back the times which we passed in liberty and happiness, when in the tranquil enjoyment of unrestrained freedom we roved through our forests, and only knew the bears as our enemy; call back our council fires, our fathers and pious priests; call back our brothers, wives and children, which cruel white men have destroyed.—Your friend? You came with the silver smile of peace, and we received you into our cabins; we hunted for you, toiled for you; our wives and daughters cherished and protected you; but when your numbers increased, you rose like wolves upon us, fired our dwellings, drove off our cattle, sent us in tribes to the wilderness, to seek for shelter; and now you ask me, while naked and a prisoner, to be your friend!

GENERAL: We have not done this, deluded man; your pretended advocates, over the great waters, have told you this tale.

INDIAN: Alas! it is a true one; I feel it here; 'tis no fiction: I was the chief of a great and daring tribe, which smiled on death with indifference and contempt; my cabin was the seat of hospitality and of love; I was first in council, and first in the field; my prosperity increased, my prospects brightened; but the white man came, and all was blasted.

GENERAL: What has been done, was the result of war.

INDIAN: Wherefore wage war against us? Was not your territory sufficiently ample, but did you sigh for our possessions? Were you not satisfied with taking our land from us, but would you hunt the lords of the soil into the den of the otter? Why drive to desperation a free and liberal people? Think you I would be your enemy unless urged by powerful wrongs? No, white man, no! the Great Spirit whom we worship, is also the God whom you adore; for friends we cheerfully lay down our lives; but against foes, our lives are staked with desperation. Had I taken you prisoner, death should have been your portion; death in cruel torments. Then why spare me? why spare the man whose knife was whetted against your life?

GENERAL: To show, by contrast, the difference of our principles. You would strike down the captive who implores your protection: we tender life and liberty to the prisoner, who asks himself for death.

INDIAN: Is this your vengeance?

GENERAL: It is. The Great Spirit delights in mercy. Be thou our friend, warrior; bury thy tomahawk deep in earth; let not jealous foreigners excite thy vengeance against us; but living as we do in one territory, let us smoke the calumet of peace, you and all your tribe, and let concord hereafter reign amongst us.—Be this the token. [*Gives a belt of wampum.*

INDIAN: Brother, I accept the token; forgive my rage, and pardon my unjust anger. Protect our warriors and wives; guard their wigwams from destruction; soften their prejudices and remove their jealousies. Do this, and the red man is your friend. I have urged you far to end my life: you have tempered your passions with mercy, and we are no longer foes. Farewell! [*Exit.*

LAROLE: Parbleu, dis general is like von great Roman. I vill speak von vord pour myself, I vill make de speech like de sauvage.

GENERAL: [*To* LAROLE.] And you, sir, it appears, are in disguise, unlike a civilized soldier; you have been taken in the ranks with Indians.

LAROLE: Sair, mon general, you sall here vat I am goin to say. I am von Frenchiman; in my contree every Frenchiman he is von soldat.

GENERAL: Well?

LAROLE: Begar, sair, I must fight vid somebody, because it is my bisness. In de Egypt I did fight 'gainst de Turc; in Europe I did fight de whole vorld vis de Grand Napoleon, and in Amerique I did fight against you vid myself. Mais, you take a me de prisonier, I can fight no more; I vill trow myself on de protection of dis contree; I vill no more fight contree de Yankee Doodel; I vill stay here and eat de ros beef vid you, and mon capitain la, he may go to de devil.

GENERAL: Admirably concluded. And you, sir, what can we do to lighten your captivity?

PENDRAGON: Why sir, if war was not my profession, I'd sell out; but it's always my maxim to obey orders, whatever they may be; therefore, shall be happy to have a brush with you in war, and equally happy to crack a bottle of Burgundy with you in peace; a flash in the pan in one way, or a puff from a segar in another; a bullet under the ribs in battle, or a country dance in a ball-room; all's one to me, if it's only fashionably conducted.

GENERAL: Well, let's into my tent and partake of some refreshment. We may not always meet as enemies.

PENDRAGON: [*To* ADELA.] Allow me the felicity of your little finger. [*Aside.*] She's struck with my figure, split me! LaRole, take notice.

LAROLE: Oh, you are de littel devil among de ladies. [*Exeunt.*

Scene II. *A Prison.*

CHRISTINE *seated on a bench; her appearance betrays grief and despair.*

CHRISTINE: At length the weary night has passed away, and day dawns, but brings no joy or comfort to my aching heart. Alas! alas! Christine, where are all the bright visions thy fond fancy painted? where is the content and love which gleamed through the casement of our cottage, when my dear father smiled on his child, and entwined around her his protecting arms: when the false Lenox, too, with honeyed lips, and tones soft as zephyrs, vow'd eternal love? Let me not think of them, or I shall go mad. Oh, what a contrast! pent up in a vile prison, and in disguise! condemned to die, and perishing unknown and unprotected. On the one side, my grave yawns for me; and on the other, a false lover, and a cruel father, drive me to despair. My brain is on fire! *[Hurries about with rapid strides. Music loud and violent.]* Ha! what is this? *[Tears the miniature from around her neck.]* Lenox, these are thy features! thy mild looks beam hope and joy upon me. *[Kisses it.]* Could such a face be false? Away with it! even now he weds another. *[Throws the miniature indignantly from her.]* So, 'tis gone, and I am left alone in darkness and despair. *[She stands transfixed with grief—muffled drum rolls—she starts.]* Ha! they come for me. Be firm, my heart!

Enter an OFFICER *and a file of* SOLDIERS.

OFFICER: Young man, your hour has arrived; the detachment waits without to receive you.

CHRISTINE: [*Faintly.*] I am ready.

OFFICER: Can I serve you in any manner? Is there no letter—no remembrance that you would wish sent to father or friend?

CHRISTINE: Oh, forbear!

SOLDIER: [*Picking up the miniature.*] See, sir, here is a miniature.

OFFICER: [*Examining it.*] By Heavens, they are the features of Captain Lenox! How came you by this? What! a thief too? 'Tis well your career is cut short.

CHRISTINE: Oh no, no! Give it me, I implore you; 'tis mine.

OFFICER: I shall restore it to the rightful owner. Come, we wait.

CHRISTINE: Lead on. A few fleeting moments, and all my troubles will be at an end. *[Exeunt.*

Scene III. *Before the Tent.*

Enter GENERAL, SOLDIERS, *&c., with papers.*

GENERAL: He has not confessed who set him on?

OFFICER: He has not, but admits the crime.

GENERAL: [*Returning papers.*] 'Tis well—see him executed according to the sentence. Hard and imperious duty, which, at once, shuts out hope and mercy! [*Exit* GENERAL.

Officer: Now to seek for Lenox, and restore to him his miniature. [*Exit.*

Scene IV. *The Camp, as in Act I, Scene III; the stage is thrown open, drums roll, and the procession enters for the execution of* Christine; *she is in the centre, between the two detachments; her coat is off, and the stock unloosened from her neck—her step is firm, until she reaches the tent of* Lenox, *when she clasps her hands and hangs down her head in despair. Procession makes the circuit of the stage with slow steps, and when opposite the tent she kneels; an* Officer *places the bandage over her eyes, and gives a sign to a detachment of four to advance; they step forward, and level their muskets at her; at the moment,* Lenox *rushes from the tent with the miniature in his hand and strikes up their guns.*

Lenox: Hold! for your lives! [*Rushes down to* Christine, *and tears the bandage from her eyes.*] 'Tis she! 'tis she! 'tis my own, my beloved Christine! [*Holds her in his arms; she faints.*

2nd Officer: What means this?

Lenox: Stand off, ye cruel executioners, would you destroy a woman?

Officer: A woman? Heavens! how did this happen?

Enter General, Adela, LaRole, Soldiers, *&c.*

Lenox: Support her, Adela, support my dear Christine! [Adela *assists.*

Christine: [*Recovering.*] Where am I? [*Sees* Lenox *and* Adela.] Hide me, save me from that horrid sight!

Lenox: Do you not know me, dear Christine?

Christine: Traitor, begone! let me die at once! Is she not your bride?

Lenox: No, by Heavens, no! 'tis my early friend, my dear companion. Could you doubt my love?

Christine: Not married? not your betrothed? O Lenox, are you then faithful?

Lenox: Could Christine doubt my vows?

Christine: I see it all—I have been deceived. Pardon me, dear Lenox; but driven to despair by your supposed perfidy, I enlisted, and rushed on my fate—which in a moment (horrid thought!) would have terminated. But you are true, and I am happy. [*Embrace.*

LaRole: Parbleu! it is a littel voman vidout de petticoat. Suppose she take a me von prisonier, O quell disgrace!

Enter Jasper, Jerry *and* Peasants.

Jasper: Where is she? where is my daughter?

Christine: My father? I dare not look upon him.

Jasper: Come to my arms, dear wanderer. Could you leave your poor old father thus? You've nearly broke my heart, Christine.

Christine: My sufferings have been equally severe; but do you pardon your child?

Jasper: I do—I do! and further prove my love, by making you happy. Take her, Lenox, she is yours; and never let father attempt to force his child into a marriage which her heart abhors.

Jerry: Well, I vow, Miss Crissy, you look very pretty in pantaloons, and make a fine soger; but after all, I'm glad to have escaped a wife who wears the breeches before marriage—so I consent that you shall have the infantry ossifer, because I can't help it; and so I'll marry Patty, the weaver's daughter, though she can't crack a bottle nor bring down a buck.

General: All things have terminated happily. Our arms have been triumphant, and our gallant soldiers rewarded with the approbation of their country. Love has intwined a wreath for your brows, Lenox, and domestic peace and happiness await you; and when old age draws on apace, may you remember the Plains of Chippewa, and feel towards Britain as freemen should feel towards all the world: *"Enemies in war—in peace, friends."*

Finis.

A Memoir of the Theatre

To William Dunlap, Esq.

"New-York, July 11th, 1832.

"DEAR SIR,

"I am happy to hear that your work on the American Drama is in press, and trust that you may realize from it that harvest of fame and money to which your untiring industry and diversified labours give you an eminent claim. You desire me to furnish you a list of my dramatic productions; it will, my dear sir, constitute a sorry link in the chain of American writers—my plays have all been *ad captandum:* a kind of *amateur* performance, with no claim to the character of a settled, regular, or domiciliated writer for the green-room—a sort of voluntary supernumerary— a dramatic writer by 'particular desire, and for this night only,' as they say in the bills of the play; my "line,' as you well know, has been in the more rugged paths of politics, a line in which there is more fact than poetry, more feeling than fiction; in which, to be sure, there are 'exits and entrances'—where the 'prompter's whistle' is constantly heard in the voice of the people; but which, in our popular government, almost disqualifies us for the more soft and agreeable translation to the lofty conception of tragedy, the pure dictation of genteel comedy, or the wit, gaiety, and humour of broad farce.

"I had an early hankering for the national drama, a kind of juvenile patriotism, which burst forth, for the first time, in a few sorry doggrels in the form of a prologue to a play, which a Thespian company, of which I was a member, produced in the South-street theatre—the old American theatre in Philadelphia. The idea was probably suggested by the sign of the Federal Convention at the tavern opposite the theatre. You, no doubt, remember the picture and the motto: an excellent piece of painting of the kind, representing a group of venerable personages engaged in public discussions, with the following distich:

> "'These thirty-eight great men have signed a powerful deed,
> That better times, to us, shall very soon succeed.'

"The sign must have been painted soon after the adoption of the federal constitution, and I remember to have stood 'many a time and oft,' gazing, when a boy, at the assembled patriots, particularly the venerable head and spectacles of Dr. Franklin, always in conspicuous relief. In our Thespian corps, the honour of cutting the plays, substituting new passages, casting parts, and writing couplets at the exits, was divided between myself and a fellow of infinite wit and humour, by the name of Helmbold; who subsequently became the editor of a scandalous little paper, called *The Tickler*: he was a rare rascal, perpetrated all kind of calumnies, was constantly mulcted in fines, sometimes imprisoned, was full of faults, which were forgotten in his conversational qualities and dry sallies of genuine wit, particularly his Dutch stories. After years of singular vicissitudes, Helmbold joined the army as a common soldier, fought bravely during the late war, obtained a commission, and died. Our little company soon dwindled away; the expenses were too heavy for our pockets; our writings and performances were sufficiently wretched, but as the audience was admitted without cost, they were too polite to express any disapprobation. We recorded all our doings in a little weekly paper, published, I believe, by Jemmy Riddle, at the corner of Chesnut and Third-street, opposite the tavern kept by that sturdy old democrat, Israel Israel.

"From a boy, I was a regular attendant of the Chesnut-street theatre, during the management of Wignell and Reinagle, and made great efforts to compass the purchase of a season ticket, which I obtained generally of the treasurer, George Davis, for eighteen dollars. Our habits through life are frequently governed and directed by our early steps. I seldom missed a night; and always retired to bed, after witnessing a good play, gratified and improved: and thus, probably, escaped the haunts of taverns, and the pursuits of depraved pleasures, which too frequently allure and destroy our young men; hence I was always the firm friend of the drama, and had an undoubted right to oppose my example through life to the horror and hostility expressed by sectarians to plays and play-houses generally. Independent of several of your plays which had obtained possession of the stage, and were duly incorporated in the legitimate drama, the first call to support the productions of a fellow townsman, was, I think, Barker's opera of *The Indian Princess*. Charles Ingersoll had previously written a tragedy, a very able production for a very young man, which was supported by all the 'good society;' but Barker, who was 'one of us,' an amiable and intelligent young fellow, who owed nothing to hereditary rank, though his father was a whig, and a soldier of the revolution, was in reality a fine spirited poet, a patriotic ode writer, and finally a gallant soldier of the late war.

The managers gave Barker an excellent chance with all his plays, and he had merit and popularity to give them in return full houses.

"About this time, I ventured to attempt a little melo-drama, under the title of *The Fortress of Sorrento*, which, not having money enough to pay for printing, nor sufficient influence to have acted, I thrust the manuscript in my pocket, and, having occasion to visit New-York, I called in at David Longworth's Dramatic Repository one day, spoke of the little piece, and struck a bargain with him, by giving him the manuscript in return for a copy of every play he had published, which at once furnished me with a tolerably large dramatic collection. I believe the play never was performed, and I was almost ashamed to own it; but it was my first regular attempt at dramatic composition.

"In the year 1812, while in Charleston, Mr. Young requested me to write a piece for his wife's benefit. You remember her, no doubt; remarkable as she was for her personal beauty and amiable deportment, it would have been very ungallant to have refused, particularly as he requested that it should be a '*breeches part*,' to use a green-room term, though she was equally attractive in every character. Poor Mrs. Young! She died last year in Philadelphia. When she first arrived in New-York, from London, it was difficult to conceive a more perfect beauty; her complexion was of dazzling whiteness, her golden hair and ruddy complexion, figure somewhat *embonpoint,* and graceful carriage, made her a great favourite. I soon produced the little piece, which was called *Paul and Alexis, or the Orphans of the Rhine*. I was, at that period, a very active politician, and my political opponents did me the honour to go to the theatre the night it was performed, for the purpose of hissing it, which was not attempted until the curtain fell, and the piece was successful. After three years' absence in Europe and Africa, I saw the same piece performed at the Park, under the title of *The Wandering Boys*, which even now holds possession of the stage. It seems Mr. Young sent the manuscript to London, where the title was changed, and the bantling cut up, altered, and considerably improved.

"About this time, John Miller, the American bookseller in London, paid us a visit. Among the passengers in the same ship was a fine English girl of great talent and promise, Miss Leesugg, afterwards Mrs. Hackett. She was engaged at the Park as a singer, and Phillips, who was here about the same period fulfilling a most successful engagement, was decided and unqualified in his admiration of her talent. Every one took an interest in her success: she was gay, kind-hearted, and popular, always in excellent spirits, and always perfect. Anxious for her success, I ventured to write a play for her benefit, and in three days finished the patriotic piece of *She would be a Soldier, or the Battle of Chippewa*, which, I was happy to find, produced her an excellent house. Mrs. Hackett retired from the stage after her marriage, and lost six or seven years of profitable and unrivalled engagement.

"After this play, I became in a manner domiciliated in the greenroom. My friends, Price and Simpson, who had always been exceedingly kind and liberal, allowed me to stray about the premises like one of the family, and, always anxious for their success, I ventured upon another attempt for a holyday occasion, and produced *Marion, or the Hero of Lake George*. It was played on the 25th of November, Evacuation day, and I bustled about among my military friends, to raise a party in support of a military play, and what with generals, staff-officers, rank and file, the Park theatre was so crammed, that not a word of the play was heard, which was a very fortunate affair for the author. The managers presented me with a pair of handsome silver pitchers, which I still retain as a memento of their good-will and friendly consideration. You must bear in mind that while I was thus employed in occasional attempts at play-writing, I was engaged in editing a daily journal, and in all the fierce contests of political strife: I had, therefore, but little time to devote to all that study and reflection so essential to the success of dramatic composition.

"My next piece, I believe, was written for the benefit of a relative and friend, who wanted something to bring a house; and as the struggle for liberty in Greece was at that period the prevailing excitement, I finished the melodrama of the *Grecian Captive,* which was brought out with all the advantages of good scenery and music. As a 'good house' was of more consequence to the actor than fame to the author, it was resolved that the hero of the piece should make his appearance on an elephant, and the heroine on a camel, which were procured from a neighbouring *menagerie*, and the *tout ensemble* was sufficiently imposing, only it happened that the huge elephant, in shaking his skin, so rocked the castle on his back, that the Grecian general nearly lost his balance, and was in imminent danger of coming down from his 'high estate' to the infinite merriment of the audience. On this occasion, to use another significant phrase, a 'gag' was hit upon of a new character altogether. The play was printed, and each auditor was presented with a copy gratis, as he entered the house. Figure to yourself a thousand people in a theatre, each with a book of the play in hand—imagine the turning over a thousand leaves simultaneously, the buzz and fluttering it produced, and you will readily believe that the actors entirely forgot their parts, and even the equanimity of the elephant and camel were essentially disturbed.

"My last appearance as a dramatic writer was in another national piece, called *The Siege of Tripoli*, which the managers persuaded me to bring out for my own benefit, being my first attempt to derive any profit from dramatic efforts. The piece was elegantly got up—the house crowded with beauty and fashion—every thing went off in the happiest manner; when, a short time after the audience had retired, the Park theatre was discovered to be on fire, and in a short time was a heap of ruins. This conflagration burnt out all my dramatic fire and energy, since which I have been, as you well know, peaceably employed in settling the affairs of the nation, and mildly engaged in the political differences and disagreements which are so fruitful in our great state.

"I still, however, retain a warm interest for the success of the drama, and all who are entitled to success engaged in sustaining it, and to none greater than to yourself, who have done more, in actual labour and successful efforts, than any man in America. That you may realize all you have promised yourself, and all that you are richly entitled to, is the sincere wish of

"Dear Sir,

"Your friend and servant,

"M. M. Noah.

Staging a Nation: Mordecai Noah and the Early Republic

Daniel J. Kleinfeld

Journalism was where Noah got his start, and due to the light-hearted tone of his editorials, it remained his most reliable source of income (Sarna 35). But no matter how entertaining his columns, he always had two goals in mind. The first was to give the young country in which he lived a distinctive identity. The second was to reconcile his intense feelings of patriotism with his strongly felt Jewish identity. Noah combined these goals by attempting, in his creation of the American identity, to fashion an America that could provide a haven for Jews who needed to escape the ingrained anti-Semitism of Europe. In the United States, Noah sought to create a land which would gather and embrace the Jews.

Noah understood that America was a polyglot nation, its character still unformed, and so sought to answer the question of what sort of person the new American would be. He sought to portray the American as a creation of the high ideals of the Constitutional Convention—combining the practicality of the Puritans, the intellectualism of the English, and the tolerance that was already a peculiarly American characteristic. Noah's America had obtained its independence from an oppressive empire in a noble revolution, and had managed to keep its independence in a final war in 1812. From the passion and energy of the fight for independence, Americans formed an image of a nation dedicated to the principles of equality and liberty. Noah's writings clearly project the belief that liberty and equality would eventually take hold, and Americans would fully live up to their ideals as a people who held freedom and tolerance as their highest values.

Equally important to Noah was to deal with his own Jewishness. Noah was always a proto-Zionist, although he shifted in belief from endorsing a separate Jewish colony in the New World to advocating immediate return of the Jews to Jerusalem. He was considered the leading spokesman for American Jews, and maintained contact with Jewish communities throughout the world in the hopes both promoting Jewish unity and encouraging mass immigration of Jews to America. Noah firmly believed, as he said in a letter to President John Quincy Adams,

> This is the only country where the Jews can be completely regenerated: where, in the employment of perfect civil & religious liberty, free from the operation & effect of national or religious prejudices, under the protection of the laws, their faculties could be developed, their talents & enterprise encouraged, their persons & property protected, and themselves respected and esteemed, as their conduct and deportment shal merit.

It was crucial for the Jews that America be a land which would meet these high political and social standards, and not fall under the domination of the anti-Semitism which had long been a part of European tradition. The belief that Americans' behavior could be changed to meet these standards, especially by education, was a central part of Noah's world view. Noah had always held that the hatred of Jews was "a prejudice founded on ignorance" (*Discourse* 7), and thus a prejudice that could be eliminated through education. Noah praised the fact that "the state, some years since, justly considering that education was the proper basis on which good citizens could be erected, . . . created a large school fund" (*Essays* 176). Noah further believed that, "Seven-eighths of the bad characters who disfigure the world . . . have been thus reduced to extremities from the culpable neglect and unpardonable indifference of parents" (*Essays* 125). With such strong views concerning the potential value of education in changing human behavior, it was easy for him to conclude that his writings could have a profound effect on America. Noah viewed what he wrote as another form of education, and education would help the American people to "estimate the real blessings of liberty, to become useful and honorable citizens, the friends of their country, of morality and virtue" (*Mechanics* 11).

Noah's first attempt to define America through his writings came in the series of essays written for the *New York National Advocate*, later published as *Essays of Howard*. These essays, written pseudononymously, dealt in a lighthearted way with various matters of "domestic economy." Included were such subjects as meal-times: "It is not necessary to eat more than two meals a day" (*Essays* 31); styles of dress: "Ladies should make their own dresses, and fabricate their own bonnets" (*Essays* 9); and the proper mating rituals: "Long courtships are insufferable" (*Essays* 62). It was these essays, in fact, which made the *National Advocate* one of New York's best-selling papers. Noah's advice, both sensible and entertaining, appealed to a wide range of readers, from men of society to housewives, and his columns were regularly read and followed. This popularity allowed Noah to begin defining the American identity, and to create an "American," a character that embodied American ideals, as Noah understood them.

The intention of Noah's columns was that they not only entertain, but also "lead to a reform which at present appears . . . desirable" (*Essays* Preface). Indeed, his attitude could be summarized by his comment, "Why not adopt new systems, and set foot a radical reform at once?" (*Essays* 69). It was of the utmost importance to Noah that Americans not be left like

> the Chinese, the oldest and most numerous people on earth, with a rich soil, a moral system, boasting of great philosophers, great mechanical ingenuity, shackled by superstition, and cramped by the influence of customs, which exist now in the same fashion as they did many thousands of years ago. (*Mechanics 12*)

Americans, of course, were not threatened by old American customs but rather by those of Europe. In *Essays of Howard*, Noah displays unceasing contempt for "the follies and extravagance of Europe" (*Essays* 40). Whether it was "merchants . . . furnished with a splendor equal to that of British nobility" (*Essays* 51), or "cards invented for the amusement of kings . . . [whose] use or abuse has caused great misery in the civilized world" (*Essays* 143), or "youths sent . . . to New York to try [their] fortune like Yorkshire boobies who go up to London" (*Essays* 78), Noah's verdict is the same: "in this country, it cannot be afforded" (*Essays* 40). Noah believed that Americans would be misled if they tried to ape the English; rather, Americans had to create their own styles, habits and customs, styles more suited to the New World. "If we agree to call a plain chip hat and muslin gown *fashionable* . . . who would dare dispute it?" (*Essays* 10).

Noah's dislike of European customs in America was not at this time in his life indicative of any nativist bias on Noah's part. Quite the contrary, Noah saw America as a land of immigrants, where anyone could become a success. In Noah's view, "A poor uneducated African . . . in this good country . . . can, by industry, lay by securely, enough to make him happy when the evening of his life approaches" (*Essays* 84). Noah's vision of America as a land embracing many different nationalities is nowhere clearer than in his column of July 31, 1819, where he describes an American city street:

> Here a party of industrious Swiss . . . There is a party from Normandy, hardy, industrious temperate; and these women with high caps, white as snow and stiffly starched, or from Provence, in the south of France; there goes an honest indifferent Dutch family, with slow pace, and crooked pipes in their mouths, looking at everything and astonished at nothing; here rolls an Englishman, with ruddy cheeks and a busy roast beef countenance; there's an Irishman and his five children, all with breeches and worsted stockings, feeling perfectly at home, though just landed on the soil. (*Essays* 101)

In Noah's vision, America was a land in which everyone may take part and be accepted. Anyone, whatever his status in Europe, could become a full member of the American community.

The ideas which Noah set forth in *Essays of Howard* were the foundation on which Noah built his concept of an America which would be receptive towards

Jews. Noah envisioned America as a polyglot nation, a new world, free from the prejudices of Europe, without a concept of one national race, and willing to accept all, including Jews. But Noah saw it as his role to make it so, to create the reality of an America which promoted tolerance. In his column of September 35, 1819, describing the Sabbath, Noah makes plain the value of religion and religious tolerance. Here he sets forth a view of America as a land where God is worshiped "not with the shouts of fanaticism, nor the fretful penances of temporal authority—not as dealing damnation to one sect and blessings to others—not as crushing one portion of his creation and elevating another: but as a just and righteous God" (*Essays* 116). Although Noah is referring here to the Sunday Sabbath rituals of Christianity, what he sees as significant about religion in America is not divisions over the day of the service, but that all religions worship one God, however differently they may worship Him. In the service of this message, Noah delivers the following strongly felt passage:

> I followed, in my imagination, the various sects, having one object in view: . . . the hymn of the choristers floated through aisles; and even the angels and cherubims joined their voices in sacred harmony of praise and devotion, while, with one voice the multitude cried aloud, "Our Father, which art in heaven, hallowed be thy name." (*Essays* 117)

While Noah's *Essays of Howard* were promoting the ideas of American religious tolerance and inclusion, Noah was putting these ideas into practice through his own political maneuverings. Among Noah's efforts to incorporate the Jews into America of that day, two are most notable. The first is Noah's support of American synagogues, discerned particularly in a speech published in 1818 under the title of *Discourse Delivered at the Consecration of the Synagogue of K. K. Sheerit Israel . . . in the City of New York.* The second was the Ararat colony, Noah's ambitious scheme for settling the Jews on Grand Island in New York. In Noah's speech to Sheerit Israel, the central theme is America as the haven for the Jews, as a land in which Jews may live without fear of persecution. What made America a more tolerant nation, in Noah's eyes, was that it was a *Christian* nation, and "the countries under control of Christian powers are sensible to the evils arising from religious oppression, and are anxiously endeavouring to establish more liberal and enlightened opinions, [as] we may learn from the countenance and protection afforded to the Jews in common with other denominations" (*Discourse* 12–13).

Although Noah acknowledged that Christian ministers were sometimes guilty of anti-Semitism, he believed that this prejudice would eventually be swallowed up by the similarities between the religions of the Jews and the Christians, since the Christians had suffered for their religious beliefs in Rome, and the Jews had always, "suffered for having proclaimed and supported the existence of one God" (*Discourse* 9). Because America was a Christian country, Jews would be able to live freely, for "between two good men professing different faiths, no difference exists . . . both have a right to worship the Almighty in his own way" (*Discourse*

28). In this country where freedom and tolerance are the standards, "for the first time in eighteen centuries, it may be said that the Jew feels he was born equal, and is entitled to equal protection" (*Discourse* 12).

However, Noah did believe that eventually Jews would leave America and return to the Promised Land. Moreover, he believed that it was not enough for the Jews to wait for God to bring them to Jerusalem. Rather, the Jews had to make an active effort to create a Zion. Noah's plan for doing so was the colony of Ararat. Ararat was to be an agricultural colony in America. The use of Ararat to the Jews was twofold. First, it was to be, at least until the Last Days, a New Jerusalem, a Jewish community in which Judaism would be preserved. Noah believed that Jews were meant to live among other Jews, that it was very important to preserve the Jewish people, and that the best way to do so was to create a land for the Jews. On occasion, the practice of Jewish rituals, such as observance of the Sabbath, came into conflict with Christian rituals. An example was the controversy over whether state employees should have Saturday or Sunday off, a controversy Noah was involved in. To Noah, every Jewish ritual was important since, "the observance of those religious tenets which make us a distinct people, the faithful performance of the covenants enjoined upon us by our patriarchs and legislators, are the sure guides to the preservation of our faith" (*Discourse* 32). The way to avoid conflicts between Jewish and Christian observances was to separate the two. This is not to say that Noah believed Jews should divorce themselves entirely from what was clearly a Christian-American culture—far from it. It is to say, however, that Noah felt the need to be, in Jonathan Sarna's words, "apart from" even while being "part of," the American culture that existed.

The colony of Ararat was to be a haven for Jews living in Europe and the Middle East who were, at the time, suffering anti-Semitic persecution. Noah had observed at the consecration of Sheerit Israel that "from the attractions of light and liberty which our dear country holds forth to the persecuted of all nations, many of our people have emigrated from Europe, and their increasing number made it necessary for their accommodation, that we should enlarge our place of worship" (*Discourse* 30). Now, he planned to enlarge this accommodation to comprehend an entire community.

But Noah's plan, as he saw it, also was of advantage to the United States. Ararat brought two central benefits for the United States. The existence of a Jewish colony in the United States would, first of all, be proof positive that the United States was willing to live up to the principles that it was founded upon. Noah made this point forcefully in a letter to Thomas Jefferson:

> Nothing, I am persuaded, can be more gratifying to you than to see the Jews in this country in the full employment of civil and religious rights, to know that they possess equal privileges, and above all to feel that to your efforts in the Independence and formation of our government, they, in great part, owe these inestimable privileges.

For the United States to give to the Jews a colony of their own would be a gesture of tolerance demonstrating America's unique commitment.

Ararat brought with it more than symbolic benefits, however. In an effort to persuade President John Quincy Adams to allot land for Ararat, Noah wrote to him that Jewish immigrants could serve America's economic interests:

> The commerce of a great portion of Europe is under their control, and by transferring their capital and enterprise to the United States, they may more fully develop our resources, point out new avenues to trade, encourage manufacturers, benefit our finances, and probably make large purchases of public lands.

Noah believed that the presence of an entire colony of Jews in America could not help but to improve the fortunes of the Union. Moreover, Noah planned to invite, "the most wealthy, intelligent, and enterprising of the nation," who would transform the Grand Island area from an unsettled wilderness to a wealthy center of trade and agriculture (Letter to Adams).

Noah did hope to gain personally by the Ararat plan, particularly from his position as Ambassador to the Jews of Europe. Noah had, for much of his life, sought to obtain an ambassadorship, and was certainly eager for the salary and prestige that would accompany the task of convincing European Jews to emigrate to the United States. Still, personal gain was not his main motive—there were far simpler ways to obtain a position than by proposing a fantastic plan to offer shelter to one of the most universally persecuted people in the world. There can be no question that he was concerned primarily with the advantages his plans could offer both to the Jews and to America.

When Ararat fell through, Noah set out on his next ambitious project, made clearest in his *Address Delivered before the Society of Mechanics and Tradesmen*. Noah set out to shape the American character in such a way as to eliminate anti-Semitism in America. America seemed fertile soil for such a project. Jews had played a significant part in the American Revolution, "holding a high rank in the army and fighting for liberty with a gallantry worthy of the descendants of Joshua, David, and Maccabeeus" (*Memoirs* 136). Jews had also fought in the War of 1812, which "found every Israelite . . . in arms, actively co-operating in the defense and support of the just rights of the nation" (*Memoirs* 138). After the war, "we see them [Jews] on the bench as judges, in the legislatures as members, and assisting the government" (*Memoirs* 136). In addition to the historical role played by the Jews of America, the American Constitution supported concepts of religious tolerance. Noah had observed that, "the most distinguished feature of our compact . . . is religious liberty" (*Memoirs* 138). Most importantly, in Noah's view, was the fact that Americans could still demonstrate the resolve to end anti-Semitism. In Europe, anti-Semitism was an inextricable part of the culture, but in America, it hadn't had time to take root, and could still be stopped.

Despite these Constitutional principles, anti-Semitism was still prevalent in America, a reality driven home to Noah by the constant anti-Semitic remarks that were shouted at him during his speeches at every political rally. What gave Noah hope, however, was his continuing faith in the power of education. While he had once believed that virtue would reign when people were educated about the evils of intolerance and the proper codes of behavior, he now held that America's animating principles were so firmly based in virtue that simply through educating students about the history of America, one could eliminate prejudice. Once Americans were sufficiently educated, the United States would become "a nation forgetting religious distinctions, shunning the horrors of religious intolerance, and uniting as one family in harmony and affection" (*Memoirs* 137). To this end, he promoted education more earnestly than ever, supporting the construction of American libraries and schools, certain that once Americans reached a certain stage of education, prejudice against the Jews would vanish, and the Jews could find haven among Christians.

At the same time Noah was working for the return of the Jews to the Holy Land. As the Ottoman Empire declined, land in the Middle East was put up for sale, including the original site of Israel, the Holy Land itself. Noah began to argue in favor of the United States purchasing the land and making it into an American Jewish colony. For the Jews, this would be the restoration of the homeland—Israel was the Promised Land, the home of David, Saul, and Solomon, the land given to the Jews by God. For the United States, a Middle Eastern colony would not only offer the financial advantages of a colony in a land rich with natural resources, but would also serve as a friendly foothold in the Middle East, one which could be used to strengthen the United States' position in a region which had long been inaccessible.

Noah seized the opportunity and wrote one of his major essays on the Jewish return to Zion, *Discourse on the Restoration of the Jews* (1845). In this essay, Noah proposed what would eventually become the standard Zionist view, that the only proper site for the New Jerusalem was the original Jerusalem. The restoration of the historical Israel to the Jews had obvious benefits for the Jews. As with previous utopian Jewish schemes, the return to Israel offered the Jews a haven from the prevalent anti-Semitism of the times, and a chance to live among fellow Jews, to practice Jewish rituals without conflict with other religious sects, and to fully develop their Jewish community. The return to the original Holy Land carried with it other significant advantages compared to previous schemes proposed by Jews who argued for a homeland, regardless of the location. Jews had emotional ties to Israel that had survived the two thousand years of exile. This was the land where their descendants had lived, where the original judges had governed. For both religious Jews and Christians, the restoration of the Jews to Jerusalem was one of the events which would help to bring about a Messianic era. Most importantly, the idea of a Jewish settlement in Jerusalem had instant credibility, as opposed to a settlement in some undeveloped American wilderness. There was no question that the Jews had a long history in Israel. The opening up of the Middle East would finally provide the opportunity to create a workable, successful Jewish colony.

Again the United States was to be instrumental in Noah's plans. After all, some entity actually had to buy the land from the Turks, and the United States seemed like the primary candidate. The two main reasons earlier used to justify Ararat were brought up again. One was the ideological victory the United States would win by suppoorting the restoration of the Jews. As Noah said of the plan for restoration:

> Where . . . can we commence this great work of regeneration with a better prospect of success than in a free country and a liberal government? Where can we plead the cause of independence for the children of Israel with greater confidence than in the cradle of American liberty? Where ask for toleration and kindness for the seed of Abraham if we find it not among the descendants of the Pilgrims? (*Discourse* 10)

Moreover, as before, Noah believed the United States would accrue direct economic benefits by aiding in the development of Israel. If the Holy Land were to become, as some proposed, an American colony, it could offer the United States substantial economic benefits. But even if it were only a friendly nation, Israel would still serve America's economic interests. As a fundamentally Western nation, it would provide an excellent outpost of the Christian West in the Middle East, allowing the flow of a trade that too long had been blocked. Once again, Noah had developed a plan which would be in the interests of the Jewish community and the United States. Of course, Noah's plan for the restoration of the Jews to the Holy Land went unheeded.

Selections from *Essays of Howard, on Domestic Economy*

Originally Published In The New-York National Advocate.
"Eye Nature's Walks."
New-York: Printed by G. L. Birch & Co. No. 39 1/2 Frankfort-Street.
1820.

Preface.

The following Essays were published in the New-York *National Advocate;* and having created some interest throughout the Union, are now collected and republished in a more compact form.

They were originally intended to lighten the labour and detail of political contests, which the times may have rendered necessary, and with a hope that they might lead to the adoption of a more economical system in all our domestic relations. After the British Classics, it would be a vain attempt to produce a standard work on the same principles: yet desultory reflections on habits, customs, and fashions, may lead to a reform which at present appears peculiarly desirable. It is unnecessary to say that the author intended to personify no individual—to satirize no family; he is incapable of such efforts, and if these essays either improve, amuse or edify, he shall feel himself amply repaid for his labour.

Essays On Domestic Economy.
October 2, 1818.
[Idleness and Luxury]

It has been frequently asked, What is the cause of the increase of pauperism in our city? How is it that our poor-house is not only crowded with age and decay, but even with youthful mendicity? How is it that so many young women become inmates of charitable institutions, and so many of them foreigners? And, above all, to what causes are we to attribute an increase of depravity, sensuality, and crime? These are serious questions, which, one day, we must seriously ask ourselves.

Volumes have been written on pauperism, which, though they may not fully apply to such cases, yet in principle, if not in extent, they have a close connexion. Mankind is the same all over the world, and the same remedies may be safely applied in like cases. *The want of industry is the foundation of the evil,* and industry in the poorer order of the community can only be promoted by example among the better educated and refined.

We have often imagined that our *domestic economy* was greatly misunderstood, if not sadly neglected, and we have frequently been tempted to attribute the cause at once to our wives and daughters: but the fear of offending, when we would only seek to reform, has ever checked our complaints. But the evil may increase until whole communities fall victims to its effects; and, though we tread on dangerous ground, we must pluck up courage to say, that our ladies, generally, are not sufficiently industrious; and having said so, we throw ourselves on their mercy for an indulgent hearing.

It is sometimes necessary to mingle in domestic concerns—to leave the arcana of governments, the asperity of politics, and the hurry of business, to look *at home*—where, after all, true happiness is only to be found; where, surrounded by family, by endearing ties, and by household gods, a true estimate of character can alone be formed. *We employ too many domestics,* and thus encourage idleness and extravagance. The labour of a house which can be effected by two persons should never employ four. Servant maids, whose time is not wholly engrossed by employment, and who have not before them the cheering and judicious example of industry in their mistresses, acquire too soon a negligence, extravagance, and listlessness, which beget indifference, pamper the body, and corrupt the mind. They are then dismissed—they try other places—and the result is the same; without stability and industry, they continue to change until they can no longer find a place, and then they swell the list of depravity, or increase the number of mendicants. The mistress who sets an example of industry to the maid, will ever derive the benefit of her labour, and the maid will reciprocally gain every thing from the example. But, says the fashionable wife, am I to rub furniture, visit the kitchen, and darn night-caps? We say, ay good dame; for it will produce health and content, economy and happiness. Why do our ladies look pale? Why are they not all florid and robust? Why do so many fall victims to disease and early death? It is because they do not take sufficient *exercise*—they do not bustle sufficiently about the house—they do not appropriate a due portion of their time to domestic concerns. What can be more engaging than to see the tidy, active wife, and the accomplished woman, blended in one person? What, in domestic life, wears an aspect so winning, as the cultivated mistress of the drawing room and the industrious mother combined? Economy is the foundation of prosperity in all things, but particularly in domestic life. Ladies should make their own dresses, and fabricate their own bonnets. Milliners and mantuamakers, it is true, would not be so much encouraged—but what then? Money would be saved, rents would decrease, provisions would be cheap, idleness unknown, and poverty unseen.

Another evil now strikes me forcibly. We have too many societies erroneously called *charitable,* which create artificial wants rather than supplying real ones; which tend to encourage pauperism instead of industry. Our wives and daughters are ambitious of the *honour* of being members of these multiplied associations, civil, ecclesiastical, and mechanical; and the annual contributions and admission fees swell in the aggregate to a sum which, in truth, the head of a family careful of his own interest cannot well afford, in addition to taxes and other burdens.

Dress is exorbitantly extravagant—simplicity is no longer known: *Fashion,* with an iron sceptre, now reigns triumphant. Cashmere and merino shawls, Leghorns at forty dollars, watches, chains, seals, rings, and other unnecessary valuables, convert our ladies into walking mines of wealth. Those who cannot afford to be in the fashion, stretch their utmost means to imitate their neighbours, and gradually become poor; when, with proper economy, they might have been comfortable. All classes of society are more or less affected by fashion, or borne away by example. Hence pauperism; want in early life, and poverty in old age. A little *resolution,* and the evil is overcome. If we agree to call a plain chip hat and muslin gown *fashionable*—if we agree that the industrious wife is the most fashionable being in the world, who dare dispute it? Here we have the remedy in our own hands; and never can the wife be made sensible of those facts, until the husband, by a proper example, *confirms* them—until they both unite to promote industry, economy, content, and happiness.

February 5, 1819.
[Decadence and Dinner Parties]

In a populous city, like ours, there are many objects of real charity, particularly during inclement seasons, when the poor seek refuge in the city, and calculate on being provided for by the humane inhabitants. Mankind have claims on each other which should not be evaded. Providence has not blessed one with wealth, that he should enjoy it alone, without contributing all that he can, with propriety and just discrimination, to alleviate the wants, and soften the condition of his fellow creature, who is born with equal feelings and rights, though not blessed with equal good fortune. A trifle spared from superfluities, the remnants of luxury, the scraps of a feast, could be made greatly subservient to charitable purposes, independent of that portion of worldly possessions which is due to the poor. We see in our papers appeals to the humane, from individuals and associations; and yet, when the season of fashions sets in, it is incredible to contemplate the sums uselessly squandered.

A few days ago, a party was given by what is called a fashionable family, in this city, to about eighty persons, fifty of whom were ladies. Three or four rooms, splendidly furnished, and extravagantly illuminated, were thrown open for the invited guests, who all arrived before *ten o'clock*, an hour when they should have been tranquilly reposing on their pillows, and their "casements" closed against the "vile squeaking of the wry-necked fife." When they had all assembled, dressed in costly extremes, it was discovered that they were all acquainted: no strangers, no assemblage of talent, no collection of genius, no foreigners of merit: to please whom an excuse was necessary to make this feast. About *midnight* the party seated themselves at supper, and it was supposed by a calculating and reflecting person present, that the spreading of the table cost no less than *five hundred dollars!!* What a sum to be destroyed in one short hour! The *substantials* on this table, consisting of a few turkeys, tongues, hams, fowls, rounds of beef and game, all cold, could have been purchased for *fifty dollars;* the residue of this immense sum was expended for whips, creams, floating islands, pyramids of kisses, temples of sugarplumbs, ices, *blanc manges,* macaroons and plumb cake; and ladies of delicacy, of refined habits, of soft and amiable manners, were at *midnight,* cloying their stomachs, after excessive exercise in dancing, with this trash; this compound of flour, starch, isinglass, vermilion, sugar, yolks of eggs, and all those deleterious articles calculated to impair the constitution, weaken the organs of digestion, and lay the foundation for permanent disease.—Suppose then they reject these flimsy substances for something more substantial? where is the delicacy of a lady, and in what light can it be seen, when she is swallowing large slices of ham and chicken, and washing them down with sour wine and water, just as the clock sounds "the drowsy" commencement of morn? Let me, however, note the expense of this party: For the table $500—the incidental expenses of lights, music, servants, additional furniture, arrangements, &c. &c. cannot be computed at less than 200 more—that is *Seven Hundred Dollars.* There were fifty ladies present—suppose that each had already incurred the expense of a ball dress, yet their pride would take the alarm at appearing twice in the same costume, without some visible variation; I will say, that for alterations and additions of ornament, for this night only, the expense of each lady was twenty dollars—that is, $1000; the gentlemen, altogether, for clothes and other necessaries, shall only have expended $300; then the cost of this feast, for all its contingencies, was $2000!! What a sum to be thrown away in one night! to be melted in a few hours, leaving "not a rack behind!" This sum would clothe, maintain and school, for the winter, nearly *sixty poor children,* and all expended in one little night!

But it may be said, where is the use of society, and of wealth, if it cannot be thus expended? Do they not, in fashionable companies in Europe, expend immense sums on entertainments, and does not this money circulate among tradesmen, and benefit the community? I answer, that the comparison is unjust.

Where wealth is so unequally distributed that one man can have an income of 2 or 300,000 dollars per annum, the circulation of that money, by any means, is correct and beneficial; but the bane here is, that others will imitate the extravagance without having the same means. Why should we imitate the follies and extravagance of Europe? In this country it cannot be afforded. There are but few incomes which are more than equivalent to support a family comfortably and handsomely; to be judiciously hospitable; to clothe and educate children; to assist the poor; and to patronize arts, sciences, and useful institutions. No man, to do his duty to his family, to provide reasonable settlements for his children, and discharge the obligations of a good citizen, can possibly afford to spend $700 for a party in one night. A merchant cannot ascertain how much he is worth—the transitory and fluctuating concerns of commerce render his pecuniary situation always doubtful. Besides, there is an evil, and a great one, in a pernicious example: persons less capable of launching into these extravagances are induced to imitate the weak displays of their neighbours; persons who depend on the precarious sales of a retail store for subsistence, give parties, live beyond their income, and become bankrupts. I like to see friends and neighbours entertained; I like judicious hospitality and rational amusement. There can be no objection to pass a profitable evening at the theatre, or to attend a ball occasionally: but incurring an expense of several hundred dollars for a feast, in one night, is beyond approbation.

In attending, also, to these nocturnal invitations, considerations of health have not had due influence. Ladies of delicate habits and constitution accept these polite passports to indisposition; and with thin shoes and silk stockings, with their flannels thrown aside, that the symmetry of the shape may not be deranged, they sally forth at inclement periods, exposed to the vicissitudes of the season, the frost and cold, and the overpowering heat of crowded rooms; they fatigue themselves with dancing, destroy the tone of their stomach with eating sweets and a commixture of food, and return shivering to their homes at two in the morning; all the next day they are tortured with headaches, and many never rise from the bed. The lists of mortality present upwards of several hundreds, victims to consumptions, annually: a melancholy sacrifice at the shrine of dissipation. What an erroneous and dangerous path is pursued to acquire happiness! Look at a young lady who is not acustomeds [*sic*] to this round of dissipation—she is all life, health, and animation; her mind is elastic, her spirits buoyant; the blood mantles in her cheeks, and gives spirit and fire to her eyes; her intellect is clear; her judgment sound; she scarcely lays her head on her pillow when sleep seals up her eyelids, and sweet dreams evince a spirit undisturbed, a constitution undecayed. Such a person is worth every thing to society, and society should do every thing to preserve such persons pure, healthy and unsophisticated.

May 6, 1819.
[Wall Street Men and Wives]

Wall-Street is a kind of commercial barometer, and I always observe the countenances of men of business in passing through this bustling street. Very lately I was stopped by a commercial quidnunc, who informed me that Mr. A, B, C, D, E and F, had failed within three days; that times were uncommonly bad and prospects very gloomy, and the result could not be foreseen. Independent of the hazards of commerce, I could account for these failures. These houses, of some ten years' standing, had commenced with small capitals, some with no capital; and instead of uniting industry, prudence, and rigid economy, a contrary course had been pursued, and the first shock overwhelmed them. Look into the houses of some of the merchants, and see them furnished with a splendour equal to that of British nobility; look at their mode of life and actual expenses, and say whether any business can bear such extravagance. Several of these broken merchants have expended for ten years past, nearly 10,000 dollars per annum, in their houses, carriages and wines; can it, therefore, be surprising, that an accumulation of such expenses should lead to ruin?

I have long observed with regret, the wanton extravagance of our merchants and traders. A store is rented at 1200 or 1500 dollars per annum, and a dwelling-house at 1000 or 1200 dollars; and a system of living corresponding with such establishments is adopted, which sets economy at defiance, and leads to ruin—and, by a pernicious example, attracts others into the same dangerous vortex. Why should men waste money? why should more money be expended than what may be necessary for the decent comforts of life? why will families plunge themselves into ruin, merely to live a few years in luxury? Is not such a course at war with common sense, and with the duty which a man owes to society and his family? Can any business prosper under an annual domestic expenditure of 10,000 dollars, together with losses in trade? These reflections I made to myself as I entered Broadway and looked into Eastburn's; not a soul was there—and not one dollar would extravagant men take from their appetites, to purchase a mental banquet at so large a storehouse; a crowd was entering the City Hotel, and, as I follow all crowds to study character, I fell into the current, which carried me up to the ball-room, where, on a long table which covered half of the saloon, a gorgeous display of rich plated ware was seen—an auctioneer was selling the ware to many ladies and very few gentlemen, and the ladies were bidding for articles, the real value of which they were ignorant of. Now, thinks I, while these amiable wives are so anxiously struggling to get rid of their husbands' money, their husbands, poor creatures, are toiling in the sun, borrowing at large premiums in Wall-street, and doing all to preserve their credit, while their unthinking companions are plunging them into deeper difficulties. One lady bid high for a plated soup tureen—"She sha'n't have it, I am determined," said a cross little woman, "I'll have it, cost what it will;"—then commenced opposition, then commenced a system of outbidding, until the article was knocked off at *twice* its value. And who suffers, said I? The husband. Surely, some reflection, some consideration, is due to a toiling, anxious, worried husband, who, while endeavouring to save a dollar in business, loses twenty by the extravagance of a wife. Why buy a plated soup tureen for forty dollars? will not one of china for five dollars do full as well? why buy plated wine coolers, plated toast racks, beefsteak plates, and gravy dishes? If you cannot afford to buy silver, then purchase china, which is more neat and economical. But the eccentricities of fashion are ruining families by wholesale, and what is wanted for unnecessary articles, would doubly pay for those which are indispensable.

If these things are not checked, we may complain of the times without producing reform, and now is the period to commence the work of regeneration, and to use firmness where persuasion fails.

May 11, 1819.
[Of Servants]

I am satisfied of one fact, from close personal observation; and that is, a very considerable and unnecessary sum of money is annually expended in this city, from the too prevailing custom of sending servants to market instead of the master going himself. Old men will be curious and prying into other people's affairs: I know it, and must abide the censure; but, as I said before, I am well off in the world, and have nothing else to do than to look out for the best means of promoting the happiness of my fellow creatures: so I brushed up my old cocked hat, seized my cane, and one bright morning in spring I took my stand near the Fly-market, to make observations on what passed in that bustling and all-important place. Upon a moderate calculation, I decided, that out of four persons who came to market, two were servants; and I had an opportunity of observing their separate expenditures. A black gentleman, with his wool nicely combed, a superfine blue coat, with watch and seals, and a large basket on his arm, brushed up to the butcher. I want four fine ribs and three of the best steaks. You must give my price, then, says the butcher. I never dispute that, said the black gentleman—come, weigh them—here's the money. Four cutlets, said he to the veal butcher—how much? Twelve shillings. There's the shiners. Put those fowls into my basket, Mr. said the sable provider, and take out the price from this five dollar note. Let me have five pounds of that salmon—how much is it? Six shillings a pound. Not dear—there's your money. Let me see what else. Three dozen eggs, sallads, cranberries—Zounds, I shall have nothing left out of my *ten dollars*. In this manner did an improvident master entrust a careless servant to cater for him, who, without system or economy, expended ten dollars, when five would have been more than sufficient. Suppose that this sum is thus daily wasted, it consumes nearly 2000 dollars per annum for marketing alone. A master of a family, instead of rolling about in bed until eight o'clock, or probably later, yawning or harmonizing with his drowsy wife, in a good comfortable snore, "making the welkin ring," should be stirring with the lark; should rouse the servants; set industry into motion; be off to market himself with his little basket; should cheapen every thing he may require, and purchase no more than what is strictly necessary, and then return from his economical duty, and find his wife ready to receive him at breakfast with cheerful looks, his table spread with frugality, cleanliness and comfort. Then the business of the day having had a happy and judicious commencement, will progress lightly and prosperously. What pride can be more false, more dangerous, more censurable, than that of feeling ashamed to purchase in person, and not by deputy, the articles indispensable for domestic consumption? Set your house to rights, is an early and a just proverb; and if husbands do not set a proper example of economy to their wives, they are not authorized to rail at their extravagance. I do not admire invidious comparisons, nor am I pleased when I see one city eulogized at the expense of another: but I do admire the Philadelphia custom, of ladies going to market; and I see no reason why ladies should not go to market, as well as to go what is called "a shopping." I can perceive no more impropriety in a lady's purchasing a nice pound of butter, a basket of fruit, or a pair of pheasants, than in purchasing a pair of shoes, or gloves, floss cotton, or a chip hat. In principle, and in practice, it is the same; both, of necessity, are indispensable. But, as I was saying, I do admire the Philadelphia ladies, who market twice a week, make all domestic purchases, and are familiar with all the arcana of higgling and purchasing on the best terms—who are they serving? Why, their families. "Many a time and oft" have I admired those bewitching faces, with pure red and white, peeping from under a drab bonnet, pacing with modest steps up and down a clean market, with a nice looking little girl behind with a basket, and a tin kettle in which the butter lies covered with fresh vine leaves and congealed with ice; a small steak, a few mutton chops, a sallad, or a fowl, the aggregate of which is not considerable, constitute their maximum of supplies, and thus is economy promoted and comfort produced. It is very injudicious to trust servants with what is the duty of masters to perform. A servant may feel some interest for his master, but not knowing his resources, he cannot study that interest with proper nicety; and it not unfrequently happens, that by trusting expenditures to their care, the "superflux" finds its way into their pockets.

May 21, 1819.
[Of Clothing]

Sauntering along in Broadway a few days ago, at a loss what to do with myself, I made a halt at Goodrich's Library, and attentively regarding the persons passing up and down that bustling street, endeavoured to read from their several countenances what were their occupations, habits and pursuits. The sun shone brightly, the air was balmy and refreshing, and the whole city in motion—happy to escape from that domestic confinement which a week of rainy weather had produced. The current increased after twelve o'clock. Here a good-looking young gentleman came out of Dubois's store with a roll of music in his hand, humming the air of "There's nothing half so sweet in life as Love's young dream." I dare say he was going to make an amatory offering of the sonnet at the shrine of some young lady's piano, and between them exchange such flattering testimonials of "Love's young dream," that the parties will become old before they realize their hopes. Long courtships are insufferable; they have made me an old bachelor. I observed a number of dandy beaux (for they spring up like asparagus in our city) with rattans in hand, and gloves of bright yellow, sunning themselves in front of the City Hotel, and with a peculiar smirk, an elegant negligee nod of the head, and a kind of drawling "How-de-do," salute the passing traveller, or the drawing-room acquaintance. These exotics worry me—they are of no possible good to society, and may do, as Iago says, to "suckle fools and chronicle small beer." What I particularly object to in them, independent of the bad example they set to an enlightened community, is the inordinate appetite which they exhibit at the routs which our good people make for them—and they can clear a waiter with the same facility that a good general and his troops clear the field of enemies. A number of young ladies stepped in casually to the library—sauntered a few moments, admired the splendid binding of the books, looked into La Belle Assemble and Fashions for April, and made their exit. Several gaily, and several neatly dressed, passed with rapid steps; some shook their reticules, and I heard some money jingle, which they were hastening to get rid of at a *fashionable* store, where articles are charged twenty-five percent higher by virtue of a *name.* One object attracted my particular attention: a lady, dressed not very extravagantly nor yet very plain, young and beautiful, was walking slowly, leading by the hand a very interesting baby of three years of age; the dear little cherub, with flaxen hair in flowing ringlets, and rosy cheeks, could hardly get along, in consequence of the heavy incumbrance and weight of dress with which her fond mamma had loaded her. I examined her attentively; she had on a cambric dress, scolloped at the bottom and exquisitely worked, and rendered, of course, unnecessarily heavy by wreaths of embroidered flowers, pantalets, silk stockings, and pink kid slippers; on her little head she wore a good sized chip bonnet, decorated with artificial flowers, and over which the little miniature woman carried a green silk parasol. I began to calculate the cost of all this finery, (for I always calculate things) and made out that the accoutrements of this dear little baby must have swallowed up nearly forty dollars. Now this is really an object of just reprehension: a love of dress in a grown female is natural, and we are often disposed to overlook occasional extravagance when it don't run into extremes; because it is reasonable that a lady should expect admiration, and dress is sometimes a great auxiliary—but to crush an infant with finery, to decorate a baby just as susceptible of propriety as a large doll, and to waste money so unnecessarily, nay, so wantonly, cannot be too severely censured. What kind of admiration does a mother expect to derive from such an exhibition? She surely cannot be looking out for a sweetheart for her daughter so early—and she can, in conscience, expect nothing from the passing observer, but an expression of "poor dear little baby, what a weak mamma you have got—how much you would ornament a parlour mantle, by being stuck up to your elbows in one of the china jars."

I don't know any extravagance which is so reprehensible as that of wasting money on the dress of an infant. First impressions are always the most lasting; and, therefore, first impressions should ever be judiciously formed. "Just as the twig is bent, the tree's inclined:" once fill the little head of a prattling child with ideas of dress—chip bonnets, parasols, and kid slippers, and a walk in Broadway for an exhibition, and the child will talk of nothing else, think of nothing else; she will grow up with extravagant attachments too early formed, and too deeply rooted, to be ever eradicated; and she will lament, even in prosperity, and more so in adversity, that a foolish and unnecessary pride in the mother, gave a direction so dangerous to her early impressions. I never enter into one of our weekly practising ball rooms, but I find it turned into an actual nursery; where mothers are stiffly seated on benches, witnessing with delight their dear little bespangled and bedizzened children, straining their feeble legs into the contortions of a *piruet* or *pigeon-wing;* and worn out with fatigue and thinly clad, the dear babies lay the foundation of a sickly constitution, by an early initiation into the arcana of amusements and rounds of dissipation. Why not dress children plain, very plain, but neat and clean? Why not let them walk in the park or on the battery; taste the fresh air;

roll on the grass, and gambol on the green; and by such proper and innocent recreations, promote health and vigour, and keep the mind wholesome? Society in its mature state, is either benefitted or materially affected by the manner in which children are brought up; and parents have much to answer for, in neglecting to adopt sound maxims and a correct course of policy in relation to them.

June 5, 1819.
[Courtship and Marriage]

I don't subscribe to all the city papers, but I read them at a Coffee House, where, for one shilling, I get a cup of strong and refreshing coffee, and have an opportunity of pursuing my old habit of studying characters at the same time. A few days ago, I amused myself with counting the marriages in my friend John Lang's Gazette, and also the paper published by little Mr. Butler—but I really was shocked to see such a falling off. It appeared to me, that in a community so extensive as ours, there are one third less marriages than are necessary to obtain a fair equilibrium of population. Why don't people marry? Why are there so many antiquated damsels and superannuated bachelors? Aye, thinks I, there's the question—but it can be solved. The errors of education, and the extravagance of fashion, for which young ladies are celebrated, frighten the young men from making advances—and the follies and personal expenses of young men, render them insensible to all the joys and comforts of matrimony; thus faults on both sides have a tendency to keep them separated, till young ladies become old, and old bachelors marry to get nurses. Why not adopt new systems, and set on foot a radical reform at once? I would begin with children at a very early age, and accustom them to simple and nutritious fare, very plain dress, and hardy amusements; the girls should be stirring and active, familiarized at an early period with domestic concerns, quick and expert at their needle—they should read judiciously and write frequently, for writing well is an elegant accomplishment. If I could afford it, a little music and dancing should also be acquired, but they should not go into company at an early age. I see, with regret, mothers dragging their daughters of twelve and thirteen years to parties and balls, under an erroneous impression that it gives them an air of ease and confidence; may be it does; it may give them too much confidence, and they may acquire an early taste for pleasure and amusements. If they are pretty, be sure of it some coxcombs will whisper flattery into their tender ears, and little misses accustomed to hear these fine things, will neglect indispensable improvements, fancy themselves all perfection, and before they arrive at an age when mothers are justified in bringing them *out,* they acquire habits and ideas which render it necessary that they should be kept at *home.*

Then the boys are very apt to be equally spoilt by the indulgence of mamma, and the tranquil compliance of father: Bob must have a superfine blue coat at forty dollars—a dandy neckcloth, and chains and seals, and because it is the *fashion,* forsooth; and money in his pocket to visit the third tier of boxes in our theatre, to eat oysters and ice cream, smoke segars, and drink brandy and water. These ruinous indulgences are seen by the sisters, and they must come in for a share of the extravagance. Bob has *this,* and I must have *that.* Example is every thing; if it be a pernicious one, it cannot fail to produce a pernicious effect. "Train up a child in the way he *should* go, and when he is old he will not depart from it."

If parents will only have firmness to resist the pressing and dangerous solicitations of their children; if they adopt a correct and wholesome system, and enforce it with unyielding strictness, in a very short time the good effects would be discernible; and what at first children violently and obstinately opposed, they will, at length, cheerfully submit to, and all will go on smooth and happy. Marriages, therefore, are rare, because the parties *fear* each other. A young man of moderate expectations, fears the extravagance of a wife, and a young woman fears that her husband would abridge her customary indulgences, and thus these fears operate to keep them apart. It cannot be necessary to bring up daughters extravagantly because the father is rich—if it is justified on the score of fitness and propriety of habits and customs, how keenly must they feel a reverse of fortune! People sometimes meet with sad reverses: I was told that several bankruptcies occurred lately in Baltimore, among merchants who had foolishly lived like nabobs; and I also heard, that their wives and daughters behaved well on the occasion, and resigned their luxuries and extravagances without a sigh. This is creditable to them certainly; but had they not been led into these extravagances, these reverses might never have happened. Avoid all *causes* of unhappiness.

The other day I saw a pretty young lady purchase a white satin reticule, with clasps, for six dollars, and a few minutes afterwards she went into Mrs. Poppleton's. Now, thinks I, she feels a little faint with walking, and intends eating a tart or a jumble, or drinking a glass of lemonade, or some such reasonable refreshment; but she purchased a huge piece of heavy plum cake, and after demolishing a good half, she thrust the remainder into her reticule, and, in a few minutes, the white satin became quite affected by the grease of the cake, and was, of course, useless. There is six dollars and a half gone at once, which would have supported twelve poor families for one day. The gentlemen, however, set bad examples; and the ladies, unfortunately, imitate them.

This coat cost me 45 dollars, said a fashionable friend to me—feel the cloth, 16 dollars per yard. What extravagance! what a waste of money!—No wonder merchants break—no wonder people marry so seldom. If a different system is not adopted, I shall begin to fear that the happiness of the community, its prosperity and increase, will be seriously affected. Dandy bachelors and antiquated belles will usurp the places which should be occupied by young married couples and smiling infants; and Hymen's torch, which should burn bright and clear, will be dimmed by the mildews of fashionable extravagance and bankruptcy.

June 30, 1819.
[City and Country]

I had occasion, the other day, to purchase some trifles in a store in Broadway, which were shown to me by a clerk, a young man fashionably dressed with a dandy coat and neckcloth, in the usual ridiculous manner. Looking stedfastly at him, I thought I recognized his countenance. Is your name Greenwood? said I. That is my name, at your service, said the young man, closing the till with a fashionable slam, and yawning in a most languishing manner. Of Orange county? Yes, of old Orange, said he; I was tired of rural felicity, and dairy maids, and stone barns, and thought I'd try my fortune at the capital, where genius and elegance always are patronized. Well, sir, is your change of residence profitable and useful? Why, sir, it's pleasant; I see a great deal of good company in the shop; have some leisure to dress, promenade, and learn French; I get a small salary, 'tis true, but I may pick up a fortune in the way of marriage; luck, you know, comes unexpected, but it sometimes comes, and that's enough.

I left the puppy. His father, old Oliver Greenwood, is an honest, practical farmer in Orange county; his house is substantial, but old fashioned, surrounded with a white paled fence, and a neat flower garden in the rear; an old oak, with its thick foliage and cumbrous branches, casts a venerable shade over his peaceful mansion; the interior is furnished neatly and with some ornament; the parlour is covered with a carpet ingeniously made and woven by the wife and daughters; a bookcase with a choice collection, a spinnet, and a few pictures of great men and scripture subjects, constituting all that is necessary for exhibition or for use. When I was some years younger I was in the habit of taking my gun and paying a visit to old Greenwood for a few days. Many a hearty meal have I taken in his hospitable mansion. Talk of comfort in our splendid drawing rooms and crowded parties! it is not known. After a morning's ramble over the well cultivated fields, and brushing off the spangled dew from the rich and perfumed clover, we returned to the house, warned by the shrill echo of the breakfast horn: our sinews braced with exercise, and our appetites rendered keen by the swelling breeze. No unmeaning ceremony or tedious compliments worried the hungry stranger; the wife was neat and cheerful; the girls plainly dressed, with rosy cheeks and sparkling eyes; they had no papers in their rich brown hair, with pins crossed in curls—no languid drawl, or vacant stare, or slip-shod shoes, or greasy morning gown: they were brisk as bees, lively as Euphrosyne, industrious as Lucretia—and their morning dresses might vie with mountain snow for whiteness. And then the breakfast: no vapid tea or cold toast, greasy butter, and chipped meat—a clear cup of coffee and cream, butter, fresh and hard from the dairy, smoked shad, boiled eggs, and sweet brown bread. These were nearly all the produce of the farm; consequently, comfort was united with economy. It was at this period that I remembered seeing the young man from whom I had just parted in Broadway. He was then dressed as a plain and respectable farmer, and was occupied in various duties about the premises, and bidding fair to become a useful citizen: the folly and indulgence of the father yielded to his caprices, and he sent him to New-York to try his fortune, like Yorkshire boobies who go up to London for the same purpose.

There is no error so pernicious in its effects as that of sending young men, fresh from the country, pure in principle and inexperienced, to reside in a populous city, and become familiar with its pleasures, its vices, and extravagances. What inducement can an honest farmer have, in thus banishing his children from independence, industry and comfort? There is, certainly, no occupation more honourable, more useful, more valuable to a country, than that of agriculture; the farmer is the defender of the soil he tills—labour nerves his arm, and patriotism warms his heart; he is most to be depended upon, because his pursuits are more steady, and more generally prosperous. Of all the characters of which our country boasts, there is not one superior to a well informed and sensible farmer; not alone a practical man, but one who has read, who knows the world, his country, and its laws. What sight is more gratifying, than that of seeing a young man of information and good qualities, between the handles of a plough? Follow him to his well stocked barn, and see him gracefully and manfully ply the flail, culling the rich treasures of Ceres; and when exercise demands a transient rest, see him seated on his sheaves of straw, and hear him talk of Greece and Rome; narrate historic facts; dwell on the history of his country, its wars, government and institutions. Why, such a man is above all price—he is useful to himself and beneficial to his country. Pursue this train of thought, and trace him to the hall of the legislature, and see him in another and more elevated capacity, giving laws to the state, redressing public grievances and healing private wrongs. How can a parent permit his son to be cut off from usefulness, and "crib" himself in a city upon a miserable stipend, dragging out a life of indolent pleasure without hope of profit or advancement. Most of our small retail stores are filled thus with the sons of farmers, who eager to escape salutary labour, and partake of the delusive pleasures of a city, are crowding to New-York, abandoning a sure road to character and independence, and giving us a portion of population which is neither useful to society nor beneficial to themselves.

July 9, 1819.
[Banks]

I have heard much of the *Savings Bank* and the name of bank, together with its operations, not being generally understood by that part of the community least informed, I was fearful that the new project in our city would not take, or that it would meet with powerful obstacles. I am extremely happy to find that I am in error, and that this admirable guardian of the poor, industrious, and economical, will most assuredly thrive and produce great blessings. I find, however, that the operations of this bank are not fully understood, and that an idea prevails that bank notes are to be issued, speculations set on foot, discounts effected, bad debts contracted, and bankruptcy hazarded. By no means, Nicholas, said I, to my old domestic, who came to me with $200 of his earnings to deposit in this bank, there is no risk in this bank, there is no loss to be incurred, for if there was, the objects of the bank, which are to preserve and secure deposits, would then be destroyed.

"Save the pence," says my old friend Benjamin Franklin, "and the pounds will take care of themselves." I took a walk to the institution, to see the operations of the new bank; I found the directors all good moral men, worthy of confidence. So far all was right; and I took my stand near the entrance, to notice the characters who approached. I first saw a pretty little servant girl, of about 16, whom I had often seen at the house of my friend, Mrs. Rosebud, in Hudson-street, and admired also for her cleanliness and good deportment. Ah, Katy, said I, my pretty maid, where are you going, and what have you tied up in that blue cotton bag? Why, Mr. Howard, said she, with a smile, which displayed her fine teeth, I have forty dollars here, which I have saved from my wages, and I am going to deposit it in the bank. Indeed! forty dollars? you have been very economical, said I. Why, said she, I receive *six* dollars a month, and I find that I can save *four* of it; now four dollars saved a month, makes very nearly fifty dollars a year. I am only sixteen, suppose I deposit fifty dollars yearly from my wages for ten years, when, if I live, I shall be twenty-six years old; what with interest accumulating upon interest, I shall have *several hundred dollars at my command:* quite a little fortune to begin the world with, and something handsome towards housekeeping, should I marry. Excellent! said I, giving her an affectionate shake by the hand, and adding a two dollar City Bank note to her stock, you calculate like a little philosopher, Katy, and you must do well. She entered the bank, and I shortly after perceived Cuff, my boot cleaner, with a row of polished boots arranged on his pole, which he was carrying home; he also stopped and took out a ragged pocket book, and counted some bank notes. What are you going to do with that money, Cuff? said I. Why, I shall deposit it in the Savings Bank, said he. I find that I can lay by $100 per year, and in ten years I shall be able to buy a little farm, and be comfortable in my old age. Excellent again! said I: here's a poor uneducated African, who toils for his daily bread, and yet in this good country, he can, by industry, lay by securely, enough to make him happy when the evening of his life approaches. See the benefit of these good institutions. A clerk from Chatham-street next approached—I had known him to be an extravagant young man—he came to make a small deposit. How now, Robert, said I, have you any thing to spare, which you are disposed to lay by? Why, sir, said he, I have been six years a clerk, and I found, after paying all my necessary expenses, that I had $200 dollars per year over, which, had I not spent extravagantly and needlessly, I should have had, at this day, upwards of $1200 to begin business with. Now, sir, I am determined to turn over a new leaf, and instead of spending my money in pleasure, I shall lay it up, and in time, secure to myself a competence. After him, came a variety of persons, with small and large deposits, and cheerfully left them at the bank, with the hope that the solid benefits which the institution held forth would induce many to follow their example. I came away highly pleased at the prospect in view, and have no doubt of its success.

There is one thing which I should not omit noticing, and that is, the importance of having the directors always as correct and honourable as the present board now is, for the trust is awfully responsible; it is not the rich, but the poor and industrious, who will suffer from the improper speculations of the directors; these should be seldom changed, and always cautiously selected, and the very best stock should be purchased for the sums deposited, so that no possible risk might be incurred. Establish confidence on a sure basis, and it never will be shaken.

July 31, 1819.
[Of Immigrants]

"Crib not thyself in cities."—Shakspeare.

For some time past, I have had occasion to remark the increase of emigrants in our city, and the strange faces, and still more strange habiliments that meet our eye at every turn. Here a party of industrious Swiss, who had forsaken their mountains and valleys, their lakes and glaciers, to breathe more freely the air of liberty in the new world; the men in "russet mantle clad," with mild looks and sunburnt complexions; the women with tight boddices, short petticoats, and their hair in long and graceful plaits, holding their ruddy children by the hand, fusby as Bacchus, and, with vacant stare, glancing their eyes over buildings, churches, gorgeous stores, and gaily dressed people, in a place where they expected to see the tall larch, the mountain pine, and hear the cry of wolves. There is a party from Normandy, hardy, industrious and temperate; and these women with high caps, white as snow and stiffly starched, are from Provence, in the south of France; there goes an honest indifferent Dutch family, with slow pace, and crooked pipes in their mouths, looking at every thing, and astonished at nothing; here rolls an Englishman, with ruddy cheeks and a busy roast beef countenance; there's an Irishman and his five children, all with breeches and worsted stockings, feeling perfectly at home, though just landed on the soil.

What is this combination of foreign habits and strange customs to produce to our country—good or evil? Good, no doubt, if prudence, industry, economy, and morality, regulate their movements. Population is the wealth of a country. The soil may be productive, the climate salubrious, the government just and free, but, without an industrious and increasing population, these blessings are unknown and unfelt. It is to the honour of the American government, that in the fourty-fourth year of independence, such is the confidence inspired in our laws and equal rights, such the hopes of industry and frugality, that the weary, the persecuted, and the enterprising of Europe, are hastening to our shores. If unnecessary wars, and conflicts of ambition, drag the peaceful tenant of the hamlet to the field of battle—if the tax-gatherer seizes upon half the gains of his labour to gild the palaces of the voluptuous—if the poor are to feed and pamper a bigotted priesthood, and oppression's iron hand weigh down their property, they sigh and turn their eyes to the western world; they collect, in time, their little means, and with Providence as a conductor, "tempering the wind to the shorn lamb," they commit themselves to the ocean, and at length, tread the soil of freedom. But it frequently happens, that hope, which is not the forerunner of certainty, bedecks our land with all the beauties of paradise; reason and reflection are lost in the pleasures of anticipation, and the emigrant expects too much from America, and relies too little on his own exertions. We have all the cardinal qualities to constitute a great empire; a free government, a fruitful soil, and a wholesome climate: these are fundamental advantages which man must improve, advance, and perpetuate, by his diligence, fidelity, and industry. Emigrants, therefore, when they intend to locate themselves in a particular spot, should, almost immediately after their arrival in port, repair to their place of destination, and enter upon their projects of enterprize and industry. Even a short residence in the city is injurious: as much money is spent in a few weeks in living and seeing all that may be curious in a populous city, as would be required to build a comfortable cottage. Let them lose not a moment—let the farmer, with his family, shun the expensive allurements and pernicious examples of a city—let him depart for his settlement, and with his axe, clear his land, build his cabin, plant his corn, and then his fortune has commenced: he is a proprietor of the soil—he is sovereign and independent: his wife labours, his girls work, his boys are hardy and industrious: their land produces corn—their cows furnish milk—their sheep clothing—their forests fuel—their hives honey—their trees maple sugar—they have fruits in abundance, and ample stores of provisions. What do they want? Nothing but health to labour, and contentment to sweeten their fare.

There is a vast quantity of rich and valuable lands in the United States that can be purchased for two dollars per acre. A farm of fifty acres, sufficiently extensive for a family, may be procured for $100—so that for a few hundred dollars, aided by economy and industry, an emigrant can become a landholder and a prosperous farmer; and how soon a few hundred dollars melt away in an extravagant city!

The consequences of this rapid emigration of industrious and moral Europeans will be wonderful in a few years. We have territory for one hundred millions of people, giving to each a farm. In a short time we shall hear the pipe of the Swiss goatherd playing in our valleys; we shall see the vine bent to the earth with clusters of ripe grape, and whitewashed cottages, flourishing villages, and manufacturing towns, springing up in the wilderness as if by magic; and this association of foreigners, this blending of habits, manners and language, will temper the genius and national disposition of the people, and give a softness, harmony, and judicious character to the American community.

August 6, 1819.
[Of Fashion]

Dame *Fortune* has been generally represented as blind and fickle, and I have often thought that *Fashion* should also be personified. If we call her a dame, she must be more fickle and eccentric than ever Fortune was.

The variety of changes to which the world has been subjected by Fashion, and the inordinate extravagance which has resulted from these useless changes, have produced incalculable evils in laying a foundation for waste and profusion, the ill effects of which are now felt. In former times a house was furnished with the utmost prudence—no useless article was ever purchased—and the high-backed mahogany chairs, the heavy carved mirrors, the bed and durable curtains, and all the ornaments of the mansion, were selected for their lasting and useful qualities. If after an absence of twenty years a friend returned to his country, his eyes were greeted with the same old-fashioned, yet ponderous furniture, which time had familiarized, nay, even rendered dear to him; he saw and recognized the old china jars, the sprigged teacups and flowered plates, the old chased sugar dish and teapot, the spinnet, the highly-polished wardrobe, in which were deposited the brocade dresses of his grandam and the embroidered waistcoats of his grandfather; all these objects revived the recollection of earlier days, of happy moments, and served to increase that attachment to *home,* in which are centered so many joys and so many enjoyments. But now the scene is altered, and the furniture of a house is changed as frequently as a coat and waistcoat. Instead of the useful and durable, we have the light, the costly, and flimsy ornaments of a drawing room: gilt vases, cut glass chandeliers, grand upright pianos, silk curtains, and all the paraphernalia of a fairy's palace. Immense fortunes are thus thrown away on these fickle, thoughtless changes, and, as Peter Trot says, "the upholsterer has scarcely done knocking up, when in comes the auctioneer and knocks down."

Thus fashion may be called fickle, expensive, and sometimes imperative; it ought to be resisted with firmness and decision. I would, by no means, be so much out of fashion as to be peculiarly strange and absurd; but to follow all its eccentricities, to be a slave to its caprices, and ruined by its changes, is to be, at once, deaf to prudence, discretion, and good sense.

It is not over the domestic organization alone, that fashion exercises a powerful influence; it extends to the person, and is equally as fickle and as costly in matters of dress and personal ornament. Look into the bureaus and trunks of modern men of fashion, and see the number of coats, waistcoats, pantaloons, hats, and boots. Why this unnecessary accumulation of clothing? Why purchase more than is absolutely necessary to make a respectable appearance? Think you it adds to the importance of a man to wear a blue coat at breakfast, a pea green at dinner, and a black in the evening? Then the ladies, though they have not as many superfluities as the gentlemen, still they have many to spare; there are many expenses which they could curtail, many little trifles which they could economise. It frequently happens, that both male and female, by following fashion with an extreme devotion, and pursuing her through every mazy course, fall into many ludicrous errors, and frequently cut a very sorry figure.

A few evenings since, I casually paid a visit to an old friend, and was surprised to find the rooms illuminated and filled with gaily dressed ladies and gentlemen. As I like innocent hilarity, I took my seat on a sofa between two smiling pretty lasses, who said many handsome things to me, though I am an old man. The conversation at last turned on fashions, taste, extravagance, and so on, to domestic economy. A young gentleman (some would have called him a buck, others a dandy) came in front of the sofa, and stood before the ladies, in an attitude inexpressibly inelegant, though it may have been fashionable: he had on a pair of petticoat pantaloons, so short that the calves of his legs were visible; a striped waistcoat, and his waist compressed by corsets to nearly the size of a wasp's; a cravat which nearly choked him; seals and keys in the usual quantity; the animal straddled before the ladies, with his thumbs elegantly hitched in the flaps of his pantaloons, and with a squeaking effeminate voice, pronounced sentence of displeasure on all those meddling busybodies, and philanthropic writers, who, having no money of their own, insolently obtruded their advice on men of fashion, and presumed to dictate.—The ladies smiled, but not in approbation, and they seemed to enjoy the appearance which this caricature of a man made, holding a glass of ice cream in one hand, and with the other occasionally arranging his bushy hair, and rendering himself more frightful.

At this period, the sky, which had been overcast, became quite black, and peals of thunder broke upon the ear, accompanied with vivid flashes of lightning. The ladies arose somewhat discomposed; but one, young and handsome, with whom I was conversing, turned from me very quickly, put her hand to her white bosom, and drew out a long black piece of iron or steel, which, in her confusion, she let fall—I stooped, picked it up, and handed it to her, observing that confusion. It is my corset bone, whispered she; I am so afraid of the lightning that I have to take it out—do keep it for me, dear sir, and don't look angry; it is the fashion, and it is English also.

Alas! what is fashion to bring us to? A young and delicate lady casing herself in iron, flying from the elements, binding and compressing her delicate frame and blasting her white skin by the rude embrace of a vile and black substance, checking respiration, obstructing the free use of her lungs and muscles, laying the foundation for cramps, pains and consumptions, and courting death, disguised in the alluring and illusive shape of *Fashion!* "Fie! O, fie!"

September 25, 1819.
[The Sabbath]

There are moments when serious reflection is a luxury—when the gay and elastic spirits, the sportive fancy, the lively and exuberant imagination, delight to dwell on pensive subjects—when the eye pierces the mind, and the soul holds communion with the heart: then the frail tenure of existence, the helpless condition, the dependant state of man, are seen and felt; then the monarch, the leader, and all those "dressed in brief authority," shrink into equal stations, and are sensible that affliction and death reaches alike the sovereign and the peasant. Whenever such feelings steal over my mind, I do not wish to check them: they "come like shadows," and leave a soft, yet melancholy, trace behind, which tempers that lively disposition which should be judiciously controlled, not effectually destroyed.

Under the influence of such sober feelings, I was seated at my window last Sunday, and contemplated the concourse of people which, in every direction, was passing to the several places of religious worship, as the bells, with "their iron tongues and brazen mouths," called them to the fulfilment of their sacred duty. What a noble and illustrious institution is that of *Sabbath!* Millions of beings, scattered over the globe, shunning, at the same moment, the allurements of pleasure, the avidity of gain, the habit of labour, and uniting in returning thanks to the Disposer of all good, for his manifold blessings, and his paternal protection. On this day, man disencumbers himself of care; all temporal concerns are forgotten, vexatious crosses are no longer remembered, his wearied limbs find repose, and all is sunshine around him. He who does not, at proper times, commune with his God, loses a great temporal luxury, and hazards his eternal happiness. You may be free in your religious opinions, and indifferent as to the strict performance of the duties of religion—you may philosophize on its mysteries, and coldly comply, for form's sake, with what morality requires—but there is more than form or fashion, or sentiment, which God requires of his creatures; and there are times when the most free and indifferent call upon him for protection and support. We may partly judge, from common relations in life, how pleasing it is to be sincerely and truly pious in our orisons: we hail the friend who has served us with gratitude—we gaze upon our companion in life with affection—we feel towards children and relations the sentiments of love and kindness: but how strongly combined should all those feelings be when addressing the Fountain of life—the Disposer of good—the merciful, indulgent and omnipotent God. Not with the shouts of fanaticism, nor the fretful penances of temporal authority—not as dealing damnation to one sect and blessings to others—not as crushing one portion of his creation and elevating another: but as a just and righteous God, whom you fear to offend—whom you approach with the confidence of a pure heart—whom you call upon for salvation and blessings with that freedom which arises from an unsullied conscience. This is, indeed, a luxury; and those in the gay throng, who think only of dress, of fashion, and of folly, instead of encouraging and maturing pious reflections, while in a place of worship, lose sight of the great object and end of religion. There is nothing in religion which is repulsive to human nature: it is alike foreign from the gloomy air of the monastery, and the fastidious injunctions of the bigot: religion is ever cheerful in its purity, and there is nothing appalling in its sacred character. Should we not then encourage it? Should we wait until the hour of tribulation arrives? Should we forget our God until affliction warns us of our helpless condition? No. In our prosperity, let us be grateful—in our adversity, resigned: gratefully receiving the good and ill with which our lives are chequered.

These sentiments were awakened by the sight of a crowded population hastening to church on Sunday. I followed, in imagination, the various sects, having one object in view: I listened to the prayer of the pious prelate; I dwelt with pleasure on the discourse of the able theologian; I saw the priest heave the censer high in air, and marked the curling smoke of frankincense hovering over the altar; the full swell of the deep toned organ, reverberating through the fretted roof, burst on the ear: the hymn of the choristers floated through the aisles, and even the angels and cherubims joined their voices in sacred harmony of praise and devotion, while, with one voice, the multitude cried aloud, "Our Father which art in heaven, *hallowed* be thy name."

October 2, 1819.
[Raising Children]

There is no subject or special duty which is of so much vital interest, and so little understood, as the *management of children.* I am confirmed in the opinion, from attentive observation, that this branch of domestic economy is very much neglected, and that children were better governed some twenty-five years ago than they are at present. Parents, as well as society at large, the interest of country, and the welfare of mankind, depend in a great measure on early impressions, on a proper impulse and direction given to children's minds; and this cannot be neglected without violating those great obligations which morality imposes.

I am excessively fond of children, when they are not rude or noisy, and can hardly have a higher gratification than in mixing in their innocent amusements, and participating in their joyful gambols. I take great delight in conversing with a sensible modest boy: and can nurse a rosy cheek'd infant for hours, if the urchin does not cry. With such feelings, I accepted an invitation from a friend to dinner, who had a large family of young children, and who seasoned his invitation by assurances that I should meet some gentlemen of intelligence, as well as being gratified with the sight of a promising family. These were sufficient inducements; and at the appointed hour I was there, for nothing is more rude than to keep a family waiting dinner beyond the hour invitation. I met with a friendly welcome; and the young ones, consisting of three boys and a girl, were severally ordered up to shake hands with me, and be exhibited. They each made some resistance, shuffled off a little, and came very reluctantly. I did not augur well from this specimen of breeding; a child should be instructed to approach a stranger with respectful confidence, divested alike of assurance or timidity. I would not judge hastily, and dinner was shortly announced. The children were almost the first seated, and there was some indecent scuffling for chairs, which required the interference of the father to stop, and which was not done without some difficulty, as mamma begged him not to create a riot. Order being restored, I began to eat my soup, but with little comfort: the young ones were again noisy and clamorous; one did not like the mutton, the other vociferously demanded the ship of a turkey, a third called for beer with an air of authority, and papa whispered the fourth to ask me to drink a glass of wine with him—an honour I would have declined, but was fearful of hurting the feelings of the father, who was thus ruining his child, by teaching him maxims of high life, and customs of mature age, while yet an infant.

We got through the dinner after some wrangling—a few tears, expostulations from the father, and opposition from the mother. The desert was introduced, and the young ones made a dash at the finest of the fruit; helped themselves plentifully; and, while two were fighting for a peach, they knocked over a butterboat with sauce for the pudding, which they safely lodged, partly in mamma's lap, and partly on my black small clothes. I was very near losing my temper on the occasion: it fretted me to see children so much neglected. However, while the urchins were busily engaged in destroying whatever they fancied, I was conversing with a gentleman who sat opposite to me, on the subject of manufactures, and the means of decreasing pauperism and giving employment to our poor; but this deeply interesting subject was interrupted by the nurse entering, with an infant in her arms, and a boy of two years old, leading by the hand. A new scene of uproar commenced: the children seized the baby; the baby squalled for fruit; the young one grasped at every thing in his way; a perfect riot ensued; and it was with great difficulty that the room was cleared, after bribing each of them with something eatable. I took my departure with pleasure, happy in terminating this unpleasant interview.

Times are strangely altered, or rather wholesome doctrines have become unfashionable. When I was a boy, my breakfast, with seven others, consisted of milk and water, or very weak coffee, which was placed in a large earthen pan, and each of us had a tin cup, and two good slices of bread and butter. All of our meals were served up in this manner, under the superintendence of one of the family, and we were dispatched to school at a proper hour. We had a reasonable proportion of delicacies reserved for us, and at night we joined the family party, who were all pleased to see us, and that was the season for mirth and judicious hilarity. Our education was not neglected; our appetites were not pampered; our minds were not ruined by extravagance; and our principles were not vitiated by bad examples. Nothing can have a better effect than adopting a system with children, and never departing from it, if the principles are sound. A very sacred and solemn duty is imposed upon parents, not only to feed and clothe their children, (for that seems to be the boundary of attention with many persons) but to preserve their minds and morals pure; to inculcate, by *precept* and *example*, lessons of prudence, economy, and industry. This can only be effected in one way: by decision and judicious severity. Unless a child *fears* his parent, he will never obey or respect him. This severity does not consist in beating a child, but keeping him at a respectful distance; admitting him only at stated periods into his presence, and at those periods conversing rationally and affectionately with him; crushing in the bud every attempt at wit, or, what is called, smart sayings, the precursors only of insolence, rudeness and ill manners: but, on the contrary, imprinting upon their waxen minds lessons of mildness, temperance and industry. Some will say that by this cold and repulsive course, you teach children to hate you; but it should be remembered that familiarity destroys respect; and where there is no respect, there is no fear; where there is no fear, there is no obedience. A child may fear his parent, but in time he will discover the good qualities of his father, account for his severity, and love him; and that very severity will induce a child to do nothing that may offend him. Let them live hardy when young; partake of rough but wholesome fare; abstain from luxuries; dress plainly; give them little or no money; teach them to earn it; give them a trade when they are able to work, or a suitable profession; see that their time is employed, and *compel* them, while under your care, to obey your commands, and they will turn out good citizens. It is a fact, which is undeniable, that seven-eighths of the bad characters who disfigure the world, who are useless to themselves, and of no credit or service to their families, have been thus reduced to extremities from the culpable neglect and unpardonable indifference of parents.

November 26, 1820.
[Card Playing]

Examining some newspapers a few days ago, I came across a journal printed in the state of Tennessee, which contained the confession of a murderer. I was tempted to read it, though aware that the crime, for which he was about to suffer, was the result of early depravity, of neglect, of idleness, or of vicious habits. There was something so simple in his narrative, that I was persuaded that he had not been a premeditated murderer, but had dipped his hands in blood under the influence of sudden passion, which, I discovered, had been produced by *a game of cards!* The origin of the quarrel is thus described by Bennet, the unhappy felon: We thought it too late to go to Mr. Stone's and return, which was about five miles; we concluded we would postpone it until morning, and go there to breakfast, and we, as *usual,* took our *grog,* and commenced a game at *cards;* at which we continued until about sunset, when our game stood thus: 6 and 6, and his deal. In shuffling the cards, I discovered him to look at the face of them, and place the jack of diamonds at the bottom of the pack. I cut the cards—Mr. Hay dealt them; and after dealing off the proper number, he slipped the fatal jack of diamonds from the bottom of the pack, and claimed the money then in stake, which was *ten dollars.* I at first thought him in jest, and laughed at him for making so bungling an out; and told him that might do in Georgia, but it would never do to win my money. He, in an elevated tone, asked me what I meant? I told him I meant turning the jack of diamonds from the bottom of the pack would not do to win my money—I was not in the habit of being cheated out of my money when I knew it. He replied, if I said he turned the jack from the bottom, I was a d—d liar and a rascal. I told him to give me no more of his insolent language, if he did, I would slap his jaws, which I would do any how if it was any where else; and if he claimed my money in that manner, to take it, and I was done with him: he had discovered himself to be a worthless rascal. He rose, with saying, "d—n you, you think your size will protect you;" at which time he seized a stick which lay on the floor, and aimed a blow apparently at my head. I made an attempt to dodge it, and at the same time threw up my left arm, on which the force of the blow lodged near my shoulder. I instantly seized the stick and demanded him to let go; I held the stick in my left hand, and gave him a severe blow.

This was the commencement of the affray, and Bennet, finally, seized a pair of smoothing irons and killed Hay with one blow, and then, in alarm, buried him secretly—was arrested, tried, convicted, and probably hanged for a murder originating in a *game at cards.*

Cards were originally invented for the amusement of a king, and their use or abuse has created great misery in the civilized world. If loss of fortune, loss of reputation, loss of peace and happiness, did not result from habits of gaming, the loss of temper alone would present an obstacle to their encouragement. In the case of this unhappy man, we have an instance of the awful effects of passion and avarice originating with cards; but this case was confined to poor and uneducated members of the community—men easily led into error; it is the higher classes from which good examples should emanate—it is polished and educated persons who should discountenance pernicious habits, and teach the ignorant the evil of depraved propensities.

Last week, Nicholas brought me a note, beautifully embossed and printed, containing an invitation to a party. It smells of musk, said the old man, as he left the room. Very true, said I—the age is a refined one indeed, we sprinkle bottles of cologne and orange flower water over our persons—we scatter rosemary and lavender among our clothes, as if nature required a perfume to sweeten her works. "An answer is requested."—*Pshaw!* what consequence is my presence or my absence? they will not order one ice cream less, nor one macaroni more. But I determined to go; society is pleasant, is necessary; I take great pleasure in seeing the young ladies judiciously dressed and ornamented, enjoying themselves sportively, innocently, happily—enlivening conversation with artless spirit and unstudied grace. I will go—and I ordered Nicholas to make preparation.

The hackman charged me two shillings more than his fare, imagining that no gentleman who wore silk stockings and silver buckles, and who was elated with the prospect of a hot supper, would hesitate to be imposed upon. I thought of the spiteful remark of Richard III. "Why were laws made if men were not rogues by nature?"—but, we are said to have a very vigilant police—yet laws are sometimes evaded. The full blaze of lights and beauty burst on my sight, while the flourish of hautboys, and the shrill violins, announced that the dancing had commenced.

In one of the drawing rooms the card tables were out, and I leaned on a chair, to observe old and young ladies and gentlemen engaged at loo, whist, and speculation. The old ladies appeared excessively anxious, and the young ones caught the inspiration; ill luck and bad play awakened feelings of cupidity, mingled with irascible expressions and illnatured looks; a kind of restlessness, a sharp, techy, wayward anxiety seemed to prevail; eyes were intensely fixed on the trump card; joy and sadness, mirth and harshness, alternately prevailed; envy, passion, and all the smothered attributes of Medusa, hovered over these parties assembled for *amusement;* if one took a heavy pool, the whole company saw it vanish with deep regret, and the brilliant eyes of the young and beautiful girls followed the golden bait, as if reluctant to part with its tempting prospects, while an envious ejaculation, and a significant shrug of the shoulder from the old ladies and gentlemen, indicated their regret at having lost the prize; those who were supposed to have played bad were snarled at, and those who were adepts sneered at: and it appeared to me as if some demon presided at these tables, to turn all the milk of human kindness into gall. And is this mode of spending time commendable, judicious, and beneficial? Where are the joys, the delight, the improvement of social converse? Where is the pleasure and gratification derived from accomplishments, from a combination of grace and talent? All lost—buried beneath a green cloth and a pack of cards. If young ladies could only see how unamiable they must appear to an indifferent spectator, when absorbed in a game of cards and bent on winning—if they could be sensible that, gradually and imperceptibly, the practice wears away the fine edge of their temper, and damps their sensibilities, introduces parsimony, and that hateful passion, avarice—they would shun the tempter as they would a hydra. How can any thing be encouraged as an amusement, under which danger lurks in so many shapes? Cards should only be introduced among old and rational people, who wish to kill an hour without a sacrifice of temper or money; but they should be banished from the young and elastic sprits, whose impetuous fancy reason cannot control, and prudence cannot pursue. Besides, the example among the higher classes is pernicious to other branches of society; for if educated and refined persons, governed by avarice and an attachment to cards, should lose their temper and wrangle, be covetous, expert, and sometimes unfair, what may be expected from the ignorant and the unlettered, with the same passions and the same weapons? Why, as in the case of Bennet, it may end in murder. Let them be banished.

February 9, 1820. [Education of Women]

When I have neither a good book at hand, nor a letter to write, nor a visit to pay, nor a walk to take, I read a political paper, which indifference will prove that I do not consider politics and religion the only two great subjects which should command attention. I would take a greater interest in politics, but I have an unconquerable aversion to disturbing the serenity of my temper with local conflicts, which, like the gratings of a file, sets one's teeth on edge, or like a glass of punch, which, when fortified with too much acid, creates a partial smacking of lips, and leaves a rough tartness on the palate. However, I now and then read a governor's message, not that I think more of a governor than any other citizen who elects himself or is elected to the office, but it is his constitutional duty to think on new projects for a whole year, and then detail them in neat paragraphs to the legislature, for which he is paid an equivalent in bank notes or specie, as the case may be. I was particularly pleased with the recommendation of our governor, to retrench the public expenditures, and lower the salaries of public officers. Illnatured politicians would say that it was a mere electioneering trick—a dash at popularity—that he should have done it before. But I say, "better late than never," and if in his search for popularity he saves the state a plumb annually, I pardon the motive for the sake of the result. I was, however, much gratified, at perceiving a recommendation for legislative aid to a *female academy* at Waterford, and another, I believe, at Catskill; the only two in this great state. The governor, though a very gallant man, and particularly attached to ladies of influence and talents, could not but look for some objections to the appropriation, and even went so far as to anticipate some ridicule on the project: this, to say the least of it, was a poor compliment to the discernment of a wise legislature, and for which his excellency should be punished by having a button pulled off his coat by the delicate fingers of some female friend. Why should a proposition of so much importance and utility be ridiculed? why should aid be denied to an object in which the community generally are so much interested.

The state, some years since, justly considering that education was the proper basis on which good citizens could be erected, governed by the laudable intention of making every peasant a scholar, created a large school fund, and such has been the happy result of the experiment, that the traveller can ride but few miles through our flourishing state without a modest schoolhouse breaks upon his sight, seated in the midst of a grove of oaks or weeping willows, on the margin of a bubbling stream, or placed like a beacon on a commanding eminence; he sees the little urchins frisking on the grass, opening their little baskets with their rural meal—exercise giving elasticity to the limbs, frugality sweetness to the temper—he hears the chiming of the bell, and soon perceives them at their studies. This is indeed a happy sight: their minds become expanded; they are taught to know the world, mankind, and the part they have to act: they are taught to appreciate their rights, and to become sufficiently enlightened to preserve their liberty: so much good is to be ascribed to the liberality of the state.

But have females no claims on the state? Is the sturdy oak to be trimmed and nourished, and the tender ivy neglected? Are we to cultivate the rose, and disregard the violet? I know it will be said, that girls may participate, and do participate in the bounty of the state, but then there are no academies exclusively for females, which receive any public patronage. I have always considered that females, after having attained a certain age, should not mix promiscuously with boys—it may create early and sometimes improper attachments—it impairs that mutual respect and delicacy which should be ever scrupulously observed between the sexes—it sometimes promotes confidence without emulation, indifference without attainments. After a young lady has arrived at the age of twelve years, her education should be completed among females only.

The happiest days I ever passed were at school with girls. We were an idle set of children—played all manner of pranks—kissed one-another in school, and snowball'd one-another out of it—tore our clothes—ink'd our fingers, and neglected our studies. The result of all this, was, that romps at eighteen left school full of wild notions, and got married. The transition was so rapid that it bewildered them, and a happy bridegroom would imprint his kiss on lips the dews from which had just been brush'd by a favourite boy of sixteen, in the schoolroom. Few girls, thus educated, ever made truly distinguished wives.

Well, then, if you must have separate schools, will you not also take such schools under your patronage and protection? Is the cultivation of the female mind—females with whom we pray to live, from whom we reluctantly part, an object of indifference? I shall however be told, that the science taught at Catskill, and the accomplishments at Waterford, are unnecessary for females; and that the state cannot assist institutions which instruct young ladies in botany, chemistry, languages and dancing. I will readily admit that extensive appropriations for these objects would be impolitic; but where the school fund is upwards of a million of dollars, surely two thousand dollars to each of these institutions will not be deemed an unfair proportion.

I am willing to allow, that a very learned woman, conversant with all the sciences, and devoting all her time to study, cannot be a very desirable companion; but then it is better to be familiarly acquainted with them all, than to be utterly ignorant of any. Chemistry and botany are connected with domestic affairs, a knowledge of which, if not absolutely necessary, may still be very useful; and a knowledge of the living languages, while it leads to the study of history, imparts a grace and a peculiar attraction to females. In short, a woman may be accomplished, without being a pedant; she may be learned, yet amiable; possessing a strong mind, yet soft manners; and these may occupy her attention, without intruding upon other indispensable avocations. Besides, a partial knowledge of the sciences, and some acquaintance with higher branches of study, may sometimes produce a strength of mind, a firmness and fortitude, which would enable the widow to bring up and instruct her helpless children without assistance, and the orphan to protect herself in this designing world. If we reason against this patronage on narrow grounds, if we are governed by unlettered sneers and uncouth jests, in withholding this assistance, we shall never reach that perfection in society which refinement and education jointly produce. Ay, but (says the rigid economist) our girls don't want that learning; make them fit to marry, teach them to knit and sew, and bake bread, and make pies, and cook a turkey, and nurse children, and rub furniture. Now, although I admit that a knowledge of these things is very pleasant and very useful, and a cheerful performance of them is highly meritorious; still, if to these a wife should possess a few auxiliary accomplishments, why, to a discerning husband, they must be very agreeable—they serve to make his home so comfortable. If I had friends to dine with me, I should not like to see my wife rush from the kitchen to the head of the table, with her pretty face flushed, her dress disordered, and her whole appearance something in the shape of a roasted lady—on the contrary, without neglecting the imperious duty of superintendence, I should wish to see her take her seat with perfect tranquillity, to be able to participate in the progressive and social converse, and, if she can, occasionally address the foreign gentleman on her right in a few words of French, and the one on her left in Spanish, and urge her hospitality in sounds familiar and grateful to their ears; she does herself an honour, communicates to them a pleasure, and me certainly a gratification. Then, in company with a gentleman of science, she rambles through the garden, points out and classifies the herbs, explains their uses and virtues, then pauses at the flowers, plucks a violet, and presents it with grace to the stranger, gives it its classic name, *"viola odorata,"* informs him that the *petals* are used to colour the syrup extracted from the violets, that it is an agreeable medicine for children; and, moreover, that the presence of *acids* and *alkalies* is discovered by using this syrup in chemical inquiries. Then she returns to the parlour, runs over a canzonet on the piano, plays with her children, and finally converses with an Italian gentleman on the beauties of Tasso and Ariosto. Can there be any thing more delightful than this melange of the useful and ornamental? Then let it be encouraged—let these two female seminaries be placed under the auspices of the state—let the education of women engage our attention as much as it did that of the Romans. What is the cost in comparison with the advantages? Nothing. If money cannot be raised for the object, then tax the bachelors—a very fair tax for such a purpose, and I do therefore hope that the good intentions which led to the recommendation, and the good results which may be confidently anticipated, may induce the members of the legislature to smile benignantly on the proposition, and open their hearts and the public purse together, and I promise that each of their wives and sweethearts shall reward them with a kiss.

June 3, 1820.
[Of Slavery]

I like to walk on the Battery—not only because it affords the finest view in the world, the most lively and animating picture of a prosperous and commercial nation—but because I see so many persons of different classes and distinctions, the wealthy and the wise, the poor and the unlettered, alike assemble to catch the fresh current of air that ripples the water—to mark the curling volume of black smoke ascending from the steamboats, the full swelling sails of the outward bound ship richly freighted, the islands studded over with trees, forts and cottages, and the little bark of the fisherman; here saunters the careless beau, and there the dashing belle; here comes a poor old man, with age bent double, to refresh himself with the morning breeze—and there is a nest of little infants, frisking on the grass with their nurses, and laving their limbs in the morning dews. The Battery may be called "the poor man's plantation," where all may participate equally of its benefits, and where the munificence of the city has provided an agreeable and healthy retreat. Whenever I wish to spend a pensive moment, to enjoy the beauties of nature, retire from the bustle of the world, I ascend the platform of the flagstaff, and, while sheltered from the rays of the sun, I amuse myself by looking through the telescope at the various objects in view.

A few days ago, while thus employed, I saw a small schooner coming in, apparently from sea, and making towards the wharf. Desirous of learning where she had come from and what she had brought, I sauntered down slowly, and on inquiry of an officer on board, learnt that she was a *prize!* In time of profound peace, how a prize could be made, was to me an enigma: but I shortly discovered that she, with three others, had been captured by a government vessel, charged with having violated the laws of our country and of humanity, in being engaged in the *slave trade.* To say I felt happy that the cupidity of these bucaniers had been punished, is but a poor expression to convey my sentiments. To the loss of property I would have added condign punishment, and deprived those agents of iniquity of their liberty by putting them into solitary confinement, where they might be able to appreciate the value of the blessings of which they so unfeelingly deprive others.

The question of slavery, like all others, may have opponents of mixed feelings. Motives of interest and of policy may supersede principles of humanity—still in the abstract it is an accursed traffic, revolting to humanity, and disgraceful to an enlightened and free community. What is there in that portion of creation that can justify the seizing and selling of them to slavery? Can the difference in complexion constitute a right to this barbarous custom? We have repeated instances that the intellect of the blacks is capable of high cultivation; we have in the history of Toussaint and Christophe, ample proofs of talent, bravery, prudence, and a capacity to govern. Why are they to be hunted like wild beasts in their native land, forced to foreign climes, and compelled to wear the chains of bondage? Have they no feelings, attachments, or sentiments? Can there be any human right to seize and enslave them? These questions never occur to those engaged in this traffic—but when they are deprived of their *property,* and punished for violating the laws of their country, the question is brought home to them.

The Arabs and the Portuguese were the two first powers engaged in the slave trade: the Arabs attacking by land, and the Portuguese by water. Other nations, allured by the thirst of gain, followed the same traffic; but there is no power originally engaged to any extent in this trade, which at this day possesses character or national resources: let Spain and Portugal be the examples. Slaves, it has been said, are bought from the victorious kings, and are prisoners—but it more frequently happens that they are *stolen*. "He that stealeth a man and selleth him, shall surely be put to death." Levit. xxiv. 16.

How can *Americans* be engaged in this traffic—men whose birthright is *liberty,* whose eminent peculiarity is *freedom?* Here was a small pilot-boat schooner, fitted (I blush to say it) from an American port, for the purpose of engaging in the slave-trade. I could not avoid, in fancy, tracing her progress: The schooner sails from this port with a prosperous breeze—she reaches the coast of Africa, and prowls along the shore—looks in beneath the crags and under promontories for a safe shelter—there she is moored—her men, armed, land from their boats and conceal themselves under the thick trees, brush and underwood:—Every country has its sports, and none more so than Africa: as the sun dips its beams into the western wave, the sound of the tamborine and cymbal is heard in the valleys and on the plains; then, with light hearts and joyous steps, the ebon-tinted happy people assemble to dance, to enjoy their village sports—then, with quick and hurried gait, with elastic limbs and active zeal, they move to the measure of their rude music. Mirth and shouts are seen and heard; the ivory teeth of each African is heightened by the contrast of their black and shining skin; their eyes sparkle with vivacity; and as they fold their wives and sweethearts in their arms, and pass through the mazes of the dance, the ancient fathers of the village, seated on the turf, view those sports with delight, in which they participated in youthful days. Just at that moment, when all is joy and mirth, the dark faces of these manhunters are seen scowling through the bushes; they rush in, with arms in hand, among the happy group, tear wife from husband, children from father, and turn the hour of gladness to mourning and desolation; then the sound of music is hushed, and the screams of despair are heard; then, chained and enslaved, these unfortunates are hurried on board the vessel, thrown like dogs into the hold, and separated from all that can render life desirable. Should we not rejoice when a slave vessel is captured, and a blow given to the cupidity of these savages?

The question, whether slaves born in our country shall be permitted to move from one state to another, which is adjoining, is not one that can bear comparison, nor has it any affinity to trading, capturing, and bringing slaves from the coast of Africa—they are distinct: one may be deplored, the other must be cursed—one may be a domestic evil, the other levels the character of a nation at once, and I hope, that every vessel engaged in this inhuman traffic, may be captured and sent in for condemnation.

The End

The Ararat Proclamation and Speech

The Buffalo Patriot
Vol. VIII Buffalo,
Tuesday, September 20, 1825 [No. 388.

Buffalo. Thursday, Sept. 15, 1825

It was known, at the sale of that beautiful and valuable tract called Grand Island, a few miles below this port, in the Niagara river, that it was purchased in part by the friends of Major Noah of New-York, avowedly to offer it as an asylum for his brethren of the Jewish persuasion, who in the other parts of the world, are much oppressed; and it was likewise known that it was intended to erect upon the Island a City called ARARAT. We are grateful to perceive, by the documents in this day's paper, that coupled with this colonization is a declaration of Independence, and the revival of the Jewish government under the protection of the United States, after the dispersion of that ancient and wealthy people for nearly 2,000 years—and the appointment of Mr. Noah as first Judge. It was intended, pursuant to public notice, to celebrate the event on the Island, and a flag staff was erected for the Grand Standard of Israel, and other arrangements made: but it was discovered that a sufficient number of boats could not be procured in time to convey all those to the Island who were desirous of witnessing the ceremony, and the celebration took place this day in the village, which was both interesting and impressive. At dawn of day, a salute was fired in front of the Court House, and from the terrace facing the Lake. At 10 o'clock, the masonic and military companies assembled in front of the Lodge, and at 11 the line of procession was formed as follows:

Order of Procession

Grand Marshal, Col. Potter, on horseback.

Music.

Military.

Citizens.

Civil Officers.
State Officers in Uniform.
U.S. Officers.
President, and Trustees of the Corporation.
Tyler.
Sewards.
Entered Apprentices.
Fellow Crafts.
Master Masons.
Senior and Junior Deacons.
Secretary and Treasurer.
Senior and Junior Wardens.
Masters of Lodges.
Past Masters.
Rev. Clergy.
Stewards, with corn, wine, and oil.
Globe {Principal Architect, with square, level and plumb} Globe
Bible.
Square and Compass, borne by a Master Mason.
Master of the Lodge.
The Judge of Israel.
In black, wearing the judicial robes of crimson silk, trimmed with ermine and a richly embossed golden medal suspended from the neck.
A Master Mason.
Royal Arch Masons.
Knights Templars.

On arriving at the Church door the troops opened to the right and left, and the procession entered the aisles, the Band playing the Grand March from Judas Maccabees. The full toned organ commenced its swelling notes performing the *Jubilate*. On the Communion table lay the Corner Stone, with the following inscription,

IN HEBREW
"Hear O Israel, the Lord is our God.—The Lord is ONE."
ARARAT
The Hebrews' Refuge, founded by MORDECAI MANUEL NOAH
In the month of Tisri, 5586, corresponding with September, 1825, and in the 50th year of American Independence.
On the stone lay the silver cups with wine, corn and oil.

The ceremonies commenced by the Morning Service, read emphatically by the Rev. Mr. Searl of the Episcopal Church. "Before Jehovah's awful Throne," was sung by the choir to the tune of Old Hundred.—Morning Prayer.—First lesson from Jeremiah, 31st.—Second lesson, Zeph. iii. 8th verse. Psalms for the occasion, 97, 98, 99, 100, 127th Psalm in verse. Ante Communion Service—Psalm in Hebrew—Benediction.

Mr. Noah rose and pronounced a discourse or rather delivered a speech, announcing the reorganization of the Jewish Government and going through a detail of many points of intense interest, to which a crowded auditory listened with profound attention. On the conclusion of the ceremonies the procession returned to the Lodge and the Masonic brethren and the Military repaired to the Eagle Tavern and partook of refreshments. The Church was filled with Ladies and the whole ceremony was impressive and unique. A grand salute of 24 guns was fired by the Artillery, and the Band played a number of patriotic airs.

We learn that a vast concourse assembled at Tonawanda expecting the ceremonies would be at Grand Island. Many of them came up in carriages in time to hear the inaugural speech. The following is the proclamation which will be read with great attention and interest. A finer day and more general satisfaction has not been known on any similar occasion.

Proclamation to the Jews

WHEREAS it has pleased Almighty God, to manifest to his chosen people, the approach of that period, when, in fulfillment of the promises made to the race of Jacob, and as a reward for their pious consistency and triumphant fidelity, they are to be gathered from the four quarters of the Globe, and to resume their rank and character among the governments of the Earth. And whereas, the peace which now prevails among civilized nations;—the progress of learning throughout the world, and the general spirit of liberality and toleration which exists, together with other changes, favorable to light and to liberty, mark in an especial manner, the approach of that time, when "peace on earth and good will to man," are to prevail with a benign and extended influence, and the ancient people of God, the first to proclaim his unity and omnipotence, are to be restored to their inheritence and enjoy the rights of a sovereign independent people: THEREFORE, I, MORDECAI MANUEL NOAH, Citizen of the United States of America, late Consul of said States for the city and kingdom of Tunis, High Sheriff of New-York, Counseler at Law, and by the grace of God, Governer and Judge of Israel, have issued this my proclamation, announcing to the Jews throughout the world that an asylum is prepared and hereby offered to them, where they can enjoy that peace, comfort, and happiness which have been denied them, through the intolerance and misgovernment of former ages. An asylum in a free and powerful country, where ample protection is secured to their persons, their property, and religious rights; an asylum in a country, remarkable for its vast resources, the richness of its soil, and the salubrity of its climate; where industry is encouraged, education promoted, and good faith rewarded. "A land of milk and Honey," where Israel may repose in peace, under his "vine and fig tree," and where our people may so familiarize themselves, with the science of government, and the lights of learning and civilation [*sic*], as may qualify them for that great and final restoration to their ancient heritage, which the times so powerfully indicate.

The asylum referred to is in the state of New York, the greatest state in the American confederacy. New York contains 43,214 square miles, divided into fifty five counties and having six hundred and eighty seven Post towns and cities, containing one million five hundred thousand inhabitants, together with six million acres of cultivated land, improvements in agriculture and manufactures, in trade and commerce, which include a valuation of Three Hundred Millions of dollars of Taxable property. One hundred and fifty thousand militia, armed and equipped, a constitution founded upon an equality of rights; having no test oaths, and recognizing no religious distinctions, and seven thousand free schools and colleges affording the blessings of education to Four Hundred Thousand children. Such is the great and increasing State to which the emigration of the Jews is directed.

The desired spot in the state of New-York to which I hereby invite my beloved people throughout the world, in common with those of every religious denomination, is called Grand Island, and on which I shall lay the foundation of a City of Refuge to be called Ararat.

Grand Island in the Niagara River, is bounded by Ontario on the North, and Erie on the South, and within a few miles of each of those great commercial Lakes. The island is nearly twelve miles in length and varying from three to seven miles in breadth, and contains upwards of Seventeen Thousand Acres of remarkably rich and fertile land. Lake Erie is about two hundred and seventy miles in length, and borders on the States of New-York, Pennsylvania and Ohio: and westwardly by the possessions of our friends and neighbors, the British subjects of Upper Canada. This splendid Lake unites itself by means of navigable rivers, with Lakes St. Clair, Huron, Michigan, and Superior, embracing a lake shore of nearly three thousand miles: and by short canals those vast sheets of water, will be connected with the Illinois and Mississippi rivers, thereby establishing a great and valuable internal trade to New Orleans and the Gulf of Mexico. Lake Ontario on the North, is one hundred and ninety miles in length, and empties into the St. Lawrence, which passing through the Province of Lower Canada carries the commerce of Quebec and Montreal to the Atlantic Ocean.

Thus fortified to the right and left by the extensive commercial resources of the Great Lakes, and their tributary streams—within four miles of the sublime Falls of Niagara, affording the greatest water power in the world for manufacturing purposes,—directly opposite the mouth of the Grand Canal of Three Hundred and sixty miles inland navigation, to the Hudson River, and City of New-York, having the fur trade of Upper Canada to the west, and also of the great territories towards the Rocky Mountains and the Pacific Ocean: likewise the trade of the western states of America; Grand Island may be considered as surrounded by every commercial, manufacturing, and agricultural advantage, and from its location is pre-eminently calculated to become in time the greatest trading and commercial depot in the new and better world. To men of worth and industry it has every substantial attraction, the capitalist will be enable [*sic*] to employ his resources with undoubted profit, and the merchant cannot fail to reap the reward of enterprize in a great and growing republic, but to the industrious mechanic, manufacturer and agriculturist, it holds forth great and improving advantages.

Deprived as our people have been for centuries of a right in the soil, they will learn with peculiar satisfaction, that here they can till the land, reap the harvest, and raise the flocks which are unquestionably their own; and in the full and unmolested enjoyment of their religious rights, and of every civil immunity, together with peace and plenty, they can lift up their voice in gratitude to him, who sustained our fathers in the wilderness and brought us in triumph out of the land of Egypt; who assigned to us the safe keeping of his oracles, who proclaimed us his people, and who has ever walked before us like a "cloud by day and a pillar of fire by night."

In his name do I revive, renew and re-establish the Government of the Jewish Nation under the auspices and protection of the constitution and laws of the United States of America, confirming and perpetuating all our rights and privileges, our name, our rank, and our power among the nations of the earth as they existed and were recognized under the government of the JUDGES.—And I hereby enjoin it upon all our pious and venerable Rabbis, our Presidents and Elders of Synagogues, Chiefs of Colleges, and Brethren in authority throughout the world to circulate and make known this my proclamation, and give to it full publicity, credence, and effect.

It is my will that a census of the Jews throughout the world be taken, and returns of persons, together with their age and occupation, be registered in the archives of the Synogogues where they are accustomed to worship, designating such in particular, who have been and are distinguished in the useful arts, in science, or in knowledge.

Those of our people who from age, local attachment, or from any other cause prefer remaining in the several parts of the world which they now respectively inhabit, and who are treated with liberality by the public authorities, are permitted to do so, and are specially recommended to be faithful to the governments which protect them. It is however expected, that they will aid and encourage the emigration of the young and enterprising, and endeavor to send to this country such, who will add to our national strength and character, by their industry, honor and patriotism.

Those Jews who are in the military employment of the different sovereigns of Europe are enjoined to keep in their ranks until further orders, and conduct themselves with bravery and fidelity.

I command that a strict neutrality, be observed in the pending wars between the Greeks and the Turks enjoined by considerations of safety towards a numerous population of Jews now under the oppressive dominion of the Ottoman Porte.

The annual gifts which for many centuries have been afforded to our pious bretheren in our Holy City of Jerusalem, to which may God speedily restore us, are to continue with unabated liberality; our seminaries of learning and institutions of charity in every part of the world, are to be increased, in order that wisdom and virtue, may permanently prevail among the chosen people.

I abolish forever Polygamy among the Jews, which without religious warrant, without both parties are of a suitable age, and can read and write the language of the country which they respectively inhabit, and which I trust will ensure to their offspring, the blessings of education and probably the lights of science.

Prayers shall forever be said in the Hebrew Language, but it is recommended that occasional discourses on the principles of the Jewish faith, and the doctrines of morality generally be delivered in the language of the coutry [*sic*]; together with such reforms which without departing from the ancient faith may add greater solemnity to our worship.

The Caraite and Samaritan Jews, together with the black Jews of India and Africa, and likewise those in Cochin China, and the sect on the coast of Malabar, are entitled to an equality of rights and religious privileges, as are all who may partake of the great covenant, and obey and respect the Mosaical laws.

The Indians of the American Continent, in their admitted Asiatic origin, in their worship of one God, in their dialect and language, in their sacrifices, marriages, divorces, burials, fastings, purifications, punishments, cities of refuge, division of tribes, in their High Priests, and in their wars and in their victories, being in all probability the descendants of the lost tribes of Israel, which were carried captive by the King of Assyria, measures will be adopted to make them sensible of their origin, to cultivate their minds, soften their condition and finally re-unite them with their brethren the chosen people.

A capitation Tax of three shekels in silver per annum, or one Spanish dollar is hereby levied upon each Jew throughout the world, to be collected by the Treasurers of the different congregations for the purpose of defraying the various expenses of re-organizing the government, of aiding emigrants in the purchase of agricultural implements, providing for their immediate wants & comforts, and assisting their families in making their first settlements, together with such free-will offerings as may be generously made in the furtherence of the laudible objects connected with the restoration of the people and the glory of the Jewish nation. A Judge of Israel shall be chosen once in every four years by the Consistory at Paris, at which time Proxies from every congregation shall be received.

I do hereby name as Commisioners, the most learned and pious Abraham de Cologna, Knight of the Iron Crown of Lombardy, Grand Rabbi of the Jews, and President of the Consistory at Paris, likewise the Grand Rabbi Andrade of Bordeaux, and also our learned and estimable Grand Rabbis of the German and Portugal Jews, in London, Rabbis Herschell & Mendola, together with the Honorable Aaron Nunez Cardoza, of Gibralter, Abraham Busnac, of Leghorn, Benjamin Gradis, of Bordeaux, Dr. E. Gans and Professor Zuntz, of Berlin, and Dr. Leo Woolf of Hamburgh, to aid and assist in carrying into effect the provisions of this my proclamation, with powers to appoint the necessary agents in the several parts of the world and to establish emigration societies in order that the Jews may be concentrated and capacitated to act as a distinct body, having at the head of each Kingdom or Republic such Presiding officers as I shall upon their recommendation appoint. Instructions to these my commissioners shall be forthwith transmitted. And a more enlarged & general view of plan, motives, and objects will be detailed in the address to the nation. The Consistory at Paris is hereby authorised and empowered to name three discreet persons of competent abilities to visit the United States, and make such report to the nation as the actual condition of this country shall warrant.

I do appoint Roshodes Adar, Feb. 7, 1826, to be observed with suitable demonstrations as a day of Thanksgiving to the Lord God of Israel, for the manifold blessings and signal protection which he has deigned to extend to his people, and in order that on that great occasion our prayers may be offered for the continuance of his divine mercy, and the fulfilment of all the promises and pledges made to the race of Jacob.

I recommend peace and union among us, charity and good-will to all, toleration and liberality to our brethren of every religious denomination, enjoined by the mild and just precepts of our holy religion. Honor and good faith in the fulfilment of all our contracts, together with temperance, economy and industry in our habits.

I humbly intreat to be remembered in your prayers, and lastly and most earnestly, I do enjoin you to "Keep the charge of the Lord thy God, to walk in his ways, to keep his statutes and his commandments and his judgments and his testimonies as it is written in the Laws of Moses, that thou mayest prosper in all thou doest, and whithersoever thou turnest thyself."

Given at Buffalo, in the State of New-York, this second day of Tisri, in the year of the world, 5586, corresponding with the fifteenth day of September, 1825, and in the fiftieth year of American Independence.

By the Judge,
A. B. Siexas, *Sec'y, Pro Tem.*

Speech

Brothers, Countrymen and Friends

Having made known by proclamation the re-establishment of the Hebrew government, having laid the foundation of a city of refuge, an asylum for the oppressed in this free and happy republic, I avail myself of that portion of my beloved brethren here assembled, together with this concourse of my fellow-citizens, to unfold the principles, explain the views and detail the objects contemplated in the great work of regeneration and independence to which it has pleased the Almighty to direct my attention. Truth and justice demand that I should candidly state the motives which have induced me to aim at higher objects than mere colonization. The world has a right to know what inducements have led to this declaration of Independence, and what measures are contemplated to carry the design into successful execution. The peace of mankind— the security of persons and property—the changes incidental to the revival of the Jewish government—the progress and effect of emigration, and all those vicissitudes arising from change of climate—new laws and new society, admonish me to be explicit in my declarations and candid in my statements. I shall not deceive the expectations of the world.

Two thousand years have nearly elapsed since the dissolution of the Jewish government, and no period has presented itself more auspiciously than the present for its reorganization. Peace exists among civilized powers, the march of learning and science has been rapid and successful, and mankind are at this day better qualified to estimate the blessings of toleration and liberal views, and better disposed and capacitated to encourage and enforce them, than at any former time. Religion generally, though divided and subdivided into various sects assumes a milder aspect and feelings of universal love and charity have superceded the darkness and bigotry of former ages. The nations of the old and new world including the children of Africa, have had their rights acknowledged, and their governments recognized. The oldest of nations, powerful in numbers and great in resources, remains isolated, without a home, a country or a government.

The Jews have been destined by Providence to remain a distinct people. Though scattered over the face of the globe they still retain their homogeneousness of character—the peculiarity of their tenets, the identity of their faith. In their prosperity and adversity they have uniformly been the chosen people—proud of their God, proud of their distinction, and even proud of their sufferings. Bending before the tribunals of power, yielding to persecution and torture, tranquil in misfortune, and resigned to fate, they patiently endured not meanly surrendered, they bravely defended their rights and the rights of their country, and have never despaired of divine protection or given up hopes of human justice.

Looking forward to a period of regeneration and to the fulfilment of the prophecies, the Jews have preserved within themselves the elements of government in having carefully preserved the oracles of God assigned to their safe keeping and the time has arrived when their rights as a nation can be recognized, when, in the enjoyment of independance, the lights of learning and civilization, and the obligation of industry and morality they can cultivate a friendly and affectionate understanding with the whole family of mankind and have no longer enemies on earth.

In calling the Jews together under the protection of the American Constitution and laws and governed by our happy and salutary institutions, it is proper for me to state that this asylum is temporary and provisionary. The Jews never should and never will relinquish the just hope of regaining possession of their ancient heritage, and events in the neighborhood of Palestine indicate an extraordinary change of affairs.

The Greeks are almost independent of the Ottoman Porte. The Turkish sceptre becomes weaker daily. Russia will march upon Constantinople. The Egyptians are cultivating the useful arts, and are encouraging commerce and agriculture. The Turks, driven beyond the Bosphorus may leave the land of Canaan free for the occupancy of its rightful owners, and the wealth and enterprize of the Jews may make it desirable for them to reclaim their former possession by and with the consent of the christian powers, who more enlightened, and consequently more tolerant, may be duly impressed with a sense of Justice due to an injured and oppressed people.

Called together to the Holy Land by the slow but unerring finger of Providence, the Jews coming from every quarter of the Globe would bring with them the language, habits and prejudices of each country. Assimilating only in religious doctrines, and divided on temporal affairs, they would present innumerable difficulties in organizing under any form of government, and the diversity of opinions and views would create factions as dangerous and difficult to allay as those fatal ones which existed in the time of the first and second Temples. It is in this country that the government of the Jews must be organized. Here, under the influence of perfect freedom, they may study Laws—cultivate their minds, acquire liberal principles as to men and measures, and qualify themselves to direct the energies of a just and honorable government in the land of the Patriarchs.

Conforming therefore to the constitution and Laws of the United States, there is no difficulty in organizing and concentrating the Jewish nation. Originally we were a race of shepherds; each man governed his own family, and to the enjoyment of domestic happiness they added the blessings of a pure religion. Israel accumulating in strength was led to Egypt, delivered from bondage and conducted to the promised land, by the illustrious legislator of the Jews and the great benefactor of mankind. The moral, political and ecclesiastical code of laws which the Almighty through Moses, presented to the children of Israel, forms, even at this day the basis of every civil and religious institution. The victorious Joshua settled the Israelites in the land of Canaan, and divided it according to tribes. After a short interregnum on his death, the government of the Judges commenced, which existed 300 years until it was merged in the kingdom which commenced with Saul and terminated after a brilliant epoch in the captivity. The government of the High Priests succeeded and continued 428 years, followed by the Maccabean Kings of Judah, and the nation became finally dispersed under Herod the Idumean.

In selecting from the primitive, the judicial, the legal and sacerdotal governments, a form best adapted to the times, and also to the condition of the Jewish people, I have deemed it expedient to re-organize the nation under the direction of the judges.

The authority of the Judges extended to all religious, military and civil concerns—they were absolute and independent like the Kings of Israel and Judah without the ensigns of Sovereignty. The Judges were immediately from the people, mingling in their deliberations, directing their energies, commanding their armies, & executing their Laws. The office, which was not hereditary, conforms in some respect to that of chief Magistrate, and is in accordance with the genius and disposition of the people of this country.

It is difficult at this period to decide with certainty on the manner and forms adopted in choosing the judges of Israel. Most of the distinguished men who had filled that station were "raised up" by divine influence. Their skill in war and wisdom in peace, their valour and experience, their capacity to govern and incidental and necessary qualifications calculated to excite public confidence were passports to office.

Dispersed as the nation now is, and no possibility of concentrating the general voice, there can be no just power to grant—no right to withhold—the office must be assumed by divine permission, and the power exercised by general consent and approbation. He who assumes this power, who takes the lead in the great work of regeneration and judges righteously, will always be sustained by public opinion. By this test I wish to be judged.

Born in a free country, and educated with liberal principles, familiar with all the duties of government, having enjoyed the confidence of my fellow-citizens in various public trusts— ardently attached to the principles of our holy faith, and having devoted years of labor and study to ameliorate the condition of the Jews, with an unsullied conscience and a firm reliance on Almighty God, I offer myself as an humble instrument of his divine will and solicit the confidence and protection of our beloved brethren throughout the world. If there be any person possessing greater facilities and a more ardent zeal in attempting to restore the Jews to their rights as a sovereign and independent people, to such will I cheerfully surrender the trust.

I cannot be insensible to the many difficulties which may present themselves in the successful progress of the great work of regeneration. The attempt may be pronounced visionary and impracticable—the reluctance of some to countenance the effort—the timidity of others, and the apprehensions of all may be arrayed against an enterprize extraordinary and interesting, but always feasible. I indulge in no chimerical views. I know this country, its soil, climate and resources, and confidently embark in the undertaking. Firm of purpose, when the object is public good, I allow no difficulties to check my progress. Urged to its consideration by strong and irresistable impulse, the project has always presented itself to me in the most cheering light, in the most alluring colors; and if the attempt shall result in ameliorating the condition of the Jews, and shall create a generous and liberal feeling towards them and open to them the avenues of science, learning, fame, honor and happiness, who shall say that I failed? I ask the trial—and will abide the result.

The Hebrew nation, with its sublime Theocracy, its moral laws, its warlike character and powerful government originated in a family of shepherds. From an ancestry not more illustrious, arose the heroes and sages of Greece, and to the neglected children of the forest was Rome, once mistress of the world, indebted for existence. From origins the most humble, and from projects the most doubtful, the world has been indebted for signal benefits and blessings. A few pilgrims, driven to our continent by European persecution, have laid the foundations of a splendid empire. We have less difficulties to encounter, because we are surrounded by civilization; and a few Jews in this happy land admonished by the past, and animated by anticipations of the future, may increase rapidly and prosperously, and under good government and wholesome laws, may fall back in time towards the Pacific Ocean, and possess a country the most fertile as it is capacious and valuable. We have long been captives in a land of strangers: we have long submitted patiently to oppression: we have long anxiously expected a temporal deliverence; but throughout the most terrible periods of calamity, we have done nothing for ourselves. The Almighty, who has covered us with the shield of his paternal love has given us moral agents, by which, with his divine aid, we are to effect our own deliverence. We have senses, judgment, powers of self-government, energy, capacity and wealth. If, with all these great requisites we still "hang our harps upon the willow," we still cover ourselves with sackcloth and ashes, and do not make one effort for independence, how can we reasonably continue to supplicate God for our restoration, who made man in his own image, and proclaimed him free? Why should the parent of nations, the oldest of people, the founders of religion, wander among the governments of the earth, intreating succor and protection, when we are capable of protecting ourselves?

The time has emphatically arrived to do something calculated to benefit our own condition, and excite the admiration of the world, and we must commence the work in a country free from ignoble prejudices and legal disqualifications—a country, in which liberty can be insured to the Jews without the loss of one drop of blood.

The present condition of our people throughout the world is not without interest and instruction. The rightful possessors of Palestine are slaves in their own territory, and the pious attachment of the resident Jews of the Holy Land, gives them the highest claims on our charity and protection. There are several hundred families in Jerusalem, Hebron, and Tiberias, three of the most ancient congregations in the world, and the number in the Holy Land may be computed at 100,000. Those on the borders of the Mediterranean are engaged in trade and manufactures; those in the interior, and particularly in Jerusalem, are poor and dreadfully oppressed. They are the great sentinels and guardians of the law and religion, and amidst the severest privations and the most intense sufferings, they have for centuries kept their eye upon the ruined site of the temple and said, "the time will come—the day will be accomplished." The Samaritan Jews, which formerly were numerous and scattered over Egypt, Damascus, Ascalon and Caesarea, are now reduced to a few hundred poor inoffensive persons, principally residents of Jaffa and Naplouse. As there is no essential difference between their doctrines and the rest of our brethren, the distinction between them should cease. The Caraite Jews, who are numerous, are principally residents of the Crimea and the Ukraine, and are a respectable body of men. They reject the Talmud and rabbinical doctrines, adhering closely to the precepts of our divine law. On the borders of Cochin China, we have a large colony of white and black Jews. Their numbers are computed at 10,000. The white Jews reside on the sea coast, and the blacks in the interior. The blacks, who call themselves *Beni Israel,* must have existed at the time of the first temple. The researches in the interior of Africa may, at some future period, give us immense colonies of Jews, which emigrated at an early period from Egypt. There are on the coast of Malabar and Coromandel, and in the interior of India, a considerable number of wealthy and enterprising Israelites. Measures will be adopted to ascertain their force and condition. Upwards of a million and a half of Jews reside in the dominions of the Ottoman Porte, including the Barbary States. In Constantinople and Salonichi, there cannot be less than one hundred thousand. They suffer much from the oppression of the Turks—are severely taxed, and treated with undisguised severity; but their skill in trade and their general quickness and intelligence as bankers, brokers and merchants, give them the entire control of commerce and the command of important confidential stations in the empire. The same character and condition may be likewise attributed to those numerous Jews residing in Egypt and in Persia; they have many wealthy men in Alexandria, Cairo, Ispahan, and the numerous cities beyond the Euphrates.

From countries yet uncivilized, we turn to those, which still withholding the rights of man from the descendants of the Patriarchs, are nevertheless more mild and tolerant in their measures, more liberal and generous to an afflicted people.

The settlement of the Jews in England was coeval with Julius Caesar; the inroads of the Saxons and Danes have obliterated much of the chronicles and traditions relative to their early existence in that country.—William the Conqueror brought with him a large colony from Normandy, and for a stipulated sum of money conferred upon them certain commercial privileges, and assigned them places to inhabit. It was in the feudal ages that the Jews of Britain were the most enlightened, tolerant and polished. Opulent in circumstances, and enterprising in the development of resources, they gave an early impetus and direction to that trade and commerce, which has since successfully extended itself to every quarter of the globe. During the reign of William Rufus and Henry II. the Jews were favored and protected, though always considered vassals of the crown, to be tolerated or pillaged according to the caprices of government. The cruelties practised towards them during the misguided periods of the crusade, caused many of the most respectable to abandon the country. Several families however, returned under an invitation from King John, to be again pillaged, proscribed and murdered; and for five hundred years their condition underwent no material change. Occasionally protected, but too frequently oppressed, deprived of the natural rights of subjects and citizens, it was not surprising if the Jews in England during those periods, acquired wealth without consideration, and power without respect. During the reign of George II a bill was introduced in Parliament for the naturalization of the Jews. It was supported by the ministry, though opposed with warmth by the people, and produced great excitement in the public mind. It nevertheless became a law; but such was the strenuous opposition manifested on the occasion, that it was considered prudent to repeal it at the ensuing session. The same legal disqualifications still exist in Great Britain; but it is gratifying to know, that the government affords to the Jews certain rights, immunities and protection, and our people in that country in addition to wealth and influence, are rapidly advancing in the career of learning and civilization, of charity and liberal feelings.

The miseries inflicted upon our nation in England, during the Crusade, extended their unhappy consequences to France. The Jews were among the earliest settlers in Gaul, and by their superior talent and advantages, endeavored to encourage and extend civilization among a rude and barbarous people. Their sufferings, banishments and massacres during the reigns of Philip Augustus, Lewis the ninth, Philip the Fair, Philip the Tall, Charles the Sixth and several successive kings, fill the sanguinary pages of history, and present a list of enormities that makes humanity shudder. In 1566, they were all banished the kingdom [*sic*], and in the succeeding year, only four families were permitted to return. In the 17th and 18th century, they were gradually permitted to re-occupy their former places of residence, though still exposed to the scorn of the ignorant and the insults of the barbarians, and such feelings were encouraged and perpetuated by an edict of the government compelling them to wear a distinctive dress.

During the French Revolution the Jews claimed from the constituent Assembly, the rights of citizens; many enlightened statesmen espoused their cause, and the decree of 1790 gave them a legal existence. Among the philanthropists of the age who raised his voice successfully in their behalf, was my venerable and pious friend, the Bishop Gregoire, to whom the Jews owe an incalculable debt of gratitude. The civil revolution in the condition of our brethren in France, gave rise to the moral one, which resulted from the proceedings of the Sanhedrin, convened at Paris, by the decree of 1806, and which presented to the world a galaxy of talent and learning which would do honor to any age or any country. The Jews in France are citizens, and the charter granted by the good king, Louis the 18th, confirmed all their rights. They are manufacturers, agriculturalists, merchants and bankers, and many of them possess distinguished talents.

The history of our people in Spain is of peculiar interest. Spain was a country dear to the Jews, and after their dispersion, the seat of learning and the birth place of our greatest scholars.

The Jews first appeared in Spain, during the reign of the Emperor Adrian, and in his time were numerous and wealthy, but like our brethren in Britain and France, their lives and property were held by a frail tenure, and the Goths exercised a lucrative oppression over this proscribed and unhappy people.

After the expulsion of the Jews from Syria and Egypt, they joined the Saracens and aided them in the conquest of Spain. Favoured by the Caliphs and united by a reciprocal hospitality toward the christians, the Jews found asylum and protection from the Saracen Monarchs, and the most brilliant epoch in our history from the destruction of the temple, may be traced to this period. In the early ages the Jews were enlightened and learned in the Law, they were the foes of paganism, the enemies of idolators; but it was under the Caliphs of Bagdad, and the Saracens of Spain that they cultivated the sciences, and established Seminaries of learning, and schools of literature and philosophy.

The revolutions in that country commencing in the eleventh century, eventuated unfortunately for the Jews, and the war declared by Ferdinand against the Saracens, was the commencement of their troubles and calamities. During the eleventh and twelth centuries many learned Rabbis appeared which did honor to the age and country.—They were not only deeply versed in cabalistical, allegorical and mystical interpretations of the law, but distinguished mathematicians, astronomers, masters of the dead and living languages, and natural philosophers.—In Toledo and Andalusia they had colleges in the most flourishing condition, and the piety and illustrious talents of Abraham Ben Esdra, Maimonides Kimchi, Jarchi Haleri, Abravenel and others, attested the brilliancy of that epoch in Jewish history. The fury of the Crusaders was perhaps more severely felt by the Jews in Spain than in any other part of the world, and more of our people abandoned that country than were brought out of the land of Egypt by Moses. Under the enlightened and liberal Moorish Kings, the Jews lived prosperously in Spain, but the destruction of the Moors caused their ruin, and to this day they have been banished the country [*sic*]. Upwards of a million of Jews speak the Spanish language, and will never cease to regret the barbarous edicts which prohibit their residence in that beautiful but neglected part of the globe.

Spain is a miraculous and providential instance of the impolicy and impiety of religious persecutions. She is weaker in resources, in character, in the means of sustaining independence and national rights, in arts and in arms, than when under the dominion of the Caliphs.

Portugal in ancient and modern times was not more liberal, tolerant, and humane towards the Jews than Spain; they banished, tortured, and burnt them, and Portugal from this proscriptive and cruel system is not more happily conditioned than her neighbor.

The Jews have resided in Rome since they were brought captive to that Capital, by Titus Vespasianous, yet, while subjected to the persecution of the Christian monarchs throughout Europe, it is pleasing to recollect and grateful to acknowledge the kindness and protection afforded them by several of the Roman Pontiffs, particularly Gregory the Great, Alexander 2d, Gregory the 9th, Clement the 5th, Clement 6th, Boniface 9th, Nicholas 2d, Alexander 6th, Paul 3d, &c. Men who practised the precepts which they preached. In modern times the Jews have been tranquil residents of that ancient City, yet at this day, they are compelled to wear a distinctive badge, to reside in a separate part of the town, and at periods to attend mass under penalty of a certain sum of money. In most of the cities in Italy, the Jews enjoy protection and privileges; they are a cultivated people, far advanced in science and polite literature, and I have long esteemed them as a learned and distinguished branch of the nation.

Many of the emigrants from Spain and Portugal took refuge in Holland, which, together with those from Germany, formed a considerable congregation, and in the 17th century they were wealthy and flourishing. The Jews in Amsterdam established colleges and academies, over which some of the greatest men of our nation have presided. It is supposed that there are nearly 100,000 Jews in Holland, mostly residents of Amsterdam. In comparison with the cruelties inflicted upon our nation by other powers on the continent, the Jews in Holland may have been considered happy and protected, yet they were neither free by law, nor by public opinion, and in many instances they were shut out from honorable and lucrative employment.

Notwithstanding these prohibitory decrees and unfortunate internal divisions existing among the nation, Holland has produced many eminent physicians, counsellors and literary men, particularly since the adoption of the constitution by the States in 1796, and the Jews are now held in estimation by the government.

In the Austrian and Russian dominions, in Prussia, Sweden, Denmark, and the Hanseatic towns, and throughout Germany, there must be nearly two millions and a half of Jews. Nearly a million of which were in Poland previous to the partition of 1772. In all those countries their condition has been ameliorated, yet they do not in all enjoy political rights, though their personal deportment acquires consideration and respect, if merited. Of late some strong edicts have been passed relative to the Polish and Russian Jews, and it is to be lamented that they still labor under strong personal and religious prejudices.

It will thus be perceived that with all the toleration of the times, with all the favourable condition of the Jews, they suffer much, and are deprived of many valuable rights.

Our religion embraces all that is pure and upright, all that is just and generous. In temperance, in industry, in patience and in all the duties of husband father friend and citizen, the Jews may claim an equal rank with those of any other religion [*sic*] denomination. If there are some who occasionally wander from the paths of rectitude, let it be remembered that they are men, and subject to human frailties. If in the narrow and crooked channels of traffic, in which peasecution [*sic*] has driven some of them, they at times have disregarded the high injunctions of purity and good faith let us call to mind that their virtues have never been accredited, while their faults have been magnified.—Shut out from more noble pursuits, they have been left without that incentive to good actions, that encouragement to upright conduct, that reward of merit which has been amply afforded to others.

Why should Christians persecute Jews? Sprung from a common stock, and connected by human ties which should be binding; if those ties are empty and evanescent where is the warrant for this intolerance? not in the religion which they profess; that teaches mildness, charity, and good will to all.—I judge religion from its effects, and when I look round and see the Seminaries of learning and institutions of charity: when I see temperance united to industry: virtue and wisdom, benevolence and good faith existing among Christians, if this be the result of their religion, God forbid that it should be destroyed. Let it flourish, I will sustain that faith in its purity; but let us be equally charitable to all. The Jews and Christians are only known by their hostility towards each other. This hostility neither religion recognizes. We should no more censure the Christians at this day for the cruelties practised towards the Jews in the early ages, than the Jews should now be made answerable for the factious policy of our ancestors, 500 generations ago. Times have undergone an important change; we all began to feel that we are formed of the same materials, subject to the same frailties, destined to the same death, and hoping for the same immortality. Here, then, in this free and happy country, distinctions in religion, are unknown; here we enjoy liberty without licentiousness, and land without oppression.

Among the many advantages which an asylum in this country promises, the pursuits of agriculture are the most prominent, and of all pursuits the most noble.

The Jews were an agricultural people, before they were a nation; the fruitful vallies of Canaan, the plains of Nineva, Greece, Persia, Egypt, and in modern times, Lithuania, the Ukraine, and Moldavia, exhibit their devotion and attachment to this pursuit. In no country on earth can they enjoy in this respect equal advantages to those which we hold forth. Land of a fertile quality well wooded and watered, may be purchased on the most reasonable terms; taxes are equalized and moderate: and by a recent act of the Legislature of this State, aliens can hold any quantity upon declaring their intention of becoming citizens. This great privilege which in other countries is denied to the Jews, is here afforded, together with every personal security. The lands they cultivate are their own; no sovereign or feudal lord, or magistrate can wrest their property from them, no tithes, no exactions, no persecutions await them; they will be called upon to contribute that moderate support to government, which is cheerfully yielded by every good citizen.— They will be themselves Lords of the Soil, and Sovereigns in their own right, eligible to office and honors, and acquiring that consideration and respect which unavoidably await correct deportment, talents and reputation.

The State of New-York is far advanced in improvements of every kind. There are upwards of six millions of acres of cultivated land, producing grain in abundance and every variety of fruit, and rich grazing meadows. A farm of one hundred acres well cultivated will, with industry, afford an ample livelihood and corresponding happiness to a family. I again repeat, agriculture is the natural and noble pursuit of man. Between the handles of the plough, in felling the oak of the forest, in the harvest and in the season of fruits, the farmer is still the same free and happy citizen, and has all the resources of life within himself. His cattle are raised in his pastures, his grain produce him bread, his sheep afford him wool, his trees sugar, his fields flax, he is his own brewer and distiller, his forests afford him fuel, he has all the comforts and frequently luxuries which wealth can give. He sees the sun rise in glory and set in majesty. He who wishes to be truly religious and be surrounded with the admonitions of piety, should be an agriculturist. To the man of capital the advantages held forth in this state, are numerous and acknowledged. To the land proprietor there is plenty and happiness; to the merchant and trader the most profitable facilities, and unceasing encouragement to the manufacturer and mechanic.

The laws and customs in Europe, present many obstacles to the Jews becoming mechanics. To be perfectly independent, they should learn some branch of the mechanic art. In this country, our mechanics are numerous, opulent and influential. Masons, Carpenters, blacksmiths, Tailors, Hatters, Shoemakers, Curriers and the more light branches of labour, are always amply encouraged, and with the acquirement of a trade, in this country no industrious man can possibly want.

The rising importance and value of our manufactories, should attract the attention of Jewish capitalists. The Congress of the United States, has, by a judicious revision of the Tariff, so regulated the duties on foreign fabrics, as to give permanent encouragement to our own. The market value of articles annually manufactured in this state alone, is computed at several hundred millions of dollars, and the investments are principally in Grist-Mills, Saw-Mills, Oil Mills, Fulling Mills, Carding Machines, Cotton and Woolen Factories, Iron Founderies, Trip Hammers, Distilleries, Tanneries, Asheries, Breweries, &c. &c.

Grand Island is surrounded by water power, and is admitted to be an eligible spot for the erection of manufactories.

The organization of a system of Finance for the promotion of emigration, affording aid to settlers, erecting and supporting institutions of charity, establishing seminaries of learning, and for all the purposes of an efficient and economical government, is not without some difficulty. Our means are ample but they are diffused, spread over the globe, and not readily concentrated.

Our law prohibited the Kings of Israel from "multiplying to himself silver and gold." This prohibition was intended to preserve the people from ruinous and oppressive taxation, and therefore limited the Sovereign to the moderate exigencies of his Court; but it appears from our prophet Samuel, and indeed from the ancient laws, of Babylon, also in force among the Greeks and Romans, that the *jus regeum* was computed at one tenth. The tithes afforded to the High priests were of similar value in cattle, first fruits, the harvest even to "Mint, Cummin and Anise." A considerable portion was also secured to the Levites. It is, however, obvious that these exactions were exhorbitant, and while they gave splendour to the government, they tended to impoverish the people.

Taxes should be equalized and always levied in correspondence with the wants of the nation. In organizing the Jewish Government, the poorest should be enabled to participate in the great and glorious act; and with this view I have imposed a capitation tax of Three Shekels of silver, which is equal to one Spanish dollar, to be paid annually, a sum within the means of the poorest, and if paid and collected will be amply sufficient to defray the expenses of the government in its incipient organization. This small tax, however, does not prevent free will offerings in our Synagogues, which the liberal and wealthy may make in the furtherance of the great objects in view.

A suitable person will be appointed to direct the finance department, and likewise such other officers as are usually named in all well organized governments. The Jewish capital throughout the world, may be estimated at a vast amount. Since the termination of the wars on the Continent, a great portion of the capital has returned to the coffers of its proprietors. A few millions of dollars judiciously invested and thrown into the Western District of this State, would realize a reasonable profit, and be of immense benefit to this thriving and populous section of our country.

During the European wars, many Jews joined the different armies, and I learn have distinguished themselves in sundry campaigns; several have been honored with important commissions, and given proofs of valour and fidelity. Such who prefer a military life, and who may at the present period have arms in their hands, may continue in their ranks; their arms must never be turned against the country they serve; but we have lost our ancient military character, and the discipline, courage, and constancy of those who have in modern times seen service, may be necessary to constitute the material from which future armies may be organized.

Wars are necessary in defence of national rights when unjustly assailed. So God has thought, and fought with us. So man now thinks. We may not have again such generals as Joshua, David and Maccabees, but in blending our people with the great American family, I wish to see them able and willing to sustain its honor with their lives and fortunes. Time which matures and brings forth many surprising events, may give us a territory beyond the Lakes, great in extent and resources; we may occupy a position of importance on the Pacific, and wherever providence may lead the nation, I wish to have its rights manfully sustained.

I have enjoined a strict neutrality in the existing war between the Greeks and Ottoman Porte. While it would afford me great happiness to aid any oppressed nation in a contest for liberty, we must not jeopardize the safety of millions living under the Mussulman Government, and who would be instantly sacrificed by their relentless rulers, upon the least succour being afforded to the revolutionists. While prudence, and a due regard to the safety of innocent people enjoin us not to mingle in this contest, it is due to the cause of freedom, not to throw obstacles in the way of its successful advancement.

The discovery of the lost tribes of Israel, has never ceased to be a subject of deep interest to the Jews. That divine protection which has been bestowed upon the chosen people, from the infancy of nature to the present period, has, without doubt, been equally extended to the missing tribes, and if, as I have reason to believe, our lost brethren were the ancestors of the Indians of the American Continent, the inscrutable decrees of the Almighty have been fulfilled in spreading unity and omnipotence in every quarter of the globe. Upwards of three thousand years have elapsed, since the nine and a half tribes were carried captive by Palmanazar, King of Assyria. It is supposed they were spread over the various countries of the East, and by international marriages, have lost their identity of character. It is, however, probable that from the previous sufferings of the tribes in Egyptian bondage, that they bent their course in a northwest direction, which brought them within a few leagues of the American Continent, and which they finally reached.

Those who are most conversant with the public and private economy of the Indians, are strongly of opinion that they are the lineal descendants of the Israelites, and my own researches go far to confirm me in the same belief.

The Indians worship one Supreme being as the fountain of life, and the author of all creation. Like the Israelites of old, they are divided into tribes having their Chief and distinctive Symbol to each. Some of their tribes it is said are named after the Cherubinical figures that were carried on the four principal Standards of Israel. They consider themselves as the select and beloved people of God, and have all the religious pride which our ancestors are known to have possessed. Their words are sonorous and bold, and their language and dialect are evidently of Hebrew origin. They compute time after the manner of the Israelites, by dividing the year into the four seasons, and their subdivisions are the lunar months, or our new Moons commencing according to the ecclesiastical year of Moses, the first Moon after the vernal equinox. They have their prophets, high Priests, and their sanctum sanctorum, in which all their consecrated vessels are deposited, and which are only to be approached by their archimagas or high Priest. They have their towns and cities of refuge—they have sacrifices and fastings—they abstain from unclean things, in short, in their marriages, divorces, punishment of adultery—burial of the dead, and mourning, they bear a striking analogy to our people. How came they on this continent, and if indigenous, when did they acquire the principles and essential forms of the Jews? The Indians are not Savages, they are wild and savage in their habits, but possess great vigour of intellect and native talent, they are a brave and eloquent people, with an Asiatic complexion, and Jewish features. Should we be right in our conjecture, what new scenes are opened to the nation—the first of people in the old world, and the rightful inheritors of the new?—Spread from the confines of the north west coast to Cape Horn, and from the Atlantic to the Pacific.

If the tribes could be brought together, could be made sensible of their origin, could be civilized, and restored to their long lost brethren, what joy to our people, what glory to our God, how clearly have the prophecies been fulfilled, how certain our dispersion, how miraculous our preservation, how providential our deliverance.

It shall be my duty to pursue the subject by every means in my power.—

I recommend the establishment of emigration societies throughout Europe, in order that proper aid may be afforded to those who may be disposed to visit this country, and also to ascertain the character and occupation of each emigrant, and supply them with passports and information. Passage in all cases should be taken for New-York.—it should be distinctly understood by emigrants of limited means, that it will be necessary to have at least, a sufficiency to support their families for six months, as by that time they may be enabled to realize the fruits of enterprize and industry, and a sufficient sum may at that period be paid into the general Coffers, to aid them in their purchase of land. No mistaken impression should exist, that the Jews must not labour in this country; we all are compelled to work, but with the same portion of industry, exercised in other parts of the world, we realize a greater portion of happiness, tranquility, and personal rights. We shall not be prepared to receive emigrants on Grand Island, until the ensuing summer, and this notice is given to prevent an indiscriminate and hasty emigration, which may defeat many good objects.

It is very desirable that education should be more generally diffused among the Jews, it is the staff of their existence—the star of their future happiness. There is no part of our religion which should be altered, nothing should be taken from the law, for if the power of innovation existed, there would be no end to the pruning knife. Our religion demands from us many temporal sacrifices which should be cheerfully yielded, as a slight acknowledgment for the protecting favours of the Almighty.

Although no law permits polygamy among the Jews, there is no religious statute which prohibits it, and from this omission, an indulgence is claimed in the eastern countries incompatible with morality. Having personally witnessed the observance of this custom among the Jews in Africa, I have deemed it important as one among the first acts of the government, to protest against the practice, and abolish it forever. The duties of Husband and Father can never be safely or honorably fulfilled, when those duties are subjected to the caprices which sensuality produce. Neither can a wife thus circumstanced ever receive that consideration, affection, and respect, to which virtuous, and good wives, are always entitled. Another and a serious evil is to be apprehended from the prevalence of this custom, in the promiscuous, and probably incestuous marriages, which accidental circumstances may produce among children of one father and several living mothers. In [civil]ized communities, the laws which ar[e par]amount, admit of no such privileges. [Our] religious divorces are too loose[ly exerc]ised, and demand the strong arm [of auth]ority; marriage is a sacred tie, and such alliances should not be lightly dissolved.

I have made it imperative on parties contracting matrimony, to read, write and comprehend the language of the country, which they respectively inhabit. Early marriages among our people, are enjoined by the strongest principles of religion, and many of those important alliances are formed even in infancy, and before the responsibility of the obligations can be duly estimated. It is thus, that ignorance may become hereditary, and a just policy calls for the adoption of measures, which may secure to children at least that portion of intelligence and education, which the times demand, and future generations will by such means be progressively improved and enlightened.

There are many subjects of great interest, which I reserve for future communications.

Thus commences auspiciously, I hope, the attempt to revive the Government of the oldest of nations, and lead them, if not to the promised, still to the happy land.

The effort may be successful, but otherwise, can never be injurious. It directs public attention to the claims of an oppressed people—it will admonish Sovereigns to be just and generous to them—it may produce a better state of toleration and religious feelings—it may place our people in the road to honor and fame—it opens to them the avenues of industry and competence, in short it makes men and citizens of them, gives them a name, a rank, an interest and a voice among the nations of the earth—thus, in fact, fulfilling the promises made to the descendents of the Patriarchs—that the Lord God, may say to an admiring and astonished world, "Behold my people Israel—here is the nation, that I have sworn to protect—I was their Shepherd—their Sun—their Shade—their Light and their right hand.—In the days of prosperity, they forgot me not, and in the hour of tribulation have I not forgotten them." "In a little wrath I hid my face from thee, but with everlasting kindness will I have mercy on thee, saith the Lord thy Redeemer."

To him who shelters and protects the whole family of mankind, the great omnipotent and omnipresent God, do I commit the destinies of Israel, and pray that he may have you all in his safe and holy keeping.

Discourse on the Restoration of the Jews

By M. M. Noah.
With a Map of the Land of Israel.
New-York: Harper & Brothers, 82 Cliff-Street.
1845.

Preface.

Delivered at the Tabernacle, Oct. 28 and Dec. 2, 1844

Within a few years the attention of the Christian world has been directed, in a peculiar manner, to the character, condition, and future prospects of the Jewish people. Ministers of the gospel, in more closely examining the predictions of the prophets, and the miraculous preservation of the chosen people, have been struck with the injustice and oppression they have met with for the last 1800 years; and how directly in opposition to the mild principles of the gospel has this spirit of intolerance been carried out. The responsibility in being agents in this persecution, or even by passive acquiescence giving countenance to it, has at length awakened a just and apostolic feeling towards Israel, which has of late been manifested in a more enlarged and liberal consideration, both in the pulpit and in the domestic circle. True, the efforts to evangelize them, contrary, as I think, to the manifest predictions of the prophets, continue to be unceasing, yet even in this there is charity and good feelings which cannot fail to be reciprocally beneficial. In the political, as well as the religious world, there are singular commotions which point to the East as the theatre of approaching revolutions of great and absorbing interests, and it has struck me forcibly that a movement from this free country in favour of restoring the Jews to their ancient heritage would have the good effect of directing the attention of the Christian powers generally to an effort of this character, which might gradually lead to important results; but, at all events, would create a better and kinder feeling for the Jews, and secure to them protection and privileges which at present they do not all enjoy. If, in our generation, this movement does nothing more, it will accomplish much good, and would cement the ties which ought to unite the Jew and Christian in kind offices and brotherly love. There are also religious movements of great interest among the Jews in Europe—propositions of reform, which, if they do not strike at the religion itself, will do much good in wearing away ancient prejudices, and approximating to the enlightened spirit of the age. We require a Sanhedrin to examine many points and customs in our religion, and to compare the written with the oral law, and prune many excrescences in Rabbinical writings, some of which strike at the pure principles contained in the Bible, which, under all circumstances, is our safest guide. In the observations which I have made, and the facts detailed in relation to the great work of restoration, let it not be understood that I speak in the name and in behalf of the Jewish people throughout the world. Early religious dogmas cannot be changed; strong prejudices of education require time and perseverance to remove; the liberal mind alone will comprehend my views, and the objects I desire to attain. I seek to commit no one who differs with me; we are a sect, not a nation; there is no council, no government, as yet, through which opinions may be concentrated, consequently we are left to form our own opinions on disputed points. I confidently believe in the restoration of the Jews, and in the coming of the Messiah; and believing that political events are daily assuming a shape which may finally lead to that great advent, I considered it a duty to call upon the free people of this country to aid us in any efforts which, in our present position, it may be deemed prudent to adopt, and I have the most abiding confidence in their good-will and friendly feelings in aiding to restore us to liberty and independence.

In a letter which I received from Mr. Jefferson as far back as 1818, he observes, "Your sect, by its sufferings, has furnished a remarkable proof of the universal spirit of religious intolerance inherent in every sect, disclaimed by all while feeble, and practised by all when in power; our laws have applied the only antidote to this vice, protecting our religious as they do our civil rights, by putting all on an equal footing: but more remains to be done, for although we are free by the law, we are not so in practice; public opinion erects itself into an inquisition, and exercises its office with as much fanaticism as fans the flames of an *auto-da-fé*. The prejudice still scowling on your section of our religion, although the elder one, cannot be unfelt by yourselves. It is to be hoped that individual dispositions will at length mould themselves to the model of the law, and consider the moral basis on which all our religion rests as the rallying-point which unites them in a common interest, while the peculiar dogmas branching from it are the exclusive concern of the respective sects embracing them, and no rightful subject of notice to any other.

"Public opinion needs reformation on this point, which would have the farther happy effect of doing away the hypocritical maxim of *'intus ut lubet foris ut moris.'* Nothing, I think, would be so likely to effect this as to your sect particularly, as the more careful attention to education which you recommend, and which, placing its members on the equal and commanding benches of science, will exhibit them as equal objects of respect and favour."

In addition to the foregoing observations from the illustrious author of the Declaration of American Independence, I find similar and stronger sentiments in a letter from President John Adams, written to me when nearly in his ninetieth year, with all the fervour, sincerity, and zeal he exhibited in the early scenes of our Revolution. "You have not," says this venerable patriot, "extended your ideas of the right of private judgment and the liberty of conscience, both in religion and philosophy, farther than I do. Mine are limited only by morals and propriety. I have had occasion to be acquainted with several gentlemen of your nation, and to transact business with some of them, whom I found to be men of as liberal minds, as much honour, probity, generosity, and good breeding as any I have known in any sect of religion or philosophy.

"I wish your nation may be admitted to all the privileges of citizens in every part of the world. This country has done much; I wish it may do more, and annul every narrow idea in religion, government, and commerce. Let the wits joke, the philosophers sneer! What then? It has pleased the Providence of the 'first cause,' the universal cause, that Abraham should give religion not only to the Hebrews, but to Christians and Mohammedans, the greatest part of the modern civilized world."

In another letter Mr. Adams says, "I really wish the Jews again in Judea, an independent nation, for, as I believe, the most enlightened men of it have participated in the amelioration of the philosophy of the age; once restored to an independent government, and no longer persecuted, they would soon wear away some of the asperities and peculiarities of their character, possibly in time become liberal Unitarian Christians, for your Jehovah is our Jehovah, and your God of Abraham, Isaac, and Jacob is our God."

I cannot mistake the liberality of my countrymen in making to them the appeal I have made in the following pages. Their agency involves no responsibility, no outlay of money, no painful efforts: the project itself is pacific throughout; it places the Jews in the Holy Land as mere proprietors, protected in their possessions as other citizens and subjects—and this is the basis of the restoration. Other events will follow in their proper course.

This discourse was addressed to Christians, and I cannot express my gratification at the deep attention and liberal feelings manifested by some thousands of the most distinguished of our citizens and the highest dignitaries of the Church who heard me: it was a practical illustration of the real freedom of our institutions, and satisfied me that, where Church and State are not united, there is no barrier that separates religious sects, and all are alike free, liberal, and tolerant.

***Discourse* etc.**

I have long desired, my friends and countrymen, for an opportunity to appear before you in behalf of a venerable people, whose history, whose sufferings, and whose extraordinary destiny have, for a period of 4000 years, filled the world with awe and astonishment: a people at once the most favoured and the most neglected, the most beloved, and yet the most persecuted; a people under whose salutary laws all the civilized nations of the earth now repose; a people whose origin may date from the cradle of creation, and who are likely to be preserved to the last moment of recorded time.

I have been anxious to appeal to you, citizens and Christians, in behalf of the chosen and beloved people of Almighty God, to ask you to do justice to their character, to their motives, to their constancy, and to their triumphant faith; to feel for their sufferings and woes; to extend to them your powerful protection and undivided support in accomplishing the fulfillment of their destiny, and aiding to restore them to the land of their forefathers and the possession of their ancient heritage. It is, I acknowledge, a novel, though a natural appeal, made, I may say, for the first time to Christians since the advent of Christianity; but the period, I believe, has arrived for this appeal: extraordinary events shadow forth results long expected, long prophesied, long ordained; commotions in the state and division in the Church; new theories put forth, new hopes excited, new promises made; and the political events in Syria, Egypt, Turkey, and Russia, indicate the approach of great and important revolutions, which may facilitate the return of the Jews to Jerusalem, and the organization of a powerful government in Judea, and lead to that millennium which we all look for, all hope for, all pray for.

Where, I ask, can we commence this great work of regeneration with a better prospect of success than in a free country and a liberal government? Where can we plead the cause of independence for the children of Israel with greater confidence than in the cradle of American liberty? Where ask for toleration and kindness for the seed of Abraham, if we find it not among the descendants of the Pilgrims? Here we can unfurl the standard, and seventeen millions of people will say, "God is with you; we are with you: in his name, and in the name of civil and religious liberty, go forth and repossess the land of your fathers. We have advocated the independence of the South American republics, we have given a home to our red brethren beyond the Mississippi, we have combated for the independence of Greece, we have restored the African to his native land. If these nations were entitled to our sympathies, how much more powerful and irrepressible are the claims of the beloved people, before whom the Almighty walked like a cloud by day and a pillar of fire by night; who spoke to them words of comfort and salvation, of promise, of hope, of consolation, and protection; who swore they should be *his* people, and he would be their God; who, for their special protection and final restoration, dispersed them among the nations of the earth, without confounding them with any!"

This, my countrymen, will be your judgment—your opinion—when asked to co-operate in giving freedom to the Jews. I am not required, on this occasion, to go over the history of the chosen people; you know it all; it is all recorded in that good Book which *we* have preserved for your comfort and consolation; that book which our fathers pressed to their hearts in traversing burning sands and the wide waste of waters, which famine, pestilence, and the sword could not wrest from them; which was the last cherished relic at night, and the first precious gift in the morning. You will find their history in the Bible.

We are the only people who can trace our pedigree to the infancy of nature, the only nation to whom a code of just and righteous laws were confided. Compare our situation with that of the various nations among whom we have lived, and we at once trace the cause of all our unhappiness. Our father Abraham was the first to proclaim the unity of God, Sovereign Architect of the world, Ruler of heaven and earth. Joseph, fourth descendant of Abraham, carried the same doctrines and religion with him among the Egyptians; honoured by Pharaoh, but hated by the people, who revenged themselves by violence and persecutions on his posterity. Moses, our great lawgiver, delivered them from the yoke of their oppressors, and conveyed them to the frontier of the promised land. Joshua, commanding the armies of Israel, entered the land of Canaan, planted his standard there, and the world beheld for the first time a regular code of civil, political, and religious laws, which exist even at this day in all their primitive force. Solomon, the third king of Israel, by his wisdom and glory advanced the people and country to the highest degree of splendour in arts, in arms, and in science; in wealth, in commerce, and letters; and created those jealousies among the neighbouring nations which led to wars, intestine commotions, and, finally, to the loss of the holy city, which fell into the hands of the Romans, and from that period Israel ceased to be a nation, and became scattered over the face of the earth.

The deep-rooted hatred of the ancient nations of the Israelites is therefore traceable to one great cause. Egypt, the worshippers of an ox or a crocodile, could not love a people who acknowledged only the true God. The Greeks, who murdered Socrates because he taught the existence of that God, equally detested the Jews, who openly proclaimed his unity and omnipotence. The idolatrous Canaanites, the conquered and defeated race, abhorred the Jews for their religious opinions. The Romans, who believed in oracles, soothsayers, and auguries, were always their fierce and irreconcilable enemies. We account, therefore, for the hatred of those nations who, attached to their idols, were the persecution of the Jews; but how are we to account for the oppression we have met with from our Christian brethren, having the same origin with us, our fellow-sufferers under Nero, Vespasian, Titus, and others? Let me probe the causes to their very foundation, by showing the errors of the first era of the Christian Church, and the departure from the injunctions, morality, charity, and good-will of the primitive founders of that faith.

I approach the subject, my countrymen, I trust, in a becoming spirit of respect for the attachment and devotion to the Christian faith of those who now hear me. Born and educated among Christians—having, through their confidence and liberality, held various stations of the public trust—I bring to the consideration of this deeply absorbing subject the most kind and apostolic feeling. Tinctured by no prejudice, governed by no ill will, controlled by no bigoted impulse, but with an enlarged and upright zeal, and a desire to promote human happiness equally among all faiths, I will endeavour to explain, for the first time in many centuries, how the chosen people understand and interpret the advent of Christianity, its application to them as a nation, the influence it has had on their destiny, and their views of its obligations.

We have the authority of early writers, of eminent Christian divines, of illustrious scholars and historians, for the declaration so often preached, until it is generally believed, that all the calamities of the Jews, their persecutions and sufferings, their degradation as a nation, their outcast and despised condition in many countries even at this day, are the results of the agency our fathers had in compassing the death of Jesus of Nazareth. We are, it has been said by them, crushed beneath the cross, and our only salvation is in believing in the divinity of him whom our forefathers had rejected. Hence the great, and eager, and natural desire to evangelize the Jews, and thus atone for what is deemed among pious Christians that great sin.

Let us calmly examine this subject. Let us look at the peculiar position of the Jewish nation when those important events occurred, and ascertain by what agencies and motives they were governed and influenced.

The sins of the chosen people, principally idolatry, for which they were denounced by the prophets, and punished by the Almighty, occurred before the Babylonish captivity, since that time those peculiar sins have not been repeated, and their constancy and fidelity as a nation, to their faith and principles, remain unquestioned at this day. The immense power and glory of the Jewish nation under David and Solomon long excited, as I have already said, the envy of surrounding nations. The return of the Jews to Palestine under the decree of Cyrus, at which epoch the history of the Old Testament closes, found them in a feeble condition under the Persian kings, and the entire people at one period were in danger of being destroyed by the cruel edict of Ahasuerus; and their unsettled position, together with the decay of their influence, gave rise to several divisions and sects, which greatly impaired their harmony and unity as a nation. The Persian Empire was at length subdued by Alexander the Great, 208 years after its conquest by Cyrus. The Jews attached themselves, with their usual fidelity, to Darius, and Alexander, exasperated at their decision in favour of his rival, marched upon Jerusalem; but, struck with the imposing character of their venerable faith, became their friend and protector, gave them many privileges, and selected several of the most distinguished as first settlers in his new city of Alexandria. On the death of Alexander, and the division of the empire among four of his generals, Judea became the theatre of war and intestine commotion, division and troubles of all kinds, cruelty, carnage, and oppression, until the Asmonean family, lamenting with deep anguish the wretched condition of their country and brethren, resolved to strike a blow for liberty, and for many years Judas Maccabees and brothers triumphed over their enemies, restored peace to Jerusalem, beautified the sanctuary, and enforced obedience to the Divine Law.

At length, after many trials and reverses, the Romans, under Pompey, laid siege to and captured Jerusalem, and the Jews passed under the Roman yoke, and all that was left to the chosen people was the privilege to pursue their religion unmolested; and, after unparalleled sufferings, Herod the Idumenean ascended the throne of Judea, persecuted and oppressed the people, and rendered himself so odious, that, to retrieve something of his former standing, he rebuilt the Temple with great splendour, but, as an acknowledgment of his tributary position, set up a golden eagle over the gates of the sanctuary. It was at this period, when the Jews had lost all power as a nation; when, broken down and dispirited, and but a shadow of their former liberty and glory remained to them; when it needed no prophetic warning to denote the final overthrow of the nation, that Jesus of Nazareth was born. They had expected some one at that period who was destined to act as their Messiah and temporal deliverer; some one who could break the Roman yoke, and change the aspect of human affairs; they sighed for liberty and vengeance, and prayed devoutly for a deliverer. Jesus of Nazareth was not the one they expected. His mission of peace and spirit of reform held forth no temporal hope to the afflicted. He had no sword or helmet to indicate the warrior or conqueror; he unfurled no banner, sounded no trumpet, prophesied no victory over the pagans, and the Jews gave themselves up to despair.

To comprehend and fully understand the peculiar situation in which the Jewish people were placed at that important crisis, we must endeavour, if possible, to place ourselves in their position. A nation once powerful, rich, and happy, prosperous and independent, the conquerors of every neighbouring power, living in the midst of luxury and civilization, enjoying a happy and equitable code of laws, with wise kings, gallant warriors, a pious priesthood, and great national prosperity, suddenly assailed by powerful pagan nations, allured by a love of gold, and tempted by the hope of plunder, contending year after year against fearful odds, their enemy strengthened by fresh levies, while their own resources were exhausted, finding themselves at length gradually sinking, a weak, decayed, defeated power, the once glorious and favoured people abandoned by hope and almost deserted by Providence, their Temple, their pride and glory, wrested from them, and the beams of the setting sun falling on the brazen helmet of the Roman centurien keeping guard near the Holy of Holies. In this distracted position, and at this period of unexampled calamity, Jesus of Nazareth found the Jews at the commencement of his ministry.

Corruptions, the natural consequence of great misfortune, had crept in among them: a portion of the priesthood forgot the obligations due to their high order; hypocrisy and intrigue had reached the high places, and Jesus appeared among them the most resolute of reformers. Denouncing the priests and Pharisees, preaching against hypocrisy and vice, prophesying the downfall of the nation, and in thus attracting followers and apostles by his extraordinary and gifted powers, he became formidable by his decision of character, his unceremonious expression of opinion, and the withering nature of his rebuke. He preached at all times and at all places, in and out of the Temple, with an eloquence such as no mortal has since possessed, and, to give the most powerful and absorbing interest to his mission, he proclaimed himself Son of God, and declared himself ordained by the Most High to save a benighted and suffering people, as their Saviour and Redeemer. The Jews were amazed, perplexed, and bewildered at all they saw and heard. They knew Jesus from his birth. He was in constant intercourse with his brethren in their domestic relations, and surrounded by their household gods; they remembered him a boy, disputing, as was the custom, most learnedly with the doctors in the Temple; and yet he proclaimed himself the Son of God, and performed, as it is said, most wonderful miracles, was surrounded by a number of disciples of poor but extraordinarily gifted men, who sustained his doctrines, and had an abiding faith in his mission; he gathered strength and followers as he progressed; he denounced the whole nation, and prophesied its destruction, with their altars and temples; he preached against whole cities, and proscribed their leaders with a force which, even at this day, would shake our social systems. The Jews became alarmed at his increasing power and influence, and the Sanhedrin resolved to become his accuser, and bring him to trial under the law, as laid down in the 13th of Deuteronomy.

In reflecting deeply on all the circumstances of this, the most remarkable trial and judgment in history, I am convinced, from the whole tenour of the proceedings, that the arrest, trial, and condemnation of Jesus of Nazareth was conceived and executed under a decided panic. That he proclaimed himself Son of God; that he declared he had been delegated from the Father to enter upon his mediatorial character, that he was a prophet, and the promised Messiah, was understood and admitted by all his friends and disciples; but still, it has appeared to me throughout that there was not sufficient testimony to come under the special and distinct provisions of the Law.

The parables and figures of the Hebrew language, and the Oriental mode of expression, frequently cloud and embarrass the real meaning intended to be conveyed. Jesus uniformly acknowledged the unity and omnipotence of God; to Him he prayed, as our Father in heaven, whose name was hallowed, whose will was to be executed on earth; he disclaimed any intention to alter the Mosaic Law, but confirmed and observed every part of it. Take, for example, one fact, for so it will be considered, which we find in the twelfth chapter of St. Mark, the twenty-ninth verse, in reply to a question put to Him by one of the scribes, as to which is the first commandment of all. "And Jesus answered him, The first of all commandments is, Hear, O Israel, the Lord our God is one Lord." With these words on his lips, with this belief in his heart, it is impossible to have convicted him of blasphemy. It is our creed, our universal prayer, the basis of our faith; how could such a declaration have been construed into blasphemy? The title of God was a title of power and dominion, and frequently was conferred by the Almighty himself on earthly rulers. "See, I have made thee a God to Pharaoh," as God Supreme said to Moses; "Son of God" was a title frequently conferred on those of distinguished piety and learning, and on those possessing the emanations of the Divinity, and this title the apostles themselves carry out in all their writings.

"The Son," "*My* Son," not the Father; the humanity, not the Divinity, the *image* of the invisible God, not the invisible God himself; and Paul says, there is one

God and one Mediator between God and man. Could the Almighty delegate a mediatorial character to any on earth? who can doubt it? God says to Moses, "Behold, I send an angel before thee to keep thee in the way, provoke him not, for he will not pardon your transgressions, for my name is in him—my spirit is in him."

It was not, therefore, altogether on the charge of Jesus having called himself Son of God that the Sanhedrin accused and condemned him; political considerations mingled themselves, and in a measure controlled the decision of the council, and this is demonstrable from the declaration of Caiaphas himself, as stated in the Gospel, "Because that one man should die than the nation should be destroyed."

"It was the sedition, and not altogether the blasphemy—the terror and apprehension of political overthrow, which led to conviction, and this political and national characteristic was maintained throughout; it was that consideration which induced the Jews to urge upon Pilate a confirmation of the sentence. It was the charge of assuming the prerogatives of Caesar, not the name of the Divinity, which overcame the well-founded objections of the Roman governor, and crucifixion itself was a Roman and not a Jewish punishment. The opprobrious insults heaped upon the Master came from Roman soldiers, and that mixed rabble which even in our days desecrate all that is held sacred.

I place these most absorbing events before you, my countrymen, as I find them recorded in the New Testament, not to contrast things sacred with those which are profane, but that you should understand the exact position of the Jews at that time, their painful situation, their prostrate condition, their timidity, their agitation, without even a ray of hope; a people so venerable for their antiquity, so beloved and protected for their fidelity, on the very threshold of political destruction.

It is not my duty to condemn the course of our ancestors, nor yet to justify the measures they adopted in that dire extremity, but if there are mitigating circumstances, I am bound by the highest considerations which a love of truth and justice dictates, to spread them before you, at the same time to protest against entailing upon us the responsibility of acts committed eighteen hundred years ago by our fathers, and thus transmit to untold generations the anger and hatred of a faith erroneously taught to believe us the aggressors. True, it may be said that the Jews declared their willingness to let the blood of Jesus be on their heads and the heads of their children. I do maintain that the assumption of responsibility in that case extended only to them and to their children. In the Commandments, God visits the iniquities of the father on the children to the third and fourth generation, and then only to those who hate him: who can have the power to go beyond the limits for the punishment of sin, real or imaginary, express or implied, which God himself has ordained? All the persecutions which the Jews have suffered at the hands of Christians have arose from the injustice of making one generation answerable for the acts of another.

The Jews, my friends, were but the instruments of a higher power, and in rejecting Jesus of Nazareth we have a great and overwhelming evidence of the infinite wisdom of the Almighty. Had they acknowledged him as their Messiah at that fearful crisis, the whole nation would have gradually sunk under the Roman yoke, and we should have had at this day paganism and idolatry, with all their train of terrible evils, and darkness and desolation would have been spread over the face of the earth. But the death of Jesus was the birth of Christianity, the Gentile Church sprang from the ruins which surrounded its primitive existence; its march was onward, beset with darkness and difficulties, with oppression and persecution, until the sun of the Reformation rose upon it, dissipating the clouds of darkness which had obscured its beauties, and it shone forth with a liberal and tolerant brightness, such as the Great Master had originally designed it.

Had not that event occurred, how would you have been saved from your sins? The Jews, in this, did nothing but what God himself ordained, for you will find it written in the Acts of your Apostles, "And now, brethren, I know that through ignorance ye did it, as did also your rulers."

It has been said, and with some commendations on what was called my liberality, that I did not in this discourse, on its first delivery, term Jesus of Nazareth an impostor—I have never considered him such. The impostor generally aims at temporal power, attempts to subsidize the rich and weak believer, and draws around him followers of influence whom he can control. Jesus was free from fanaticism; his was a quiet, subdued, retiring faith; he mingled with the poor, communed with the wretched, avoided the rich, and rebuked the vainglorious. In the calm of the evening he sought shelter in the secluded groves of Olivet, or wandered pensively on the shores of Galilee. He sincerely believed in his mission; he courted no one, flattered no one; in his political denunciations he was pointed and severe, in his religion calm and subdued. These are not characteristics of an impostor; but, admitting that we give a different interpretation to his mission, when 150 millions believe in his Divinity, and we see around us abundant evidences of the happiness, good faith, mild government, and liberal feelings which spring from his religion, what right has any one to call him an impostor? That religion which is calculated to make mankind great and happy cannot be a false one.

While the Almighty raised up, enlarged, and extended the Gentile Church, gave to it power and dominion, he threw the mantle of his Divine protection over his chosen people, and has preserved them amid unheard-of dangers to this very day, numerous as they have been, but still distinct as a nation, preserving the Abrahmaic covenant, walking in his statutes, and obeying his commandments; the same people whom he had brought out of Egyptian bondage, and to whom he had given the land of Israel as an inheritance for ever, and who is now leading us back in peace and happiness to repossess our ancient and promised heritage. Can the human mind imagine a miracle such as this which we have before us? Do you now perceive, Christians and brethren, why it was not designed by the Almighty that the Jews at that crisis should have acknowledged the Messiahship of Jesus of Nazareth? "The secret things are for the Lord."

Fully appreciating, therefore, as I do, the pious and benevolent objects of the Society for Evangelizing the Jews throughout the world, and desirous that those societies should continue to feel an interest both in the temporal and eternal welfare of Israel, I do not think—pardon me for saying—that their success has been commensurate with the great efforts they have made, and the means expended in the advancement of the objects in view. My desire now is, that, feeling the same interest, and directed by the same zeal, those societies should unite in efforts to promote the restoration of the Jews in their *unconverted* state, relying on the fulfillment of the prophesies and the will of God for attaining the objects they have in view after that great advent shall have arrived.

A change of religious faith, even among the least faithful, is a plant of slow progress; but among a people specially chosen and signally preserved amid the ruins of the world and the downfall of every other nation of antiquity, is an effort of insurmountable difficulty. It is impolitic to send converted Jews to preach Christianity to Israel. However sincere they may be, they never inspire confidence among their brethren. A distrust in their sincerity precedes every effort they may make. Equally impolitic—I say it respectfully—was the appointment of a converted Jew as Bishop of Jerusalem, to commence his labours of conversion on a spot so dear to the Jews, to which they are so faithfully, so devotedly, so sincerely attached; a place to which they journey in their last pilgrimage to die *as* Jews, and be buried near their kings, prophets, and judges in the valley of Jehoshaphat. If your efforts are still to be devoted to evangelizing as well as restoring, send pious and sincere Christians to them, who entertain a kind and benevolent feeling for the Jews; and if they should not succeed in accomplishing all they desire, the messengers, at least, will be well, and kindly, and courteously received, and their mission treated with confidence and regard.

But a difficulty presents itself in the work of evangelizing which probably has not heretofore occurred to you. Let us suppose it to be as successful as the labourers in the vineyard would desire, what church is to receive us? If we join the Protestant, the Catholic will say, "We are the elder brother of the Christian Church; we spring from your fathers; the first fifteen bishops of our Church were Jews; we separated under the walls of Jersualem, and, after a painful pilgrimage of 1800 years, if you are satisfied to believe in what we believe, come to us, to the communion of saints, to the remission of sins." The Protestants will say, in their usual mild and tolerant spirit, "We keep pace with the enlightened spirit of the age: here is the Bible, which was intrusted to your safe keeping, and we restore it to you unchanged; with us you will find that liberality and charity go hand in hand, free from idolatry, from the remnants of paganism, free from the control of temporal power." The Unitarian will say, "'*In medio tutissimus.*' Come to our Church, thou pillar which standest alone amid the destruction of empires; we believe with you in the unity and omnipotence of God; we do not ask you to abandon the laws of Moses, should you ever adopt the Gospel of Jesus. Come with us." The Methodist, the Presbyterian, the Universalist, the Baptist, the Socinian, the Quaker, and other churches, each have peculiar doctrines. I complain not of this: in the multitude of sects there is safety, but how are we to choose? In the divisions of the Christian Church, how are we to find the true one? I stood recently in front of a noble church in a neighbouring city, adorned with all the splendour of architecture, and all the embellishments of pious taste. It was surrounded by a frightful mob, which had set fire to it. They brandished their incendiary torches, and threw them flashing in the middle of the aisles; they covered the altar with straw, and heaped it with missals and hymn-books. The flames spread rapidly in every direction, until they reached and curled round a magnificent altar-piece—a triumph of the art. The whole church was one bright sheet of fire: the devouring element stormed, and rushed, and roared, until it encompassed the broad and stately dome. I saw the golden cross by which it was surmounted encircled with myriads of bright sparks, while the flames played round its base—that cross, *In hoc signo vincit,* melting before the consuming heat. At length the whole dome fell, and cinders, murky clouds, and flames ascended high in the air: then the ruffians sent up a shout which gave alarm to the host of heaven—a shout of exultation that a Christian church, in a land of religious freedom, had been destroyed by men calling themselves Christians. This is one of the stumbling blocks to the Jews which we cannot overleap, though in our way it lies. When did the chosen people ever fire any structure raised to the honour of God?

But, my friends, why not ask yourselves the great and cardinal question whether it is not your duty to aid in restoring the chosen people as Jews to their promised land? Are we not the only witnesses of the unity and omnipotence of God? Are we not the only witnesses of the truth of the Bible, preserved as such by the great Sovereign Architect of the world? The predictions of the restoration of Israel, distinctly intimated by prophesy, are as full as were the predictions of our overthrow and desolation. Has not God threatened and punished, and will not his promises of favour be fulfilled? Has he cast off his people, or has he merely visited their transgressions with punishment? "Behold," saith the Lord, "I will take the children of Israel from among the heathen whither they be gone, and will gather them on every side, and bring them into their own land, and I will make them one nation, in the land upon the mountains of Israel. Then shall they know that I am the Lord their God, which caused them to be led into captivity among the heathen: but I have gathered them in their own land, and have left none of them any more there. Neither will I hide my face any more from them, for I have poured out my Spirit upon the house of Israel, saith the Lord. Thus the redeemed of the Lord shall return, and come with singing into Zion; they shall obtain gladness and joy, and sorrow and mourning shall flee away. Then shall Jerusalem be a crown of glory in the hand of the Lord; she shall no more be termed forsaken, nor her land be termed desolate.'

In almost every page of the Bible we have, directly and indirectly, in positive language and in parables the literal assurance and guarantee for the restoration of the Jews to Judea. We have gone through the fiery ordeal according to prediction; we have suffered the curses, and now await the period of the blessings. The past has been dark and dreary, the future is full of hope and splendour. God himself has been our ruler, our lawgiver, our leader, and to this hour our true friend. In the midst of appalling dangers his eye has been upon us, his protecting shield has been before us. To us he committed the lamp which has illumined the world, and we have held it with a steady hand for a light to the Gentiles.

No, no, my friends; what would be to us our blessings, our redemption, our salvation, without our restoration? Our land is blighted with the curse, shall it not enjoy the blessing? It long hath mourned, shall it not rejoice?

Innumerable are the promises which present themselves wherever the eye is turned. "The remnant of Jacob," saith the prophet, "shall be in the midst of many people, as a dew from the Lord, as showers upon the grass." And Isaiah, rapt in the contemplation of the glorious future reserved for his brethren of the Jewish Church, says, "Lift up thine eyes round about and see: all they gather themselves together, they come to thee: thy sons shall come from afar, and thy daughters shall be nursed at thy side."

We find the current strong and impulsive in every chapter of that illustrious prophet. "And the Lord shall set up an ensign for the nations, and shall assemble the outcasts of Israel, and gather together the dispersed of Judah from the four corners of the earth. Cry out and shout, inhabitants of Zion, for great is the Holy One of Israel in the midst of thee."

Again: listen to the prophet relative to the restoration and the rebuilding of Zion. "Behold, I will gather them out of all countries whither I have driven them in my anger, and in my fury, and in great wrath, and I will bring them again to this place and I will cause them to dwell safely, and they shall be my people, and I will be their God, and I will make with them an *everlasting* covenant, and I will *not* turn away from them to do them good, and I will plant them in thy land, assuredly with my whole heart, and with my whole soul: for thus saith the Lord, Like as I have brought all this great evil upon this people, so will I bring them all the good that I have promised them. I, the Lord, have called thee in righteousness, and will hold thine hand, and will keep thee, and give thee for a covenant of the people, for *a light of the Gentiles:* I am the Lord. *That* is my name, and my glory I will not give to another." "Fear not, for I am with thee; be not dismayed, for I am thy God. Behold, all that were incensed against thee shall be ashamed and confounded. Arise, shine, for thy light *is* come, and the glory of the Lord is risen upon thee, and the Gentiles shall come to thy light, and kings to the brightness of thy rising." "Whereas thou hast been forsaken and hated, so that no man went through thee, I will make thee an *eternal* excellency, a joy of many generations. Violence shall no more be heard in thy land, wasting nor destruction within thy borders, but thou shalt call thy walls salvation, and thy gates praise. Thy people, also, shall be all righteous; they shall inherit the land *forever.* The branch of my planting, the work of my hands, that I may be glorified. And the sons of strangers shall build up thy walls, and their kings shall minister unto thee; for in my wrath I smote thee but in my favour I had mercy upon thee. For the nation and kingdom that will not serve thee shall perish, and I will bless them that bless thee, and curse them that curse thee."

On these unfulfilled predictions, my friends, rest the happiness of the human race; and you are heirs to this new covenant, partners in the compact, sharers in the glory. Understand these prophesies distinctly: they relate to the literal, and not to the spiritual restoration of the Jews, as many believe. Some think that these prophesies were fulfilled at the restoration of Babylon; but you will find in the eleventh of Isaiah, beginning at the eleventh verse, these words: "And it shall come to pass in that day, that the Lord shall set his hand *again* the *second* time to recover the remnant of his people, which will be left (not in Babylon, but) from Assyria, and from Egypt, and from Pathros, and from Cush, and from Elam, and from Shina, and from Hamath, and from the islands of the sea"—the whole world.

Above all, you that believe in the predictions of your apostles—you who believe in the second coming of the Son of Man—where is he to come to? By your own showing, to Jerusalem, to Zion, to the beloved city of hope and promise; He is, according to your own evangelists, to your own belief, to come to the Jews, and yet you would convert them *here;* you strive to evangelize them, in the face of all that is sacred in the promises of God and the predictions of his prophets, that they shall occupy their own land as *Jews.* In your zeal you forget the solemn, emphatic, brief declaration of your Redeemer, which you should remember as the shades of darkness draw around you, and the light of morning breaks upon your sight, *"Salvation is of the Jews."*

Within the last twenty-five years great revolutions have occurred in the East, affecting in a peculiar manner the future destiny of the followers of Mohammed, and distinctly marking the gradual advancement of the Christian power. Turkey has been deprived of Greece, after a fearful and sanguinary struggle, and the land of warriors and sages has become sovereign and independent. Egypt conquered and occupied Syria, and her fierce pacha had thrown off allegiance to the sultan. Menaced, however, by the superior power of the Ottoman Porte, Mehemet Ali was compelled to submit to the commander of the faithful, reconveying Syria to Turkey, and was content to accept the hereditary possession of Egypt.

Russia has assailed the wandering hordes of the Caucasses. England has had various contests with the native princes of India, and has waged war with China. The issue of these contests in Asia has been marked with singular success, and evidently indicate the progressive power of the Christian governments in that interesting quarter of the globe. France has carried its victorious arms through the north of Africa. Russia, with a steady glance and firm step, approaches Turkey in Europe, and when her railroads are completed to the Black Sea, will pour in her Cossacks from the Don and the Vistula, and Constantinople will be occupied by the descendants of the Tartar dynasty, and all Turkey in Europe, united to Greece, will constitute either an independent empire, or be occupied by Russia, who, with one arm on the Mediterranean, and the other on the North Sea, will nearly embrace all Europe. The counterbalance of this gigantic power will be a firm and liberal union of Austria with all Italy and the Roman States, down to the borders of Gaul: but the revolution will not end here. England must possess Egypt, as affording the only secure route to her possessions in India through the Red Sea; then Palestine, thus placed between the Russian possessions and Egypt, reverts to its legitimate proprietors, and for the safety of the surrounding nations, a powerful, wealthy, independent, and enterprising people are placed there by and with the consent of the Christian powers, and with their aid and agency the land of Israel passes once more into the possession of the descendants of Abraham. The ports of the Mediterranean will be again opened to the busy hum of commerce; the fields will again bear the fruitful harvest, and Christian and Jew will together, on Mount Zion, raise their voices in praise of Him whose covenant with Abraham was to endure forever, and in whose seed all the nations of the earth are to be blessed. This is our destiny. Every attempt to colonize the Jews in other countries has failed: their eye has steadily rested on their own beloved Jerusalem, and they have said, "The time will come, the promise will be fulfilled."

The Jews are in a most favourable position to repossess themselves of the promised land, and organize a free and liberal government; they are at this time zealously and strenuously engaged in advancing the cause of education. In Poland, Moldavia, Wallachia, on the Rhine and Danube, and wherever the liberality of the governments have not interposed obstacles, they are practical farmers. Agriculture was once their only natural employment; the land is now desolate, according to the prediction of the prophets, but it is full of hope and promise. The soil is rich, loamy, and everywhere indicates fruitfulness, and the magnificent cedars of Lebanon, show the strength of the soil on the highest elevations; the climate is mild and salubrious, and double crops in the low lands may be annually anticipated. Everything is produced in the greatest variety. Wheat, barley, rye, corn, oats, and the cotton plant in great abundance. The sugarcane is cultivated with success; tobacco grows plentifully on the mountains; indigo is produced in abundance on the banks of the Jordan; olives and olive oil are everywhere found; the mulberry almost grows wild, out of which the most beautiful silk is made; grapes of the largest kind flourish everywhere; cochineal is procured in abundance on the coast, and can be most profitably cultivated. The coffee-tree grows almost spontaneously; and oranges, figs, dates, pomegranates, peaches, apples, plums, nectarines, pineapples, and all the tropical fruits known to us, flourish everywhere throughout Syria. The several ports in the Mediterranean which formerly carried on a most valuable commerce can be advantageously reoccupied. Manufactures of wool, cotton, and silk could furnish all the Levant and the islands of the Mediterranean with useful fabrics. In a circumference within twenty days' travel of the Holy City, two millions of Jews reside. Of the two and a half tribes which removed east of the trans-Jordanic cities, Judah and Benjamin, and half Manasseh, I compute the number in every part of the world as exceeding six millions. Of the missing nine and a half tribes, part of which are in Turkey, China, Hindostan, Persia, and on this Continent, it is impossible to ascertain their numerical force. Many retain only the strict observance of the Mosaic laws, rejecting the Talmud and Commentaries. Others, in Syria, Egypt, and Turkey, are rigid observers of all the ceremonies. Reforms are in progress which correspond with the enlightened character of the age, without invading any of the cardinal principles of the religion. The whole sect are therefore in a position, as far as intelligence, education, industry, undivided enterprise, variety of pursuits, science, a love of the arts, political economy, and wealth could desire, to adopt the initiatory steps for the organization of a free government in Syria, as I have before said, by, and with the consent, and under the protection of the Christian powers. I propose, therefore, for all the Christian societies who take an interest in the fate of Israel, to assist in their restoration by aiding to colonize the Jews in Judea; the progress may be slow, but the result will be certain. The tree must be planted, and it will not want liberal and pious hands to water it, and in time it may flourish and produce fruit of hope and blessing.

The first step is to solicit from the Sultan of Turkey permission for the Jews to purchase and hold land; to build houses, and to follow any occupation they may desire, without molestation and in perfect security. There is no difficulty in securing this privilege for them. The moment the Christian powers feel an interest in behalf of the Jewish people, the Turkish government will secure and carry out their views, for it must always be remembered that the one hundred and twenty millions of Mussulmen are also the descendants of Abraham. There is but a single link that divides us, and they also are partners in the great compact. The Jews are, at this day, the most influential persons connected with the commerce and monetary affairs of Turkey, and enjoy important privileges, but hitherto they have had no protecting influence, no friendly hand stretched forth to aid them. The moment the sultan issues his *Hatti Scherif,* allowing the Jews to purchase and hold land in Syria, subject to the same laws and limitations which govern Mussulmen, the whole territory surrounding Jerusalem, including the villages Hebron, Safat, Tyre, also Beyroot, Jaffa, and other ports of the Mediterranean, will be occupied by enterprising Jews. The valleys of the Jordan will be filled by agriculturists from the north of Germany, Poland, and Russia. Merchants will occupy the seaports, and the commanding positions within the walls of Jerusalem will be purchased by the wealthy and pious of our brethren. Those who desire to reside in the Holy Land, and have not the means, may be aided by these societies to reach their desired haven of repose. Christians can thus give impetus to this important movement; and emigration flowing in, and actively engaged in every laudable pursuit, will soon become consolidated, and lay the foundation for the elements of government and the triumph of restoration. This, my friends, may be the glorious result of any liberal movement you may be disposed to make in promoting the final destiny of the chosen people.

The discovery and application of steam will be found to be a great auxiliary in the promotion of this interesting experiment. Steam packets to Alexandria leave England every fortnight; a line of packets are established between Marseilles and Constantinople, stopping at the Italian ports, and at Athens and Smyrna, thus bringing the Jewish people within a few days' travel of Jerusalem. Our Mediterranean and Levant trade, hitherto much neglected, will be revived, affording facilities to reach Palestine from this country direct.

While many who are now present may suppose that we shall not live to hear of the triumphant success of this project, yet, my friends, it may be nearer than we imagine. Let us unfurl the standard, leaving the result to Him whose protecting influence overshadows us all—who is infinite in wisdom, unbounded and unrestricted in power. The Jews suppose that the period of the restoration, which they so ardently desire and pray for, must be determined by the will of God alone, and that their agency in bringing about this great advent is not required, and consequently, they wait patiently, without making those preliminary efforts so essential to the consummation of that great object. We never yet have been fully sensible of our duties and obligations as agents of a higher Power. Providence has endowed us with mind, with reason, with energy; blessed us with ample means to carry out his expressed wishes, laws, and ordinances. If we do not move when he disposes events to correspond with the fulfillment of his promises and the prediction of his prophets, we leave undone that which he entails upon us as a duty to perform, and the work is not accomplished, the day of deliverance has not arrived. He has spoken—he has promised. It is our duty, if the fulfillment of that Divine promise can be secured by mortal means and human agency, to see it executed. Will the dews of heaven produce a harvest without the labour of the husbandman?

But we cannot move alone in the great work of the restoration. The power and influence of our Christian brethren, which now control the destinies of the world, must be invoked in carrying out this most interesting project.

I am persuaded that the great events connected with the millennium so confidently predicted in the Scriptures, so anxiously desired by liberal and pious Christians, so intimately blended with the latter days—that consummation of a great and providential design in the union of the Jews and Gentiles, and the fulfilment of the prophecies—can alone be looked for *after* the restoration of the Jews to the land which the Lord gave to them for an everlasting possession. It is your duty, men and Christians, to aid us peaceably, tranquilly, and triumphantly to repossess the land of our fathers, to which we have a legal, equitable, perpetual right, by a covenant which the whole civilized world acknowledges. That power and glory which were once our own, you now possess; the banner of the Crescent floats where the standard of Judah was once displayed: it is for you to unfurl it again on Mount Zion. It will redound to your honour—it will perpetuate your glory. You believe in the second coming of Jesus of Nazareth. That second advent, Christians, depends upon you. It cannot come to pass, by your own admission, until the Jews are restored, and restored in their unconverted state. If he is again to appear, it must be to his own people, and in the land of his birth and his affections—on the spot where he preached, and prophesied, and died.

From the days of Constantine, when Church and State were first united, when the Christian religion was used as an instrument to carry out political objects, all has been confusion—the admixture of pagan worship, in which the mildness, charity, simplicity, and beauty of primitive Christianity were wholly lost. The sun of that faith, as I have already said, only rose at the period of the reformation, and has gone on gradually shedding its mild rays over the whole world. It only rose for us, for since that period we have enjoyed comparative tranquility. But free by law, we are not so by public opinion. Prejudice still scowls upon us, denying us that estimation, that influence, that portion of worldly honours and rights which should appertain to the good citizen of every faith. We are not yet fully incorporated in the family of mankind. Christians by profession are not all Christians in practice; they have assumed to themselves the right to proscribe, the right to denounce, the right to punish, the right to hate, the right to judge, the right to condemn: and the afflictions under which the chosen people have suffered, from an assumption of these rights, have entailed an awful responsibility upon Christians. "Vengeance belongeth to me," saith the Lord; but it has been wrested from him by man. Where is the warrant for this persecution of the Jews—this innate feeling of hostility and prejudice against them—on the part of Christians? Not in the gentle spirit and forgiving kindness of their great Master. His example was more benign, his practice more charitable. He forgave the Jews with all his heart for any wrongs done to him; he prayed for them, loved them, and declared that he died for them; and yet those who profess to walk in his meek and lowly steps refuse to feel as he felt, to forgive as he forgave, and to love the children for the Father's sake. We have lost all—country, government, kingdom, and power. You have it all—it is yours. It was once ours—it is again to be restored to us. Dismiss, therefore, from your hearts all prejudice which still lurks there against the favoured people of God, and consider their miraculous preservation as a light and beacon for the great events which are to follow. They are worthy of your love, your confidence, and respect. Is it nothing to have had such fathers and founders of their faith as Abraham, Isaac, and Jacob; such mothers as Sarah and Rebecca, Leah and Rachel; such illustrious women as Miriam and Deborah, Ruth and Esther? Is it nothing to have been deemed worthy by the Almighty to have had a path made for them through the waste of waters; to have been led to Sinai, and there received the precious and Divine gift of that law which we all revere and hold sacred at this day? Is it nothing to have erected the Temple of Jerusalem, where the priesthood and Levites presented their votive and expiatory offerings to the Most High? Is it nothing, my friends, to have outlived all the nations of the earth, and to have survived all who sought to ruin and destroy us? Where are those who fought at Marathon, Salamis, and Platea? Where are the generals of Alexander—the mighty myriads of Xerxes? Where are the bones of those which once whitened the plains of Troy? We only hear of them in the pages of history. But if you ask, Where are the descendants of the million of brave souls who fell under the triple walls of Jerusalem? where are the subjects of David, and Solomon, and the brethren of Jesus? I answer, Here! Here we are—miraculously preserved—the pure and unmixed blood of the Hebrews, having the Law for our light, and God for our Redeemer.

How we have suffered, my friends, for steadily adhering to a belief in his unity, I need not pain you by recapitulating. Even to this day persecution has not sheathed its bloody sword. But if the Jews- for eighteen hundred years have been assailed by the sword, by the rack, and the Inquisition, their great, and abiding, and absorbing faith has sustained them in the midst of those trials. When bound to the stake by men who claimed to be Christians, and the flames hissed and cracked around them; when, exhausted and dying, they called upon God to sustain them in their extremity, a still, small voice, pure and angelic, whispered in their ear, "Fear not, Jacob, for I am with thee."

Countrymen and citizens, thank God, your hands and hearts are free from the stains of such iniquity. If you have wronged Israel, it has arisen only from the prejudices of early education. Dismiss such feelings; be better acquainted with the Jew, and learn to estimate his virtues. See him in the bosom of his family, the best of fathers, and the truest of friends. See children dutiful, affectionate, and devotedly attached, supporting their parents with pride and exultation. See wives the most faithful, mothers the most devoted. Go with me into the haunts of misery, where the daughters of misfortune walk the streets of this great city, and see if among them all you find *one* Jewess. Come with me to the prisons, where crime riots and vice abounds, and examine whether a Jew is the tenant of a dungeon. Go into your almshouses, and ascertain how many Jews are recipients of your bounty. See them all, the friends of virtue and of temperance, obedient to the laws, and devoted to the country that protects them. Are we not, then, worthy of your confidence and esteem, discharging, as we do, every moral obligation imposed upon us? Vice and misfortune belong exclusively to no sect. Human nature is frail and fallible, and we should temper all our prejudices with mercy and charity.

Call to mind, therefore, whenever a feeling of prejudice is found lurking about your hearts against the chosen people, how much the world is indebted to the Jews. When you read the sublime Mosaic records, and see in them the wisdom and providence, the power and forgiving kindness, the confidence and affection of the Almighty, call to mind that Moses was a Jew. Whenever you pour out your hearts in devotion with the inspired Psalmist, and your whole soul is rapt in delight and devotion in dwelling upon his divine muse, remember also that *David* was a Jew. Whenever that mighty prophet, whose poetic soul was warmed by an ethereal fire, and who bears you on the wings of hope and exultation, of joy and rapture, remember that Isaiah was a Jew. But do not confine yourselves to the great army of kings and prophets of the Bible. Go to your own New Testament, and—ask whether the Gentiles have *ever* had such evangelists as Judah furnished; and yet Paul, the mighty man of mind, of faith, and fervour, was a *Jew*—"A Hebrew of Hebrews."

And John, too, the gentle, the loving, and beloved, was likewise a Jew; but there is yet another, on whom all your affections are centred, to whom all your hopes and aspirations are directed, to whom you look for grace, and mercy, and salvation—Jesus of Nazareth was a Jew, and told you, in language which should sink deep into your hearts, as a commanding, imperative, and unrepealed precept and admonition, "Verily, I say unto you, inasmuch as ye have done those charities unto one of the *least* of these my brethren, ye have done it unto me."

I have referred to this country as the most suitable spot, from its character and institutions, from which a project of this kind might with security and success be undertaken, but has it ever occurred to you, my friends, that the eighteenth chapter of Isaiah might possibly have reference to America in connexion with the restoration of the Jews? Indulge me a moment in examining that short but singular chapter.

"Ho to the land" (it is translated *wo,* but evidently erroneously: it is *Ho,* or *Hail)*—"Hail to the land, shadowing with wings, which is beyond the rivers of Ethiopia."

The prophet, in this vision, was in Palestine, having Europe on his right, Africa on his left, and in front the Mediterranean Sea, and on looking down on the northern coast of Africa, speaks of a land "which is beyond the rivers of Ethiopia." That land is America; there is no other land which lies beyond the rivers of Cush known as Africa. But all lands spoken of in the Bible have a distinctive name; how is it that the Prophet Isaiah only speaks of it as "a land?" It was not discovered at the period of the prophecy, and, consequently, could have no name: it is our western world, and can mean no other. "Hail to the land, shadowing with wings." The arms of no country are so emphatically "wings" as those of the United States. It is an eagle in the act of flying with outspread wings, peculiarly conspicuous as an armorial ensign and living description of our land, which, under the shadow of her wings, offers a shelter for the persecuted of all nations. "That sendeth ambassadors by sea." This country cannot send ambassadors but by sea. On all the other continents they can be sent by land, *"even in vessels of bulrushes."* Here "vessels," not ships, is the term used by the prophet. The true translation is, in vessels "impressing on the face of the water," answering to our steamboats; for the Hebrew word *gomey* is translated bulrushes: it is so, but it has two other meanings: one is, a rush of waters; the second is, *impresseth,* which is translated *yegomey,* meaning an impetus, a forcible propelling power; the third meaning is, the weed bulrush, which grows in the water; and, by-the-way, it may also be mentioned that our live oak is cut by men in water and among the bulrushes. These swift messengers, therefore, to carry ambassadors, may be construed into steam vessels. Here, then, we have the explanation of that verse. The land lying beyond the rivers of Ethiopia is America; the shadowing with wings is the American ensign, the emblem of its protective influence; "which sendeth ambassadors by sea," denotes the only country that must send those messengers on the ocean; and the vessels of bulrushes either applies to the light, fast-sailing vessels peculiar to our country, or our steam vessels. Thus far, I think, our country is fully indicated and shadowed forth in the vision of the prophet: "Go, ye swift messengers, to a nation scattered and peeled." This nation, it cannot be doubted, is the Jewish nation; "to a nation" means evidently "from a nation terrible from their beginning." It will be asked, In what respect have the Americans been "terrible from the beginning?" The most remarkably so of all the nations of the earth.

The Americans were not known for several hundred years, and their population, character, and resources, gradually developed, as other nations have been known, they sprang into immediate political existence from a state of vassalage to a condition of freemen; they were terrible to the foes of liberty, terrible to the kings and potentates of the world, terrible to the enemies of a republican form of government, terrible to their foes in war, terrible by their example to the despots of the earth, terrible, therefore, "from the beginning," because we may say we are but yet in the beginning, being only in the 68th year of American Independence. I ought, however, to say, that the word terrible means also "wonderful," which is equally applicable. The prophet, after saying that the Lord would take his rest, meaning that he would wait the issue of things in relation to the chosen people, abide his time, but still keep them as a dew in harvest, then comes to the concluding verse of this remarkable vision: "In that time shall the present be brought unto the Lord of hosts, a people scattered and peeled, and *from* a people terrible from their beginning hitherto; a nation meted out and trodden under foot, whose land the rivers have spoiled, to the place of the name of the Lord of hosts, the Mount Zion." For an explanation of what is meant by "whose land the rivers have spoiled," if you refer to the 8th chapter of Isaiah, the 7th and 8th verses, you will discover that rivers means conquerors rushing over and despoiling their land—a frequent occurrence in Judea.

I am right in this interpretation, and that this is the land which is beyond the rivers of Ethiopia, what a glorious privilege is reserved for the free people of the United States: the only country which has given civil and religious rights to the Jews equal with all other sects; the only country which has not persecuted them, selected and pointedly distinguished in prophecy as *the* nation which, at a proper time, shall present to the Lord his chosen and trodden-down people, and pave the way for their restoration to Zion. But will they go, I am asked, when the day of redemption arrives? All will go who feel the oppressor's yoke. *We* may repose where we are free and happy, but those who, bowed to the earth by oppression, would gladly exchange a condition of vassalage for the hope of freedom: that hope the Jews never can surrender; they cannot stand up against the prediction of our prophets, against the promises of God; they cease to be a nation, a people, a sect, when they do so. Either the Messiah of the Jews has come, or he is yet to come. If he has come, we must cease praying for him to come; if he has not come, we are bound to seek him, not here, but in our own land, which has been given to us as a perpetual inheritance, and which we dare not surrender without at once surrendering our faith. We must not stop to ask whether the Jews will consent to occupy the land of Israel as freemen. Restoration is not for us alone, but for millions unborn. There is no fanaticism in it; it is easy, tranquil, natural, and gradual. Let the people go: point out the path for them in safety, and they will go, not all, but sufficient to constitute the elements of a powerful government; and those who are happy here may cast their eyes towards the sun as it rises, and know that it rises on a free and happy people beyond the mountains of Judea, and feel doubly happy in the conviction that God has redeemed all his promises to Jacob. Who can be an infidel when he looks on the Jews, and sees in them, and the Bible yet firmly in their grasp, the consummation of all the Divine promises made to them as a nation? I should think that the very idea, the hope, the prospect, and, above all, the certainty of restoring Israel to his own and promised land, would arouse the whole civilized world to a cordial and happy cooperation. Mankind would spring from the couch of ease and slumber to see the ensign displayed, and would exclaim, "The day has come! the promise is fulfilled!"

Let me therefore impress upon your minds the important fact, that the liberty and independence of the Jewish nation may grow out of a single effort which this country may make in their behalf. That effort is to procure for them a permission to purchase and hold land in security and peace; their titles and possessions confirmed; their fields and flocks undisturbed. They want only PROTECTION, and the work is accomplished. The Turkish governments cannot be insensible to the fact that clouds are gathering around them, and destiny, in which they wholly confide, teaches them to await the day of trouble and dismemberment. It is their interest to draw around them the friendly aid and co-operation of the Jewish people throughout the world, by conferring these reasonable and just privileges upon them, and when Christianity exerts its powerful agency, and stretches forth its friendly hand, the rights solicited will be cheerfully conferred. When the Jewish people can return to Palestine, and feel that in their persons and property they are as safe from danger as they are under Christian governments, they will make their purchases of select positions, and occupy them peaceably and prosperously; confidence will then take the place of distrust and, by degrees, the population in every part of Syria being greatly increased, will become consolidated, and ready to unfold the standard when political events shall demonstrate to them that the time has arrived.

Let it, however, be kept in mind, that the restoration will be at first limited and partial; the government which they may form will be transitory and contingent; the great war prophesied in Ezekiel against Gog, prince of Rush, Meshech, and Tubal, the power which now controls Archanez, Refath, and Togartnah of the Scriptures, that is to say, the Germans, Sclavonians, Sarmatians, and Turks of our day, is *Russia;* the descendants of the joint colony of Meshech and Tubal, and the little horn of Daniel. Russia, in its attempt to wrest India from England and Turkey from the Ottomites, will make the Holy Land the theatre of a terrible conflict. Tarshis, "with the young lions thereof"—evidently Great Britain, with her allies—will come to the rescue. Then will ensue the battle so sublimely described by the prophet: the fire and hailstones; the purification and victory; the advent of the Messiah, and the thousand years of happiness and peace which are to ensue. Worldly as we may seem, and recurring to events which will grow out of the political destinies of Europe, we must still remember the overruling hand of Providence in the direction of these great results. What he has predicted has literally come to pass; what remains to be fulfilled will assuredly as literally be fulfilled. Skepticism and infidelity fade before the pure light of prophecy, prediction, and Divine assurance contained in the good Book, that book of life, and love, and hope, and promise, which some are weak enough to reject and repudiate. Remember, therefore, my countrymen, you whose aid is invoked to assist in the restoration, that we are to return as we went forth; to bring back to Zion the faith we carried away with us. The temple under Solomon, which we built as Jews, we must again erect as the chosen people. You believe that the Messiah has come; you are right in believing so; you have the evidences in the power and dominion, the wealth, the happiness, the glory that surrounds you. He has come for you, but how for us? We are still the peeled, banished, scattered, and oppressed people; the oil on the surface of the ocean, which mingles not with the heaving billows. For us he is yet to come, and will come. For two thousand years we have been pursued and persecuted, and we are yet here; assemblages of men have formed communities, built cities, established governments, rose, prospered, decayed, and fell, and yet we are here. Rome conquered Greece, and she was no longer Greece. Rome, in turn, became conquered, and there are but few traces now of the once mistress of the world; yet we are still here, like the fabled Phoenix, ever springing from its ashes, or, more beautifully typical, like the bush of Moses, which ever burns, yet never consumes. You believe that Jesus of Nazareth was the Messiah, and you are Christians; were we to believe the same, we should still be Jews.

With this difference only, what is it that separates the Jew and the Gentile? Our law is your law, our prophets are your prophets, our hope is your hope, our salvation is your salvation, our God is your God. Why should we change? Why surrender that staff of Jacob which has guided our steps through so many difficulties? We can never be separated from our Shepherd; we believe in all that he had promised, and patiently await their fulfilment. Come, therefore, to our aid, and take the lead in this great work of restoration. Let the first movement for the emancipation of the Jewish nation come from this free and liberal country. Call to mind that Moses was the first founder of a republican form of government, and that the first settlers on this continent adopted the Mosaic laws as their code, and strictly enforced them.

In the appeal I have made to my fellow-citizens this evening, let it not be supposed that I mean to exclude from a participation in the great and good work, the beloved friend and companion of man; second in creation, but first in zeal and true religion. Their agency is ever of the highest importance in good works. When surrounded by the excitements of the busy world, intent on gain, and eager in the pursuit of fortunes, when the mind is wholly engrossed in temporal objects, then, in, the watches of the night and the stillness of the morn, the wife awakens the husband to a sense of religious delinquency, and calm admonition gradually but imperceptibly leads him into the path of duty and high moral obligations. Like the woman in the evangelists, who freely and happily used her box of precious ointment, all that she says and urges is the fulfillment of the most sacred duties drops like oily balsam upon the heart, soothes while it influences, and subdues while it controls. Jew or Gentile, women are ever the pillars of the Church.

And now, with the most grateful acknowledgments for the liberal attention you have honoured me with this evening, I do commend you all to the gracious protection of that Divine Providence in whom we all hope, who is all love, all mercy, and all mighty.

Address Delivered at the Hebrew Synagogue,

in Crosby-Street, New-York, on Thanksgiving Day to Aid in the Erection of the Temple at Jerusalem

By M. M. Noah.
Jamaica:
Printed by R. J. De Cordova,
66, Harbour-Street, Kingston.
1849.

M. M. Noah's Address.

About two years ago, a messenger arrived in this city from Jerusalem, having been commissioned from the Hebrew Congregation at Hebron to visit the United States, to collect aid for the suffering poor of that venerable city. He came from the neighbourhood of the cave of Macphelah, where Abraham and the founders of our faith lie burried, and asked in their name, and by their immortal memory, charity for our poor brethren, who have for many centuries piously and carefully watched that sacred spot. Some questioned the expediency of allowing our charity to travel so far from home; many gave in the name of Him who said the poor shall never depart from the land; but he asked only the aid of his brethren. The reception which he met with here, from members of the oldest congregation in America endorsed his mission to other cities, and the Pilgrim returned to the Holy City, bearing with him some remembrance from the land where the Jew and the Gentile are equally free, In a letter which I received from the American Consul at Jerusalem, he said that he had met the Rabbi, who stated that he had brought with him from the country $18,000 for the poor families of Hebron. The fidelity with which he discharged that duty, induced the Rabbis and Trustees of the Congregation of BETH-EL, at Jerusalem, to send him again to this country on a mission of still greater interest.

It may not be generally known to our people that since the destruction of our Temple, upwards of 1,800 years ago, Israel has been without a place of worship, dedicated with all the solemnities of our faith, and erected with suitable magnificence, to the Divine Architect of heaven and earth. The Jews in their own land, on that land which God gave to them as an inheritance for ever, by a deed consecrated and confirmed by ages, were not permitted to erect a Synagogue, from that final moment of the destruction of the Temple, even to the present day.

The army of the Roman Conqueror captured and carried away the nation to be sold as slaves. A few only of the faithful, hid in tombs and caverns, secreting themselves beneath the fallen columns of the Temple, remained on a spot endeared to them by so many blissful reminiscences, and by the promises of the great hereafter. The Roman Centurions pursued them—the Greeks persecuted them—the Persians destroyed them, and, in after ages, the followers of Mahomet visited them with fire and sword, and the Crusaders trampled upon their necks: yet they refused, under these unprecedented calamities, to abandon the home of their fathers, and their ancient heritage, the rich gift of the Almighty. With the laws of Moses, which they had preserved; with the sacred rolls, written by Esdras, now in their possession, which they bore from the flaming ruins; they read the law in chambers—in caves—confined rooms and deserted places; for, among their Pagan persecutors, they did not dare to worship openly that God whose protecting mercies the civilized world now unites to invoke. The mosque of the Musselmen reared its domes and minarets on the site of our Temple—Christians erected magnificent churches and rich-endowed chapels on our soil; while our people, the rightful inheritors of all that land of promise, crawled in abject submission to the walls of the Temple, to bewail their hard destiny, to pray for the peace of Jerusalem, and weep on the solitary banks of the Jordan. They never despaired of the fulfillment of those promises which God had made to them; that still small voice continually whispered in their ears, in accents soft as the cherub's voice, "Fear not, Jacob, for I am with thee."

Centuries rolled—nations arose, flourished, decayed, and fell—yet the Jewish People still existed, increased in numbers, and, under every privation and persecution, preserved their identity, their faith, and their nationality.

At length a sign is given; the thunders begin to roll all over Europe; the cry is everywhere heard in despotic government—"to arms;" the people are at war with their kings, and the kings are overthrown; Priestcraft and fanaticism are overthrown; the Sun of Liberty begins to rise; the chains of the Jews are unloosed, and they are elevated to the rank of men; the fires of superstition had burnt out, and the age of reason had revived. The Sultan of Turkey, following the march of civilized nations, says to the Jews in his dominions—"You are free; you have my permission to erect a Synagogue in Jerusalem; and messengers are dispatched at they were in the days of Solomon, to ask for aid from their brethren throughout the world, to erect of magnificent place of worship, the first that has been erected in the holy city since the advent of Christianity.

Friends and brethren, do you understand that sign? Is it not pregnant with great events? Is not this another seal broken? We can erect a Synagogue, and build a Temple here, and it excites no attention; but when the trumpet sounds from Mount Zion, every ear is opened, every heart throbs, I know full well, that there are many Jews throughout the world, who look upon the restoration of their brethren to the holy land as a possible event in the great changes which may hereafter occur—but they take little interest in the signs of the times. Happy in the enjoyment of every comfort here, they only think of their brethren in the holy land when their charitable feelings are appealed to; but when the great events of the restoration which are to fulfill the prophecies are talked of, they cling to the home of their birth, and the country of their adoption, and say, "my destiny is here." Be it so. I do not blame them; for great sacrifice of life and treasure await the first movements of Restoration. We are safe; but let us feel for those brave hearts, who will not forsake their ancient heritage—who cling with ardent devotion to the sacred soil, and who turn their eyes of hope toward Zion, and say, "The time will come, the hour will arrive." Let us furnish them with the means of living until the Trumpet again sounds on the walls of Jerusalem—let us aid to erect a Temple worthy of their faith, their devotion, and their constancy.

The Jews, I regret to say, know little of the Holy Land and of their brethren who reside in it. It is now the object of Christian research, of Christian veneration; and no learned pious and liberal Christian visits that sacred spot, who does not feel that the Chosen People of God are at this day the greatest miracle on earth, and have ever been the constant uniform object of Divine Protection. The fate of a nation may depend on many causes: one becomes weakened by unjust and unnecessary wars; another falls from want of energy, character, good faith and industry, a third is without courage to sustain its rights; and a fourth is ignorant, imbecile, and bigoted. The rise, progress and fate of the Jewish nation, exhibited no such defects of character. We sinned against God because it is the nature of man to be sinful. He punished us as the parent does his child: but, in the midst of our stubbornness, our disobedience, and hardness of heart, we did not forget the Unity and Omnipotence of that Divine Architect of the Universe, and He pardoned us: His arm always has guided us, and amid the vicissitudes of 6,000 years, the nation never has been lost; from the day and the hour that God declared us to be his people, down to the present time, we have remained the same people—distinct from all others. Shepherds of the land of promise—slaves in Egypt—a mighty power in Canaan—the revolted tribes captured at Samaria and blended with other nations,—still Judah and Benjamin remained, and were still the chosen people. The whole world of idolatry united to crush us, but the handful of God's chosen servants could not be subdued or won to apostacy. By the rivers of Babylon they wept in captivity, but could not forget Jerusalem or the songs of Zion; the fiery furnace could not subdue them, and Pagan Kings, awe-struck at their self-sacrificing piety end [sic] fidelity, set them free. After seventy years of bondage, the faithful were restored to Zion. Punished for their sins thus severely, the Children of Israel reposed 400 years in their land of milk and honey, waiting for that Prince which God promised to send them, to consolidate and rule over the nation as their temporal Sovereign. But their glory was again destined to be dimmed—their light extinguished, and darkness once more enshrouded the people. The ambitious, conquering Romans appeared in great force under the walls of Jerusalem, and summoned them to surrender.

We have heard of many wars and sieges—of gallant victories and brilliant defences, of intense sufferings and indomitable valor; but where does the page of history inscribe deeds of bravery and personal sacrifice equal to the siege of Jerusalem? Had the Jews been united at that siege—had not the embers of faction been fanned into a flame. and its defenders divided and at war with each other—Titus Vespasian could never have entered the Holy City. The testimony of Josephus is not always free from impartiality when he treats of Vespasian and Titus. He described their triumphs after the destruction of his nation, with that cowardly complacency which charactized the courtier; he was a traitor and fought against his people in the ranks of the enemy, and yet he admits that the Jews performed prodigies of valor. "They cried to their besiegers from walls crumbling to ruins, that they courted death which was preferable to a shameful slavery, and that they would exert themselves to the last to prove to the Romans that no boundary was to be affixed to their determined resistance." The siege of Jerusalem lasted 166 days; and after unheard-of sufferings, the flames of their Temple lighted the funeral pile of the nation. and 1,100,000 souls were buried in the ruins. From that day they have been in a perpetual state of martyrdom, suspended between life and death. What bloody vicissitudes, what scenes of grief, what barbarities, what ravages, what disasters, what injustice, have not been exercised by the different nations of the globe, against a people devoted to slavery and abandoned by fortune!—Pagans, Mahommedans, and Christians, have by turns occupied the Holy Land, and deluged it with blood. Still our people refused to abandon the country which God had given them. Sentinels on the ramparts, they watched for us, prayed for us. We were driven out among the nations of the earth; our home was nowhere; our people everywhere. Who has done this? Who brought Abraham from Ur to the Chaldess? Who sent Joseph a slave in Egypt? Who authorized Moses to lead the people through the Red Sea? Who gave the law in thunder on Mount Sinai? Who raised a long line of prophets who poured forth a living stream of eloquence and divine song. which even the present age cannot hear unmoved? Who preserved Daniel in the lions' den? Shadrach, Meschech and Abednego in the fiery furnace? Our God, your God, who made bare His holy arm in the eyes of all the nations. Shall we not sustain each other when so divinely sustained and protected? Shall we turn a deaf ear to the supplications of our brethren at Jerusalem, who have stood by their faith so triumphantly? I hope not.

It has been said that the Jews are indolent, are disinclined to labor, are only employed in studying the law, and devoting all their hours to prayer, and prefer leading a life of dependence and want to one of prosperous active industry. I thank them that they do so! Amid our worldly cares, one [sic] pursuits of gain, our limited knowledge of our holy faith, our surrender of many cardinal points—probably from necessity, I am thankful that there is a holy band of brotherhood at Zion, whose nights and days are devoted to our sublime laws, our venerable institutions. I wish them to remain so; I think it our duty and our interest to share our means with them—to repay them with the bread of life, for aiding us with the bread of salvation. Jerusalem should ever be an object of the warmest attachment in our sight. To see the Holy Land sovereign and independent under its rightful proprietors; to know that the Temple will again be rebuilt; to hope to see the standard of Judah once more unfurled on Mount Zion; to die on that spot, and to be buried near David and Solomon in the valley of Jehoshaphat, should be our highest ambition, our earnest hope, our incessant prayer.

There are some who may consider the permission extended to the Jews in Jerusalem to build a Temple, or a magnificent synagogue, a concession of little importance: but taken with other extraordinary signs of the times, it has a most important bearing. We may be unmindful and indifferent in relation to those signs; but there is a Divine hand which directs, a Divine agency which controls these movements; there are Divine promises yet to be fulfilled; Divine attributes which are yet to be made apparent to the unbeliever. Since the establishment of christianity, the world has not seen a revolution equal to that existing at the present moment in Europe: one hundred millions of people are in arms against their sovereigns. It is a struggle indeed for liberty and human rights; but religious as well as civil liberty; the blow is equally aimed at priestcraft, at that powerful union of church and state, which for centuries has kept the world in bondage. The allied Sovereigns may succeed in overpowering the people and maintaining their thrones and sceptres; but great concessions will be made to the wishes of the people to avoid hurricanes of frightful outbreaks:—the people are no longer in chains. To the Jews, this great revolution has been a wonderful manifestation of God's providence and watchfulness; it has made them men, citizens, a people, a nation—it has given them rank, position, power,—it has elevated them to the highest offices. Look back 1800 years on Rome, the proud mistress of the world, and see the Jewish captives in chains following the triumphant car of the victorious Titus; see them sold in bondage; see them the architects of the Colliseum and the Pantheon, the servile laborers everywhere. When Rome fell, and christianity arose, see them even more fiercely persecuted, the inmates of the dungeons of the inquisition, and the victims of the Auto de Fe; see the chosen people, whose only sin was their belief in one God, locked up at night in the Ghetto, like animals in a cage, and look at them now in Rome: declared to be free by law, and possessing equal rights with their fellow-citizens. See them in France and Germany, and in every country in Europe, filling the highest situations in the governments, the proudest elevations on the benches of law and science, and diffusing everywhere the lights of their deep philosophy, and the fruits of their close and ardent study. And has this great advent been brought about by human agency? I believe it not;—it is part and parcel of those promises—the first step in the fulfilment of that great event which is to manifest to the whole world the power, the unity, the omnipotence of the Lord God of Israel, one God and the God of all Creation, and that He alone is the King of Kings, Redeemer of the World, and the Sole Judge of the Earth.

Other great revolutions are also in progress—quietly, slowly, but securely—the age of Reason and Philosophy among Christians. In every direction, there appear to me evidences of a progressive but mighty change in the fundamental principles of that faith, which it is our duty and our interest to watch, as developments of the deepest importance to our future destiny as a nation. I have noticed the liberal feelings everywhere evinced toward the Jewish people, and interest in their spiritual character, as much as in their temporal welfare. I see everywhere a change manifested toward us as a sect. There are closer affinities developing themselves among christians. They are gradually unloosing the chains of a religious prejudice against us, and feel a deeper interest in our fate and final advent. Few adhere at the present day, to the spiritual restoration of the Jews, while the multitude admit that this restoration must be literal. The promises of God to the Chosen People are now more fully recognized, and evangelizing them is postponed until after the great events contingent on our restoration as an independent power. Reason and Truth begin to resume their empire, as the shackles of ecclesiastical power become weakened, and man defends his right to think, to speak, and to act freely and openly upon all matters appertaining to the Christian faith.

The result of this religious freedoms manifest itself in gradually withdrawing from the great founder of the Christian faith, the divine attributes conceded to him by his disciples and followers. Since the Reformation, this change has been gradually unfolding itself. But professing Christians did not dare to express their doubts even to themselves; they were unbelievers ever, but only in the deep recesses of the heart. But now Reformers, Socialists, Communists, Philosophers, openly express their doubts. All Germany is deeply tinctured with this belief, and other Luthers are springing up, declaring their unchanged belief in the sublime morality of Jesus of Nazareth—their entire confidence in him as an eminent and illustrious reformer, teacher, prophet, brother; but denying his divine issue, his participation in the Godhead, and his right to share with the Almighty the attributes of divinity. The Jews are deeply interested in the extent sion [sic] and preservation of Christian morals. To us and to the world, it would be a deep calamity to see our laws, our principles, our doctrines abrogated, which have been so beneficially spread throughout the world, under another name. If we were enfeebled and broken down, and had not the power to enforce and carry out the doctrines of our faith, still happily they have not been lost to the world, but flourish under another denomination. "Do unto others as you would desire others to do unto you:—love your neighbour as yourself:"—deal justly to all men, honor your parents, be faithful to the governments that protect you, be merciful, be charitable, and love God with all your heart and soul—these are Jewish precepts. advanced as such by a great Jewish reformer, and ingrafted upon the religion adopted by his followers and friends; and their divine origin is unchanged.

If it is asked why has not Judaism preached against Christianity, when Christianity has, for 1800 years, been incessantly preaching against Judaism. The answer is this. Our cause is in greater hands; in good time, He will give the world the unmistakable evidence that He alone is the Great Redeemer, and that salvation is alone with him. Our unwillingness to preach against Christianity grew out of the fact, that in pulling down the landmarks of that faith, we should assail and endanger many of our own cherished principles and doctrines; and although disbelieving the divine attributes claimed for Jesus of Nazareth, we could not deny or reject his principles, and he always avowed the faith which we avow.

Without wishing to unsettle any of the principles which sustain the Christian religion, we have asked what would be the effect of separating from the character of Jesus of Nazareth the divine characteristics claimed for him? The world would become Unitarians; men would openly become converts to that faith with sincerity, as their hearts would be thereby released from harassing and perplexing doubts, and Christianity, in all its high moral attributes. There is enough in the character of Jesus to give him a rank among the highest practical moralists divested of all faith in his divine attributes; more, much more than in the character of Mahomet, who claimed none of those attributes. Jesus declared that "God was a spirit, and those who worshipped him must worship Him in spirit and truth;" we declare no more.

We must watch these changes closely as they occur; whatever doubts may shake the faith of Christianity, whose doubts can never reach us—we are now as we ever have been, as we ever hope to be,—one God, one faith, one people. We have no mysteries, no revelations which are not natural and reasonable. In this position we have stood for ages, and it is a platform which will endure forever, and on which all religions can s[t]and. We must seek, however, to take advantage of the times and the changes throughout the world, as they may relate to our temporal prosperity. We cannot at this moment tell what important results may grow out of this permission to build a magnificent Synagogue in Jerusalem. One right conferred, one prejudice removed, leads to the enjoyment of other rights, to the removal of other prejudices, and finally the nation begins to lift up its head; education completes the great work, and the Jews of Jerusalem, the great defenders and expounders of the law, become enlightened and liberal citizens, qualified to be intrusted with higher powers.

Let us not believe that, although our faith is admitted to have a divine origin, that salvation is for the Jews exclusively. Salvation for Gentiles, is equally included; He who made the whole earth, will protect all His children in it. We are the altar of the Sanctuary, on which it is said, a fire shall animate and revive all Creation alike—the Gentile shall stand before its light, and rejoice in the warmth which it imparts. Had it not been for Christianity and Mahometanism, which sprung up upon the ruins of our nation, and raised aloft our prostrate banner, Paganism would still have flourished, every God would have been worshiped but the true and living one; the heathen would have triumphed at this very day, and all would have been darkness and desolation. From among a few of our own people has God raised up a new sect, which, with the descendants of Joshua, maintained in part His divine precepts. This intermediate power, though intolerant and presecuting [sic] has still stood between us and utter destruction, and now eight millions of the chosen people—the same people who were at Sinai, at Babylon and at Zion, stand forth in the presence of all the earth, the miracle of God's Providence; and Christian and Mussulman will march before them in the great advent of the Restoration, surrendering their trust, giving up their guardianship, and crying aloud, with our great prophet, "Prepare ye the way of the Lord, make straight in the desert a highway for our God," and this advanced guard will bear on their banner, as they pass beneath the triple wall of Jerusalem, that verse from Scripture, which has ever been our guide, "Yet I am the Lord thy God, from the land of Egypt, and thou shalt know no God but me; for there is no Saviour besides me." Oh, children of Israel you know not the great destiny which is in store for you! Study to deserve it, study to meet it and to merit it, by the practice of many virtues, by toleration and good faith, mercy, charity and forgiveness.

The world call us a proud people. If there is a nobility on earth; if pure and unadulterated blood, descending from such ancestors as Abraham, Isaac, and Jacob, Moses, David, and Solomon, which courses through our veins, give us a claim to national distinction, we have a right to be proud of such ancestry, but that pride should be limited to imitating their wisdom and cultivating among ourselves that nationality which alone embraces the elements of our restoration. The designs of the Almighty are brought about by human agency, He inclines the hearts of men to execute His great purposes on earth; wars, revolutions, changes in the political world, the dismemberment of nations, the downfall of kings, the elevation of the people, the light of knowledge, the march of science, and the triumph of liberal opinions, are all His works, through His inscrutable decrees.

This permission to lay a corner stone once more in Jerusalem, to erect a magnificent temple to His honor and to His worship, by His ancient and faithful people, and which we are this day called upon to aid, is another great sign of His divine power and will, foreshadowing the great promises hereafter,—the assurances that we shall yet be independent and worship Him on Zion in freedom and tranquility.

But I have often heard my co-religionarians say, painfully heard them say, that the promises of restoration though [sic] repeatedly made, are surrounded with many difficulties; that the land so remote, would never repay the sacrifices in reassembling the people from the four quarters of the earth; and that when assembled, bringing with them the languages and usages of many countries, it would be greatly embarrassing to organize the government and we should be subjected to neighbouring wars and internal difficulties—in short, that we were content with our present condition, and required no change. Such sentiments, I know, do prevail, but not among all; it is the fruit of toleration, of comfort, of ease, of wealth; but there are hearts which are yet to be touched with the pure love of liberty, when the time arrives. But the work is not to be accomplished by us; our will, our wishes, our doubts, and our scruples, are empty and evanescent; there is a higher power, and a stronger arm, which will direct the movements of the great advent, which will show us the path; our cloud by day and our pillar by night. Are we not His chosen people, has He not blessed us, when shadowed beneath His protecting mantle, and punished us when we forgot His holy ordinances? And do we not await His promises of final national regeneration? How can we doubt the future, in contemplating the past! Has He not said "all the house of Israel, even all of it, and the cities shall be inhabited, and the wastes shall be builded?" has He not said, "I will settle you after your old states, and will do better for you than at your beginning, and you shall know that I am the Lord?" Has He not said, "For I will take you from among the heathen, and gather you from all countries, and will bring you into your own land?" But you shrink from the desolation of Judea, and fear that the land will for ever wither under its ancient curse. Even there we have been anticipated by the mercy of divine forgiveness. "I will multiply the fruit of the tree, and the increase of the field, that ye shall receive no more reproach of famine, and they shall say, this land that was desolate, is become like the Garden of Eden; I the Lord have spoken it, and I will do it." Shall we ourselves become infidels, and doubt the promises of the Almighty? God forbid. Let us therefore prepare for that great change which will fill the whole world with wonder and astonishment. Other nations, in breaking the yoke of the oppressors and becoming rulers in their own land, bring with them their national characteristics. An ignorant people cannot make an enlightened government, but when the trumpet sounds for us on Zion, every country on earth will give up its great men among the Jewish people, and a combination of talent, wealth, enterprise, learning, skill, energy, and bravery will be collected in Palestine, with all the lights of science and civilization, and once more elevate those laws which Moses had consecrated to liberty and the republican forms of government. Let us commence the great work, and leave its consummation to our great Shepherd and Redeemer.

I hope you will agree with me, that it is a privilege to be permitted to contribute our mite to the erection of this great Synagogue, near the site of the temple, that all Israel should aid in its completion. It will possess one advantage—it will be orthodox. The Jewish religion should never change its original form or type, reforms create schisms, and promote divisions; besides impairing the unity of our faith; religion is of the heart. There must be the seat of devotion; forms and ceremonies are all empty without sincere piety.

I must confess that I should like to see some changes in our ritual and ceremonies. While admiring the beauty and sublimity of the Hebrew language, I should still be gratified, if we could introduce in our prayers, a portion of the language of the country, in order that we may better comprehend the great responsibilities of our faith. We might also curtail many repetitions, and introduce some beneficial changes; but where are the limitations and boundaries to these reforms, when we once introduce the pruning knife? Where is our authority to change of modify those forms and ceremonies, the native purity of our faith, which we have sustained for four thousand years through the severest sufferings and privations? There are great dangers in all innovations on an established religion, and it is preferable to pursue the plain beaten paths so long adopted by our ancestors, than to venture upon unexplored regions, and carry out reforms which finally efface the landmarks of our ancient faith. Yet if this is pursued by other congregations, we shall be gratified to know, that there i8 one congregation in Jerusalem, which will never change its ancient laws and customs; and therefore we can more cheerfully and more liberally extend our aid in the erection of this new Synagogue, under the conviction that it will be founded on a rock which will last for ages. The accommodations to the pious, which a new and extensive place of worship will afford, will attract a greater number of our people to Jerusalem from the surrounding countries. Admonished by the signs of the times, and by the expectation of important events, we find the aged Jews, with some little means, coming down the Danube, from the Red Sea, and over the mountains of Circassia, journeying toward Jerusalem; there in holy meditation and prayer, to spend the remnant of their days, and to sit under the wall of the Temple and pray for the peace of Israel, and when they die, surrounded by the learned and pious, to be buried in the consecrated earth, near the ashes of the great prophets, the sublime Psalmist, and the illustrious of our fathers and ancestors. If there is any consolation in the last hours of life among the truly pious of our faith, it is in knowing that they are to be buried under the shadow of Mount Zion; to be near when the trumpet shall arouse the quick and the dead, at the day of the Great Atonement. I never hear the name of Jerusalem, without thinking of that mighty man, whose consecrated fingers struck the wires of his ravishing harp and gave alarm to the hosts of Heaven—that beloved of God, that Warrior, Poet, King—stern in his friendships, sublime in his orisons, he whose heart melted in his love and adoration of the Lord—the good, the great, the illustrious David. Who can read his psalms without feeling all the pride of religious faith in knowing that he too was a Jew? What a privilege it is to stand by his tomb—what a blessing to lie near him even in death!

I have said that the building of this new Synagogue in Jerusalem would be considered throughout the world as a remarkable sign, particularly among a people who, though separated and dispersed in the four quarters of the world, are united by the most extraordinary bonds of sympathy, like the magnetic shock, it reaches every extremity; like the flash of electricity which conveys intelligence in every direction, the Jews will hear of it and will see the hand-writing on the wall. we have been preserved miraculously for great and startling events; God's dealings with his People have been most wonderful; we have passed through the promised punishments; shall we not enjoy the promised blessings? When and how this great advent is to be brought about, is still in the heart and hand of that great Spirit, who depresses and raises up, who breaks down thrones and elevates the oppressed and persecuted; as the great French historian has said "Providence moves through time, as the gods of Homer through space—it makes a step, and ages roll away." To the Christian world, which has a common origin with us, and still clings to the Jewish nation as the favored and chosen people of God, this little expressive sign will not be without its impression—it is one blast of that silver trumpet, which at the dawn of day was sounded from the eastern portals of our temple. Here is the Church of the Holy Sepulchre, in which Christians offer us their pious orisons to the memory of Him who, while on earth, deserved all that the best feelings in the heart could bestow; there are the minarets of the Mosque of Omar, built on the site of our Temple; and there in simple grandeur, in one corner of Mount Zion, is the new Synagogue of the Jews—the parent and his children, all were happy on the same spot, all wafting the orisons to that Heaven where sits in divine majesty the Lord of Hosts and the God of Israel.

It is not the least curious in the erection of this new edifice in Jerusalem, that we can direct the builders to the spot where all the materials of Herod's Temple yet lie in silent grandeur. Beneath the Mosque of El'Aska, the great chambers, the immense granite pillars, the magnificent marble columns with exquisitely carved tops and bases, the richly ornamented gates, the reservoirs still with water, in which the Priests and Levites bathed, are at this day to be found. not crumbling in ruins, but erect and majestic, and have been explored within the last two years by one of our people, now a resident of this city, proving, beyond doubt, the error of that prediction, which declared that not one stone of that temple shall stand upon another. At this particular crisis of affairs in Europe, this small sign will arouse the Jews in every direction. They have been busy amid these revolutions. It was not to be expected that a people of their literary, political and commercial influence—the bankers of Europe, the merchants of England, the statesmen of France, the philosophers of Germany, the agriculturists of Poland, the poets of Italy, the artists, mechanics and soldiers everywhere, could see these mighty events developing themselves on the Continent, without participating actively in their progress and results. They too will hear the distant sound of that trumpet, whose notes will float around the horizon, and will know who is moving in the great work.

The laying of the corner-stone of the new Temple will attract an immense number of the faithful to Jerusalem to witness the ceremony, it will not be built as the old one, on the return of our people from Babylon, with the sword in one hand and the trowel in the other. The building and the builders will be protected and assisted by all religious denominations. For many years I have cherished the hope that I might have it in my power to visit the Holy City—that my country would enable me to say to my people, with the prophet Isaiah, "Hail to the land, shadowing with wings which lies beyond the ruins of Ethiopia, which sendeth ambassadors by sea in vessels of bulrushes." Hail to the house of the Jew, as well as the Gentile.

It would be to me the proudest day of my life, if I could be present at laying the corner-stone of the new Temple of Jerusalem—if I could realize all the associations which spring from the spot, where Daniel and Solomon lived—where Isaiah prophesied, and where the Maccabees conquered.

Friends and Brethren, will you not contribute a small portion of that wealth which God has blessed you with to aid in the erection of the new building on Zion?—Will you not assist our poor brethren in Jerusalem, who are looking to you for aid in this interesting project? Will you not give a trifle that you might have the gratification of saying, "I assisted to erect this ediface dedicated to the Most High in his own—his cherished city, Jerusalem? I know you will. When was an appeal made to the charitable feelings of the Jew to aid his brethren, that it was not cheerfully, liberally, responded to? All have an interest, an inheritance in Jerusalem; Jew and Gentile, all expect to unite in pious zeal, in holy charity, in mutual forgiveness, on that day, when the nation is to be gathered together. The honored messenger, now here, the Rabbi Echiel Cohen, who is to convey the fruits of your bounty to the Holy Land, will be, I hope, enabled to say, "I met my people in the Western World, with hands that had hearts in them—who felt and who prayed for the peace of Jerusalem, who gave me the gold of Ophir, as we gave Solomon of blessed memory to erect the Temple, which yet lives in our hearts, and the prayers and blessings of the faithful await them." Send him not away to the banks of the Jordan without purse and without scrip. Let us give our mite, no matter how small. I know full well, my friends, how many claims you have upon your bounty—strong and natural ones; engraft this one upon the rest; you will not feel its pressure; but it will be to you a grateful, pleasing remembrance, when this contemplated edifice is completed, that you have an interest in its erection and your names will be impressed upon the hearts of a people whose lives are devoted to piety and whose prayers are offered for our temporal happiness and eternal salvation.

Selected Bibliography

WORKS BY MORDECAI NOAH

Noah, Mordecai. *The Fortress of Sorrento; a petit historical drama in two acts*. New York: D. Longworth, 1808.

———. *Shakespeare Illustrated; or The Novels and Histories on Which the Plays of Shakespeare Are Founded. Collected and Translated from the Originals by Mrs. Lenox . . . With Critical Remarks and Biographical Sketched of the Writers*. Philadelphia, 1809.

———. *Correspondence And Documents Relative To The Attempt To Negotiate For the Release Of The American Captives At Algiers; including remarks on our relations with that regency*. Washington City, 1816.

———. *Oration, Delivered by Appointment, Before Tammany Society of Columbian Order, Hibernian provident society, Columbian society, Union society of shipwrights and caulkers, Tailors', House carpenters', and Masons' benevolent societies. United to celebrate the 41st anniversary of American independence. . . .* New York: J. H. Sherman, 1817.

———. *Discourse, Delivered At The Consecration of the Synagogue of K.K. Shearith Israel . . . in the City of New York on Friday the 10th of Nisan, 5578, corresponding with the 17th of April, 1818*. New York: C.S. Van Winkle, 1818.

———. *She Would Be A Soldier, Or The Plains of Chippewa; An Historical Drama, In Three Acts*. New York: Longworth's dramatic repository, Shakespeare Gallery, 1819.

———. *Travels in England, France, Spain, and the Barbary States, in the years 1813-1814, and 1815*. New York: Kirk and Mercein, 1819.

———. *Essays of Howard, On Domestic Economy*. New York: Birch and Co. 1820.

———. *An Address Delivered Before the General Society of Mechanics and Tradesmen of The City of New York at the opening of the Mechanic Institution, on November 25, 1821*. 1821.

Kerr, John (claimed by Noah as an alteration of his *Paul and Alexis or The Orphans of the*

Rhine). The Wandering Boys; or The Castle of Olival. Boston: Richardson and Lord, 1821.

———. *Marion; or, The Hero of Lake George: a drama in three acts, funded on events of the revolutionary war.* New York: E. Murden, 1822.

———. *The Grecian Captive, or The Fall of Athens. As performed at the New York theater.* New York: E. Murden, 1822.

———. *A Statement of Facts Relating to the Conduct of Henry Eckford, esq., as connected with the National Advocate.* New York: J. W. Bell and Co., 1824.

———. *Discourses on the Evidences of the American Indians Being the Descendants of the Lost Tribes of Israel. Delivered Before the Mercantile Library Association. . . .* New York: J. Van Norden, 1827.

———. *Discourse on the Restoration of the Jews: Delivered at the Tabernacle, Oct. 28 and Dec. 2, 1844.* New York: Harper and Brothers, 1845.

———. *Mordecai Noah's Discourse on the Restoration of the Jews.* Republished in extract with an introductory note by D.S. Blondheim. Baltimore: The Lord Baltimore Press, 1845.

———. *Gleanings from a Gathered Harvest.* New York: C. Wells, 1845.

———. *Gleanings from a Gathered Harvest.* New York: H. Long and Bro., 1847.

———. *A Letter Adressed to the Southern Deleates of the Baltimore Delegates of the Baltimore Democratic Convention, on the Claims of the "Barnburners" to be Admitted to Seats in that Convention.* New York, 1848.

———. *Address Delivered at the Hebrew Synagogue in Crosby-Street, New-York, on Thanksgiving Day to Aid in the Erection of the Temple at Jerusalem.* Jamaica, 1849.

———. *Address Delivered at the Re-opening of the Apprentice's Library, and Reading Rooms, at the Mechanics' Hall, 472 Broadway, September 23d, 1850. . . .* New York, 1850.

SECONDARY SOURCES

Adler, Selig, and Thomas E. Connolly, eds. *From Ararat to Suburbia: The History of the Jewish Community of Buffalo.* Philadelphia, 1960.

Allen, Lewis F. *Early History of Grand Island. The City of Ararat—its corner stone. Mordecai M. Noah. Read before the Buffalo historical society club. Mar. 5, 1866.* Buffalo: Thomas' Buffalo City Directory for 1867, 1867.

———. *Founding of the City of Ararat on Grand Island—by Mordecai M. Noah. Read before the Society, March 5, 1866.* Buffalo: Buffalo Historical Society Publications, Vol. 1, 1879.

———. *The Story of the Tablet of the City of Ararat.* Buffalo: Buffalo Historical Society Publications, 1921.

Anthony, Irwin. *Decatur.* New York: Charles Scribner's Sons, 1931.

Barnett, Morris. *The Yankee Peddler; or, Old Times in Virginia.* St. Louis, 1841.

Beard, Charles A., and Mary. *The Rise of American Civilization.* New York, 1930.

Beardsley, Levi. *Reminiscences, New York, 1852.* New York, 1852.

Berton, Pierre. *Flames Across the Border: The Canadian-American Tragedy, 1813–1814.* Boston: Little, Brown, 1981.

Billington, Ray A. *The Protestant Crusade 1800-1860.* New York, 1964.

Bingnam, Robert W. *The Cradle of the Queen City.* Buffalo, 1931.

Blau, Joseph L. and Salo W. Baron. *The Jews of the United States 1790-1840: A Documen-*

tary History. New York, 1963.

Blumenthal, Walter Hart. *In Old America: Random Chapters on The Early Aborigines. With a foreword by George Alexander Kohut.* New York, 1931.

Bobbe, Dorothie. *De Witt Clinton.* New York, 1933.

Bowers, Claude G. *The Party Battles of the Jackson Period.* Boston, 1932

Brackenridge, H. M. *History of the Late War between the United States and Great Britain; Comprising a Minute Account of the Various Military and Naval Operations.* Philadelphia, 1844.

Breck, Charles. *The Fox Chase. A Comedy.* New York, 1808.

Brown, T. Alliston. *History of the American Stage . . . Biographical Sketches . . . 1733 to 1870.* New York: Dick and Fitzgerald, c. 1870.

———. *History of the New York Stage, from the First Performance in 1732 to 1901.* 4 vols. New York: Dodd, Mead and Co., 1903.

Burk, John Daly. *Female Patriotism; or, The Death of Joan of Arc.* New York, 1798.

Carlson, Oliver. *The Man Who Made News.* New York, 1942.

Cember, Esther. "Mordecai Manuel Noah: American Diplomat in Barbary 1813-1815: A Reappraisal." Unpublished M.A. thesis. Columbia U, 1968.

Clarke, L. H. *Report of the Trial of An Action on the Case, Brought by Sylvanus Miller, esq., Late Surrogate of the City and Country of New York, against Mordecai M. Noah, esq., editor of the National Advocate, for the Alleged Libel. Tried at the City Hall, in the City of New York, before the Circuit court held on the first judicial district in the state of New York, by his Honor Samuel R. Betts, on . . . the 12th day of December, 1823.* New York: J. W. Palmer and Co., 1823.

Coad, Oral Sumner. *William Dunlap.* New York, 1917.

Congdon, Charles T. *Reminiscences of a Journalist.* Boston: James R. Osgood and Co., 1880.

Cowell, Joe. *Thirty Years Passed Among the Players.* New York: Harper and Bros., 1844.

Crouthamel, James L. *James Watson Webb: A Biography.* Middletown, 1969.

Daly, Charles P. *The Settlement of Jews in North America.* Ed. Max J. Kohler. New York, 1893.

Davis, Moshe. *The Emergence of Conservative Judaism.* Philadelphia, 1963.

———. *With Eyes Toward Zion.* New York, 1977.

"Document: Recollections of the War of 1812 by George Hay, Eighth Marquis of Tweeddale." [Introd. Lewis Einstein]. *The American Historical Review* 32 (Oct. 1926–July 1927): 69–78.

Dunlap, William. *History of the American Theater.* 2d. ed. Repr. New York: Burt Franklin, 1963.

———. *A Trip to Niagara; or, Travellers in America.* New York, 1830.

Eaton, Walter P. *The Actor's Heritage: Scenes from the Theater of Yesterday and the Day Before.* Boston: Little, Brown and Co., 1924.

Edwards, Charles. *Reports of Chancery Cases Decided in the First Circuit Court of the State of New York.* Vol. I. New York, 1833.

Fox, David R. *The Decline of Aristocracy in the Politics of New York.* New York, 1919.

Fox, Louis H. *New York City Newspapers, 1820-1850: a Bibliography.* University of Chicago Press: Chicago, 1928.

Friedman, Lee M. *Pilgrims in a New Land.* Philadelphia: The Jewish Publication Society of America, 1948.

———. *Mordecai Manuel Noah as Playwright.* New York: Historia Judaica, 1942.

Gappelberg, Leonard I. "M. M. Noah and the Evening Star: Whig Journalism 1833-1840"

Unpublished Ed.D. thesis. Yeshiva U, 1970.

Gelber, Dr. M.M. *Zur Vorgeschichte des Zionismus* (German). Vienna, 1927.

Godbey, Allen H. *The Lost Tribes Theory. Suggestions toward Rewriting Hebrew History.* Durham, 1930.

Goldberg, Issac. *Major Noah: American-Jewish Pioneer.* Philadelphia: The Jewish Publication Society of America, 1936.

Goldstein, Israel. *A Century of Judaism in New York.* New York, 1930.

Govan, Thomas. *Nicholas Biddle: Nationalist and Public Banker 1786-1844.* Chicago, 1959.

Grice, C[harles]. E. *The Battle of New Orleans, or Glory, Love and Loyalty.* New York, 1816.

Grimsted, David. *Melodrama Unveiled: American Theater and Culture 1800-1850.* Chicago: University of chicago Press, 1968.

———. *The Rise of the Jewish Community of New York.* Philadelphia, 1945.

Gutmann, Harry Kroll. *Mordecai Manuel Noah, the American Jew.* Cincinnati, 1931.

Hamilton, James A. *Reminiscences of James A. Hamilton.* New York, 1869.

Hamlin, C. H. *The War Myth in United States History.* New York, 1927.

Hanson, Willis T., Jr. *Early life of John Howard Payne.* Boston, 1913.

Harap, Louis. *The Image of the Jew in American Literature: From Early Republic to Mass Immigration.* Philadelphia, 1974.

Harrison, Gabriel. *John Howard Payne.* Philadelphia: J.B. Lippincott and Co., 1885.

Haswell, Charles H. *Reminiscences of an Octogenarian of the City of New York (1816-1860).* New York: Harper and Brothers, 1896.

Havens, Daniel F. *The Columbian Muse of Comedy: The Development of a Native Tradition in Early American Social Comedy, 1787–1845.* Carbondale: Southern Illinois University Press, 1973.

Hendrick, Burton J. *The Jews in America.* New York, 1923.

Hershkowitz, Leo. "New York City 1834-1840: A Study in Local Politics." Unpublished Ph.D. thesis, New York U, 1960.

Hoover, Merle M. *Park Benjamin: Poet and Editor.* New York, 1948.

Hornblow, Arthur. *A History of the Theatre in America: From Its Beginnings to the Present Time.* 2 vols. Philadelphia: J.B. Lippincott and Co., 1919.

Hone, Phillip. *The Diary of Phillip Hone, 1828-1851.* Ed. Allan Nevins. New York: Dodd, Mead and Co., 1927.

Hopkins, Samuel M. *Reports of Cases Argued and Determined in the Court of Chancery of the State of New York.* Albany, 1827.

Hudson, Frederic. *Journalism in the United States, from 1690 to 1872.* New York: Harper and Brothers, 1873.

Hunt, William. *The American Bibliographical Sketch Book.* New York: Nafis and Cornish, 1848.

Irwin, Ray W. *The Diplomatic Relations of the United States With the Barbary Powers, 1776-1816.* Chapel Hill, 1931.

Itzkowitz, David C. *Peculiar Privilege: A Social History of English Foxhunting 1753–1885.* Hassocks, England: Harvester, 1977.

Jackson, Andrew. *Correspondence of Andrew Jackson.* Ed. John S. Bassett. Washington, 1928-33.

James, Marquis. *The Life of Andrew Jackson.* New York, 1938.

July, Robert W. *The Essential New Yorker: Guilan Crommelin Verplanck.* Durham, 1951.

Judah, Samuel B. *Gotham and the Gothamites: A Medley.* New York, 1823.

Kallen, Horace M. *Zionism and World Politics.* New York, 1921.

Karp, Abraham J. *Beginnings: Early American Judaica.* Philadelphia, 1975.
Karp, Abraham J., Ed. *The Jewish Experience in America.* New York, 1969.
Karp, Abraham J., Guest Curator. *Mordecai Manuel Noah, the First American Jew.* Yeshiva University Museum, 1987.
Kass, Alvin. *Politics in New York State 1800-1830.* Syracuse, 1965.
Kelly, Alfred H. and Winfred A. Harbison. *The American Constitution: Its Origins and Development.* New York: Norton, 1970.
Kerr, John. *The Wandering Boys: or, The Castle of Olival.* Boston: Richardson and Lord, 1821.
King, Charles. *The Life and Correspondence of Rufus King.* New York, 1900.
Kobre, Sidney. *Development of American Journalism.* Dubuque, 1969.
Memoirs of Lieut.-General Scott, LL.D. Written by Himself. New York, 1864.
Korn, Bertram W. *American Jewry and the Civil War.* Philadelphia, 1961.
———. *Eventful Years and Experiences: Studies in Nineteenth Century American Jewish History.* Cincinnati, 1958.
Korn, Bertram W., Ed. *A Bicentennial Festchrift for Jacob Rader Marcus.* Waltham, 1976.
Lamb, Mrs. Martha J. *History of the City of New York.* New York: A.S. Barnes and Co., 1880.
Lebenson, Anita Libman. *Jewish Pioneers in America 1492-1848.* New York, 1931.
Lewis, Alfred H. *Peggy O'Neal: A Novel.* Philadelphia, 1903.
Logan, Olive. *Before the Footlights and Behind the Scenes.* Philadelphia: Parmelee and Co., 1870.
Lossing, Benson J. *History of New York City.* New York: George E. Peine, 1884.
Lynch, Denis T. *An Epoch and a Man; Martin Van Buren And His Times.* New York: Horace Liveright. 1929.
Mackenzie, William L. *The Life and Times of Martin Van Buren.* Boston, 1846.
———. *The Lives and Opinions of Benj. Franklin Butler . . . and Jesse Hoyt . . . with Anecdotes or Biographical Sketches . . . .* Boston: Cook and Co., 1845.
Makover, Abraham B. *Mordecai M. Noah: His Life and Work From the Jewish Viewpoint.* New York: Bloch Pub. Co., 1917.
Mangum, Willie Person. *The Papers of Willie Person Mangum.* Ed. Henry T. Shanks. Raleigh, 1950-1956.
Marcus, Jacob R. *The Colonial American Jew.* 3 vols. Detroit, 1970.
Marcus, Jacob R., ed. *Critical Studies in American Jewish History.* Cincinnati, 1971.
———, ed. *Memoirs of American Jews.* Philadelphia, 1955.
Margolis, Max L., and Alexander Marx. *History of the Jewish People.* Philadelphia, 1927.
Martineau, Harriet. *Society in America.* 3 vols. New York, 1837.
Meserve, Walter J. *An Emerging Entertainment: The Drama of the American People to 1828.* Bloomington: Indiana University Press, 1977.
Meyers, Marvin. *The Jacksonian Persuasion.* New York, 1957.
Moise, L.C. *A Biography of Isaac Harby with an Account of the Reformed Society of Charleston, S.C. 1824-33.* Charleston, 1931.
Moody, Richard. *America Takes the Stage: Romanticism in American Drama and Theatre, 1750-1900.* Bloomington: Indiana University Press, 1955.
———. *Eminent Israelites of the Nineteenth Century: A Series of Biographical Sketches.* Philadelphia: Edward Stern and Co., 1880.
Moses, Montrose J. *The Fabulous Forrest.* Boston, 1929.
———. *Representative Plays by American Dramatists.* New York, 1918.
Mowatt, Anna Cora. *Autobiography of an Actress; or, Eighty Years on the Stage.* Boston:

Ticknor, Reed and Fields, 1854.
Murdoch, James E. *The Stage; or, Recollections of Actors and Acting.* Philadelphia: Stoddart, 1880.
Mushkat, Jerome. *Tammany.* Syracuse, 1971.
Musser, Paul H. *James Nelson Barker.* Philadelphia, 1929.
Myers, Gustavus. *History of Tammany Hall.* New York, 1901.
Nevins, Allan. *The Evening Post: A Century of Journalism.* New York, 1922.[Nichols, J. Horatio.] *The Essex Junto. A Comedy in Four Acts. By a Citizen of Massachusetts.* Salem, 1802.
Northall, William Knight. *Before and Behind the Curtain; or, Fifteen Years' Observations Among the Theatres of New York.* New York, 1851.
———. *Philadelphia, A History of the City and Its People.* Philadelphia: S.J. Clarke, 1912.
O'Brien, Frank M. *The Story of The Sun.* New York, 1918.
Odell, George C.D. *Annals of the New York Stage.* New York: Columbia University Press, 1927-1928.
Parton, James. *The Life of Horace Greely.* Boston, 1889.
[Paulding, James Kirke.] *The Diverting History of John Bull and Brother Jonathan. By Hector Bull-us.* New York, 1812.
———. *The Diverting History of John Bull and Brother Jonathan. By Hector Bull-us.* New Edition. New York, 1835.
———. *The History of Uncle Sam and His Boys.* Bound in James Kirke Paulding. *The Diverting History of John Bull and Brother Jonathan. By Hector Bull-us.* New Edition. New York, 1835.
Phelps, H.P. *Players of a Century: A Record of the Albany Stage.* Albany, 1880.
Phillipson, David, ed. *Letters of Rebecca Gratz.* Philadelphia, 1929.
Pollock, Queena. *Peggy Eaton.* New York, 1932.
Power, Tyrone. *Impressions of America: 1833, 1834, 1835.* 2 Vols. London: Bentley, 1836.
Pratt, John Webb. *Religion, Politics, and Diversity: The Church State Theme in New York History.* Ithaca, 1967.
Quinn, Arthur Hobson. *A History of the American Drama from the Beginning to the Civil War.* 2d ed. New York: Appleton, 1943.
Raisin, Max. *Mordecai Manuel Noah, Zionist, Author and Statesmen.* Warsaw, 1905.
Rees, James. *The Dramatic Authors of America.* Philadelphia, 1845.
———. *The Life of Edwin Forrest. With Reminiscences and Personal Recollections.* Philadelphia: T.B. Peterson and Bros., c. 1874.
Reissner, Hans G. *Eduard Gans: Ein Leben im Vormaerz.* Tuebingen, 1965.
Remini, Robert. *Martin Van Buren and the Making of the Democratic Party.* New York, 1970.
Rezneck, Samuel. *Unrecognized Patriots: The Jews in the American Revolution.* Westport, 1975.
Rosenbloom, Joseph. *A Biographical Dictionary of Early American Jews.* Kentucky: University of Kentucky, 1960.
Rourke, Constance. *American Humor: A Study of the National Character.* New York: Harcourt, 1931.
Rutland, Robert A. *The Newsmongers.* New York, 1973.
Sabin, Joseph. *Catalgue of the Library of Edwin Forrest Collins.* Philadelphia, 1863.
Sackler, Harry. *Major Noah: A Play.* New York, 1928.

Sarna, Jonathan D. *Jacksonian Jew: The Two Worlds of Mordecai Noah.* New York: Holmes and Meier, 1981.

Schappes, Morris U., ed. *A Documentary History of the Jews in the United States 1654-1875.* 3rd ed. New York, 1971.

Scharf, John T. and Thompson Wescott. *History of Philadelphia, 1609-1884.* 2 Vols. Philadelphia: L.H. Everts, 1884.

Sefer ha-Yashar. The Book of Yashar. Trans. Mordecai Noah. New York: Hermon Press, 1972.

Seller, Maxine. "Isaac Leeser: Architect of the American Jewish Community." Unpublished Ph.D. thesis, U Pennsylvania, 1965.

Shaw, Ronald E. *Erie Water West: A History of the Erie Canal 1792-1854.* Lexington, 1966.

Shulman, William Louis. "The National Advocate 1812-1829." Unpublished Ed.D. thesis. Yeshiva U, 1968.

de Sola Pool, David. *Portraits Etched in Stone: Early Jewish Settlers 1682-1831.* New York, 1952.

de Sola Pool, David and Tamar. *An Old Faith in the New World.* New York, 1955.

Stern, Malcolm. *Americans of Jewish Descent.* Cincinnatti, 1960.

Thomas, E.S. *Reminiscences of the Last Sixty-Five Years.* Hartford, 1840.

Trowbridge, J.T. *My Own Story.* Boston, 1903.

Van Deusen, Glyndon G. *Horace Greely: Nineteenth Century Crusader.* Philadelphia, 1953.

———. *The Jacksonian Era.* New York, 1959.

———. *Thurlow Weed: Wizard of the Lobby.* Boston, 1947.

———. *William Henry Seward.* New York, 1967.

The War. 1.20 (1813): 86–88.

Wemyss, Francis Courtney. *Chronology of the American Stage from 1752 to 1852.* New York: William Taylor and Co., c. 1852.

———. *Theatrical Biography; or, The Life of an Actor and Manager.* Glasgow: R. Griffen and Co., 1848.

Werner, M.R. *Tammany Hall.* New York: Doubleday, Doran, and Co., 1928.

Wikoff, Henry. *The Reminiscences of an Idler.* New York: Fords, Howard, and Hurlbert, c. 1850.

Williams, Stanley T. *The Life of Washington Irving.* 2 vols. New York: Oxford University Press, 1935.

Wolf, Edwin and Maxwell Whiteman. *The History of the Jews of Philadelphia from Colonial Times to the Age of Jackson.* 2d ed. Philadelphia, 1975.

Wolf, Simon. "Mordecai Manuel Noah: A Biographical Sketch." *Selected Essays and Papers.* Cincinnati, 1926.

———. *The American Jew as Patriot, Soldier, and Citizen.* New York, 1895.

Wood, William B. *Personal Recollections of the Stage . . . During a Period of Forty Years.* Philadelphia: Henry Carey Baird, 1855.

Index

About the Editors

MICHAEL SCHULDINER is Professor of English at the University of Alaska, Fairbanks. He is the author of two earlier volumes and is the editor of *Studies in Puritan American Spirituality*.

DANIEL J. KLEINFELD is a director with credits in New York, Moscow, and St. Petersburg. He has most recently worked with The New York Fringe Festival and The Soho Repertory Theatre.

Recent Titles in Contributions in American Studies

In the Public Interest: The League of Women Voters, 1920–1970
Louise M. Young

The Rhetoric of War: Training Day, the Militia, and the Military Sermon
Marie L. Ahearn

Restrained Response: American Novels of the Cold War and Korea, 1945–1962
Arne Axelsson

In Search of America: Transatlantic Essays, 1951–1990
Marcus Cunliffe

Prophetic Pictures: Nathaniel Hawthorne's Knowledge and Uses of the Visual Arts
Rita K. Gollin and John L. Idol, Jr., with the assistance of Sterling K. Eisiminger

Testing the Faith: The New Catholic Fiction in America
Anita Gandolfo

Blowing the Bridge: Essays on Hemingway and *For Whom the Bell Tolls*
Rena Sanderson

In Praise of Common Things: Lizette Woodworth Reese Revisited
Robert J. Jones

Melville and Melville Studies in Japan
Kenzaburo Ohashi, editor

Yesterday's Stories: Popular Women's Novels of the Twenties and Thirties
Patricia Raub

Preserving Charleston's Past, Shaping Its Future: The Life and Times of Susan Pringle Frost
Sidney R. Bland

Feast of Strangers: Selected Essays of Reuel Denney
Tony Quagliano, editor

www.ingramcontent.com/pod-product-compliance
Lightning Source LLC
Chambersburg PA
CBHW020947310726
48980CB00001B/94

* 9 7 8 0 3 1 3 3 1 0 4 4 7 *